What people are s

Anti-He

Lozier's book is a cocktail that mixes passion with politics, direct action with drunkenness, and self-deception with longing in his quest for belonging inside the alienating features of modern society. In doing so, he delivers a love letter to anyone curious enough to listen.
David Redmon, award-winning director of Mardi Gras: Made in China

In *Anti-Hero*, Lozier reminds us that Antifa activists and others on the radical Left are not as one-dimensional as political talking heads would like you to believe. And ultimately, if we want to overcome hatred and build a better society, we need to remember the simple truth that we are all more alike than different as human beings.
Gabriel Nadales, author of *Behind the Black Mask, My Time as an Antifa Activist*

Anti-Hero

Memories of a Black Bloc Anarchist

Anti-Hero

Memories of a Black Bloc Anarchist

A. J. Lozier

Winchester, UK
Washington, USA

JOHN HUNT PUBLISHING

First published by Zero Books, 2022
Zero Books is an imprint of John Hunt Publishing Ltd., No. 3 East St., Alresford,
Hampshire SO24 9EE, UK
office@jhpbooks.com
www.johnhuntpublishing.com
www.zero-books.net

For distributor details and how to order please visit the 'Ordering' section on our website.

Text copyright: A.J. Lozier 2020

ISBN: 978 1 78904 828 5
978 1 78904 829 2 (ebook)
Library of Congress Control Number: 2020951030

A CIP catalogue record for this book is available from the British Library.

Design: Stuart Davies

UK: Printed and bound by CPI Group (UK) Ltd, Croydon, CR0 4YY
Printed in North America by CPI GPS partners

We operate a distinctive and ethical publishing philosophy in
all areas of our business, from our global network of authors to
production and worldwide distribution.

For Brianne, whose radical, revolutionary love burns
brighter than a Molotov cocktail.

Acknowledgments

This book would not have been possible without the loving support of so many friends, family and mentors who have selflessly given of themselves throughout my life.

I want to thank my mother and father, Jack and Laura Lozier, who endured so much hardship and provided me with a loving, stable home despite impossible odds. I have to especially thank my father for regaling me with stories of the 1960s which inspired my actions for so many years, even though he probably wishes he hadn't.

Thank you to my second-grade teacher, Ms Keller, who recognized my writing talent and read my first story to the whole class.

I want to thank my friends who read excerpts of my book and provided suggestions along the way, especially Stephen Smajstrla, Alan Suderman, Brent Furl and Tyler Woerner.

Thank you to my family, Brianne, Poete and Lennon, who always believed in me and gave me the time and space to write this book, which has consumed many hours over the past 2 years.

Thank you to David Redmon and Marcelo Andrade, whose courage, passion and dedication to the causes of global justice continue to inspire me to this day.

Thank you to all the members of Alcoholics Anonymous, who helped me achieve sobriety and to become a better person.

Finally, I want to thank everyone who was a part of my life story and appear in these pages under different names. Thank you for being yourself, and for helping shape the person I am today.

Preface

It was an icy cold morning in DC. I awoke on the floor of a stranger's basement, exhausted after a 20-hour bus ride and only a few hours of sleep. My body ached from sleeping on the hardwood floor, and I craved coffee. But despite the physical discomfort and exhaustion, my heart thumped with excitement the moment I opened my eyes and remembered where I was. It was the morning of January 20, 2001 – the day of George W. Bush's inauguration.

I had not come to DC to *celebrate* the inauguration. Far from it. I was one of tens of thousands who had traveled into the city to protest the most contested election in memory. My memory, anyway, as I was only 22 years old. It was only the second election in which I had been eligible to vote. Not that I was necessarily sad about Al Gore's defeat, either. My vote had gone for Ralph Nader of the Green Party.

The year before, I attended protests at both the Republican and Democratic national conventions. I believed both political parties were bought and paid for by multinational corporations. Even my vote for Nader was cast grudgingly. My belief that all electoral politics were doomed to failure was growing deeper by the day.

This protest was particularly significant for me, because it represented a moment of stepping over the line. For the first time, I was going to participate in the anarchist "Black Bloc." While the origins of the Black Bloc went back at least to the 1980s in Europe, it had first come to prominence in the United States during the 1999 protests against the World Trade Organization (WTO) in Seattle. While tens of thousands of protesters participated in nonviolent civil disobedience and marches, a few hundred radicals dressed in all black covered their faces and proceeded to shatter the windows of corporate businesses

1

in the financial district. They were not interested in symbolic protest. They sought to dismantle the capitalist system by force.

While I only learned about the protests in Seattle through the evening news, I had spent the previous year maneuvering myself into the center of the action. Through various online channels I had acquired the phone number for a contact at the anarchist "spokescouncil meeting" which had been held in DC the night before. Prior to receiving this phone number, I had to provide references from within the leftist community. Fortunately, my experience at a direct action in Los Angeles the summer before, where I was arrested and spent 10 days in jail, passed muster with this crew. I was given a time and location for the "convergence."

There was no need for the dress code to be explained to me. My friends and I, who had traveled together from Austin, were already dressed mostly in black when we woke up that morning, and we had black bandanas stuffed into our pockets. As we walked the several blocks across the city toward 14th and K, we spoke little but considered quietly the supplies we had brought in our backpacks. Vinegar and extra bandanas, to diffuse the effects of tear gas; water bottles, to wash our eyes should we be pepper sprayed; a knife in my pocket, which could be used to slash the tires of a police cruiser should the need arise.

When we turned the final corner on 14th Street, we saw a large sea of black in the park, over 500 anarchists and a large, black banner with white lettering: *Class War Now*. We tied the bandanas around our faces and picked up the pace as we headed toward the park, lest we get picked off by the police.

We hardly had a chance to step foot in the park before the march began, immediately spilling into the streets. My friends and I hurried to catch up and join the middle of the crowd. I was surrounded by black-masked faces, large banners, drums and passionate chants. *Whose streets? Our streets!* I was filled with a sense of exhilaration, adrenaline and power like I had never known. *This is my moment,* I thought. *I am stepping across the pages of history. I am part of a revolution that will change the world forever.*

Four years later, not only had we not stopped Bush's first inauguration, he was being sworn in for a second term. In the interim, I participated in dozens of actions like the one described above, even organizing a few of my own. I traveled far and wide, participating in militant protests all across the United States, as well as Canada, Mexico and even Venezuela. I was part of the international editorial committee of IndyMedia. org, writing and publishing articles about the events around the world which I considered part of a growing global revolution against corporate capitalism. My commitment to anarchism deepened, and at one point I was a guest on John Zerzan's radio program in Eugene, Oregon.

During this period, the world was undergoing changes of its own. The morning of September 11, 2001, when the planes struck the World Trade Center buildings, I had been in the midst of final preparations for a massive convergence in Washington DC for the International Monetary Fund (IMF)/World Bank protests, which had been scheduled for the twenty-eighth. My crew and I had constructed shields out of heavy plastic cut from garbage cans. I still have a scar on my index finger from when the box cutters slipped during their construction. The IMF/World Bank meetings were canceled, but we went to DC anyway. Our still sizable anarchist Black Bloc was quickly surrounded by a heavy contingent of riot police who were in a particularly intolerant mood and escorted us along the entire parade route.

I was among the first to protest the invasion of Afghanistan, picketing in front of the White House the very night the invasion was announced. As rumblings surrounding Iraq began to emerge, the "anti-globalization" movement I had been a part of evolved into an "anti-war" movement. February 15, 2003 was, and still is, the largest coordinated protest in world history. I had been to many large protests before, but what was striking about this one was that it was not one but many, spread all around the globe. And each one was large enough to set records in its own right. There were over 10,000 at the one I attended in Austin, Texas, but something like 5000 in Dallas and 7000 in Houston on the same day. This was completely unheard of. That is to say nothing of the hundreds of thousands that turned out in San Francisco and New York, or the estimated one million in Rome.

And yet, our protests accomplished nothing. The invasion of Iraq continued as planned. Not only that, but Bush was re-elected the next year. I remember feeling deep despair. If a protest of that size could not change things, what would? Taking inspiration from the nineteenth-century anarchist organizer Joe Hill – whose dying words were "don't mourn, organize!" – my friends and I worked tirelessly to re-energize resistance in Austin in the period before and after George W. Bush's re-election. Through a combination of creativity and hard work, we managed to mobilize approximately 10,000 people once again in the streets of Austin to protest George W. Bush's inauguration. Obviously, we didn't stop the gears of capitalism or the war machine from turning for even one second. We did, however, manage to help a 19-year-old girl get arrested for assaulting a police officer.

Another small peak was followed by an even more profound crash. And here, I believe, we began to lose our way. The fractures in ideology that had followed our movement since Seattle in 1999 only became more pronounced. It was as if our utter failure to evoke any change in the world around us forced us to turn our criticisms inward. Identity politics spiked, and spokescouncil meetings transformed from a strategy for planning mass actions into miserable forums for endless self-critique. Finally, our actions became more desperate. We disrupted the speech of a visiting right-wing intellectual at the

University of Texas with air horns. The topic of his speech was the suppression of free speech on college campuses. Four more of us were arrested, all young people who – unlike the older and more seasoned among us – were either less cognizant of where the lines were, or more willing to cross them because they didn't fully understand the consequences.

The irony of this final action was not lost on me. This speaker had come to UT's campus to expose an emerging trend among the left to suppress free speech. Our response was, to put it bluntly, to suppress his free speech. We couldn't stop globalization, we couldn't stop war, but we could stop someone from speaking. What had we become?

This was the last protest I ever attended.

My purpose in writing this memoir is to document my own involvement in the militant anarchist movement over a 5-year period from 2000 – 2005. I attempt to recall the events that shaped my thinking, and the thinking that shaped my actions. This was both a complicated and exciting time for me and thousands of others around the world. My experiences were deeply tied with my own upbringing, my youth, my longings, my insecurities, my insights as well as my blind spots. My hope is that my own account will help others who are trying to understand the radical left we see today.

On the one hand, I believe the black-clad "Antifa" are not the villains they appear to be. Like I was, they are mostly young people trying to take a stand for justice and leave their mark on this world and on history. But on the other hand, and just as importantly, they are not the heroes they consider themselves to be. Their actions are often reckless and violent, and more tyrannical than libertarian. They are the tip of the spear of a radical left that has become yet more extreme since my involvement in street politics ceased nearly 15 years ago. Far from being a revolutionary movement, fighting for the rights of workers and the protection of the environment, they promote a paralyzing identity politics which has accomplished little more than strengthening the mirror image of white identity politics on the far right.

The Antifa today, similar to the "Black Bloc" during the Bush era that preceded them, remain a guilty pleasure of the left. When they are not seen as heroes, they are at the very least "anti-heroes." While many liberals may not explicitly endorse their actions, secretly they are rooting for them. The famous incident where Richard Spencer was punched in the face at Donald Trump's inauguration was widely praised on social media. Similarly, the Antifa presence at Charlottesville was described, at best, as a necessary evil to combat the militant presence of neo-Nazi's and white supremacists. The familiar trope of the radical left-wing militants "protecting" the vulnerable was peppered throughout various news articles and social media posts.

This cautious praise, however, is highly selective. For every positive story of the Antifa protecting nonviolent protesters or punching an almost universally unsympathetic character in the face, there are dozens of other videos of the Antifa in Portland, for example, physically intimidating and harassing drivers because they unilaterally decided to "shut down traffic" for whatever cause. Or physically attacking conservative speakers and their guests on college campuses. These videos seem only to be shared by those on the right, but they are consumed voraciously.

As an active participant in dozens of Black Blocs in the early 2000s, I rarely felt we received the attention we deserved. The Antifa of today does not suffer from this problem. On the contrary, their ubiquitous presence at virtually every protest has contributed to a new phenomenon – the rise of militancy by right-wing groups who are increasingly confronting Antifa on the streets, often borrowing their own tactics. To the untrained eye, it is sometimes difficult to differentiate Antifa from the right-wing groups who oppose them. Both come armed, both come dressed in armor, both come ready to do battle. The pressure on ordinary Americans to "pick sides" seems to increase by the day. The voices of those who call for civility and nonviolence are either becoming quieter, or simply more difficult to hear.

It does not take a genius to realize this cycle of escalation and violence is leading all of us toward a darker future. It was this realization that inspired me to write this book. The crux of our problem is we no longer see our political opponents as human beings. In our minds, we paint them as comic book villains. This attitude is lending increasing license to those who are able to justify unleashing physical violence upon the other. And yet, in many ways the other is nothing more than the mirror image of ourselves. Different parents, different professors or different friends might have easily led us to fight on one side versus the other. I believe my story is one of many that reveal this difficult truth.

While I am no longer a radical, I am still a liberal. I am as concerned as anyone about the rise of right-wing populism in the United States and abroad. White nationalism or outright fascism *is* witnessing a rebirth. Massive technology companies are the new monopolies, rolling back the progress social movements made a hundred years ago. Now, more than ever, we need strong leadership from the left to refocus our attention on the issues that matter most. However, I do not believe this will be possible so long as we continue to turn a blind eye to the basic immorality of Antifa's actions. Yes, protest is important. Even civil disobedience may be warranted in certain cases. However, wanton property destruction is indefensible. Pitched battles with police and political opponents create enemies where we should be creating allies. Labeling anyone who questions your tactics a "fascist" shuts down debate. Violent self-righteousness is the enemy of a free and open society. Most importantly, if we are concerned about the escalation of militancy on the right, we must begin by looking at our own movements. We must be willing to admit where we are wrong and let go of the fear that doing so will make us more vulnerable.

There is, after all, strength in vulnerability. At various times throughout history, we have been reminded of this by people like Jesus and Mahatma Gandhi. Do unto others as you would have them do unto you. Be the change you want to see in the world. Are these teachings naive in the twenty-first century? Are the stakes suddenly higher than they have ever been before? I do not think so. These teachings have only been necessary because they are contrary to human nature. The idea that "the ends justify the means" has always come easily to us. We must constantly be reminded, therefore, that this is never the case – not in our personal lives, not in politics. What we do is who we become. And who we become is the world we will create.

Chapter 1

The year was 1994. I was 16 years old and had just gotten my hands on a pair of white cassette tapes containing recordings from the 1969 Woodstock Music Festival. My dad had borrowed them from a friend because he had an idea about coming up with his own Christian version of *With a Little Help from My Friends*. My dad was not a musician. When his project fizzled out, I picked up the tapes and popped them in my Walkman and started to listen.

I was mesmerized. I listened for hours, and when the final track ended, I listened again. The music was great, but that wasn't my favorite part. What captured my attention the most were the segments in between the songs, the crackling announcements on the PA, and most of all, the roar of the crowd. I imagined the sea of bodies, hundreds of thousands of them, joined together in a common cause, sharing the same dream of peace and love. And not just that, but the conscious feeling, at least I imagined, of being a part of a moment in time, an event in history. The feeling that their lives really mattered, perhaps not individually, but collectively.

My dad was only 14 years old in 1969, when Woodstock was taking place, and probably was not even aware it was happening. He did go see the movie, however, when it hit the theaters a year later. His own father, a former marine, decorated Korean War veteran, had recently abandoned his wife and children without warning – saying he was going out to buy cigarettes and never returning. My grandma was left to raise five children on her own, my dad the oldest. My grandpa was a loud, opinionated alcoholic who was disgusted by the whole anti-war movement, Civil Rights, hippies, Beatles, etc. My dad must have known how much he would have disapproved of everything about Woodstock, and perhaps that had something to do with how the movie affected him. It was something of a conversion experience.

All the way until her death in 2011, my grandma always regretted letting him go see Woodstock.

Soon after seeing the movie, my dad started growing his hair long, and made friends with people who smoked pot and took LSD. He was living in Corpus Christi, Texas, and had an acute sense that he was living on the periphery of all the "action" of the day, which he knew to be taking place in big cities like San Francisco, New York or even Dallas. But he became the biggest hippie he could, seeking out role models.

He never was able to attend an anti-war protest. Besides, Woodstock was, in some ways, the last big hurrah of the anti-war movement, the momentum tapering off significantly after that. So, my dad's participation was limited mainly to fashion (long hair and bell bottoms) and drugs. By his own account, he tried virtually any substance he could get his hands on – PCP, cocaine, uppers, downers. But mostly he stuck with smoking pot and was never a big drinker – his memories of his father a natural deterrent.

Still, he was getting into enough trouble that my grandma felt the need to make a change, and she and her sister moved their families to Dallas. My dad managed to finish high school, got a decent job in a machine shop and bought a van. He was extremely proud of this van. I clearly remember finding an old Polaroid of him sitting in the open side door of the van, his long blond hair glistening in the Texas sun, and a Tupperware bowl of marijuana in his hands. I remember looking at it intently, and deciding I wanted to be just like him.

One day in the late 1970s he was driving around Dallas in that van with a friend in the passenger seat, when his friend called out "Girls!" My dad whipped the van around and they pulled up next to the group of high school girls walking home from school. He asked if they wanted a ride (which must have seemed creepy) and when they declined, my dad parked. They started talking, and I suppose things were going well because my dad ended up pulling some bean bags out of the van and dropping them in the front yard of whatever house they had parked in front of. My dad, his friend, my mom Laura and her best friend, Kathy, sat in the stranger's yard and talked for hours until the owner of the house came out and asked them to leave.

My dad was initially more interested in Kathy than Laura. Some months later, Kathy was pregnant. At some point my dad lost interest in Kathy soon after his first son Justin was born, however, and turned his attention to Laura. After dating for a while, they went to see The Incredible Melting Man at a nearby Drive-In theater (7 percent on Rotten Tomatoes). It was there, so I am told, I was conceived. They were married in April 1978, and I was born November the same year.

What happened to Kathy, and his son Justin, who was only about a year older than me? It's difficult to say. My dad says that Kathy had no interest in him participating in his son's life. I'm sure her account might be a little different. Nonetheless, I would not learn that I had a half-brother until I was in my early teens, and I would only meet him once.

I am not sure whether my parents were happy in their first year of marriage. I know my dad smoked a lot of pot, and my mom took downers. The impression I get is that my mom was rather depressed. One day my dad came home and found her reading the Bible. She said, "I don't think we are living right." My dad became very angry and left to go hang out with some friends.

Evidently her statement worked on him, however, because when he woke up on Good Friday, 1980, something had changed in him too. He suddenly knew that the resurrection and all of the stories about Jesus were true, and of his own volition – not being in a church and not answering an "altar call" – my dad said a prayer and gave his life to Christ. He had been "born again."

Most Christians, upon conversion, feel compelled to give up their old drug habits – but not my dad. Since his conversion was largely self-directed, he immediately set to interpreting Christianity in his own way. "Jesus probably would have smoked pot," I can almost hear him saying. Nonetheless, he was on fire, almost manic in his newfound enthusiasm and faith.

It was some days later he was hanging out with some friends, smoking pot with them and telling them about Jesus. They were not all that interested, and, frankly, annoyed. Finally, one of them said, "Look man, we're about to take some acid. I'm sure you're not into that anymore." A phrase from the New Testament popped in my dad's head, to "tarry with them." His thinking was that Jesus was someone who did whatever those around him were doing, to not separate himself or place himself "above" what the common man did with his time. So, my dad decided to stay and take acid with them. My dad took two hits, which he clearly remembers were on little pieces of paper that looked like dragons.

Sometime later (impossible to say how much time had really passed) my dad noticed the acid did not feel that strong. He said as much, suggesting the LSD "these days" wasn't nearly as strong as it had been in the 60s. He bragged, "I could probably take five more and be fine." Evidently there was plenty to go around, as one of his friends handed them the bowl containing the hits and said he was welcome to it. My dad took five more hits, for a total of seven.

I doubt my dad realized how high he became in the next couple of hours. He continued talking about Jesus, to the point where his friends asked him to leave. He remembers walking back home, feeling an acute sense that God was on his right hand, Satan on his left, as though he was walking a tightrope between good and evil.

He arrived home to my mom completely out of his mind.

I was a year old, asleep in my crib on the second floor. My dad began talking about how he should burn the apartment down. He went upstairs, and my mom, desperately afraid he might do something to me, followed him. He was ranting incomprehensibly about his father, and how he would prove he was not afraid. He looked at my mom, and he remembers her becoming transfixed, appearing to him as an angel. She whispered something, and he heard "do it." In his mind, it was an invitation to overcome fear, once and for all. A leap of faith. He jumped – actually he dove – headfirst down the stairs.

He never lost consciousness. As he lay at the bottom of the stairs, he realized he no longer had feeling or movement from the waist down, and the movement in his hands was impaired as well. He would eventually learn that he had become a quadriplegic instantly, but this would not become clear until after a long and torturous night in the hospital, enduring all manner of hallucinations and paranoid delusions.

After finally coming down, probably the hardest crash of his life, my dad learned definitively that the accident had left him permanently paralyzed. While he would retain some limited movement in his arms and hands, he would never walk again. He lay in the hospital for days, contemplating his life, and whether or not he had any desire to continue living it.

My mom stayed with him, getting a job as a waitress to support me while he spent months in a rehab facility. His occupational therapist encouraged him to think about his next move, how he might be able to support himself, and his family, financially. His previous work in a machine shop was no longer an option for him. A day or two previous he had typed a letter to his father. Almost like pulling an idea from a hat, my dad said, "Well, I can type. I guess I'll become a computer programmer."

With support from the government, my dad began taking classes at a community college, working to earn an associate degree in computer programming. It was a daily struggle for him, squeaking by with Cs or the occasional B. He failed COBOL twice, before finally passing with a D.

At this time, we were living with my mom's father in Dallas, mere blocks from where my dad had met my mom and her friends as they were walking home from school. The college was just down the road, and my dad was able to commute back and forth in his electric wheelchair. I'll never forget the day my dad graduated. I was 5 years old, and I rode in his lap all the way to the college. It was a bright sunny day, and my dad was wearing a black robe, and I held the cap in my hand to keep it from blowing away. I remember running my fingers through the yellow tassel, feeling proud.

My dad's father, my grandpa, came to the graduation. I remember him standing in the aisle and snapping a photo as my dad received his diploma.

Life got better after this. My mom, dad and I got our own apartment, a huge step up from the government subsidized one we lived in previously, or having to live with relatives. It wasn't long after this that I became interested in computer programming myself. My dad gave me the computer he used in college, and I began writing my own games and business applications to keep track of my meager allowance. By middle school, I formed an underground hacker group at my school and gave myself the nickname "Blackbeard." I never did anything particularly nefarious, but I was for some reason drawn to the idea of a secret underworld.

Religion was a huge part of our lives. My dad never quite accepted his diagnosis. Instead, he became convinced he would be miraculously healed one day. I remember going to many churches, anytime a noted "faith healer" came to town. In most cases, the healers seemed not to notice my dad. It was evidently much easier to heal people with back pain or stiffness in their joints. In the cases the healers did notice my dad, and laid hands on him, they would eventually conclude that either "God's time is not our time," or worse, that his faith was not yet strong enough.

As I grew older, my faith wavered. I read the Bible voraciously but could not understand why the God of the Bible seemed so different from the God I experienced in these churches. How was it fair that God expects us to believe, when those living in the days of either the Old Testament or the New Testament had witnessed inarguably miraculous displays of power? I had never seen the sea parted, nor manna from heaven, nor water turned to wine. I had never seen the blind made to see, or the lame made to walk.

It was around the time that I first laid hands on the Woodstock tapes that I gave up my faith entirely. I was lying in bed, quietly struggling with God in my mind.

"God, if you're real, you can do anything. Nothing could be simpler than you showing me that you exist. Please, show me you exist! Give me something! Anything!"

I waited quietly in the darkness, and there was no answer to my prayer – only more darkness, more silence. "That's it," I decided. I became an atheist on the spot.

I kept my decision a secret from my parents. I couldn't imagine having this conversation with them. Or, if I did, I couldn't imagine it ever ending. My parents could never fully love and accept me if I was not a Christian.

In the place of my loss of faith, I was looking for something to fill the void. Something to give me a sense of belonging and purpose. I listened to the Woodstock tapes again and again, longing to go back in time and join them. Interestingly enough, I learned a 25-year reunion concert was taking place in New York that August. I wanted to go, but it was impossible. I had no money of my own, and there was no chance my parents would help me pay for it. Besides, who would I go with? And so, like my dad I did the next best thing – I went to Target and bought some tie-dye T-shirts and beaded necklaces. My hair was growing long. When I walked into my first class of my Sophomore year in high school, a guy in the back said "Hey, Woodstock!" I gave him the peace sign. The nickname stuck for most of that year.

Chapter 2

Deciding to become an atheist at age 16 gave me permission to experiment with drugs, which I think I had been dying to try for most of my life. One would think being the son of a quadriplegic dad, whose disability was the direct result of drug use, would be a clear deterrent. It might have been, if it were not for the fact that my dad talked openly with me about his many drug experiences, often tinged with an air of glamor and nostalgia.

Marijuana was my dad's favorite drug, and in fact he continued to smoke until I was 7 or 8 years old. The smell was a familiar one to me and evoked a sense of calm and deep thought. Much of my experience of "church" as a child was not in actual buildings, but in people's houses. My mom and dad were part of a loose group of individuals, informally called "The Brothers," who would get together on weekends, smoke pot and discuss the Bible. But my dad's love of pot predated this period by a decade or more.

My dad told me stories about how he would smoke a joint before work, or before going out in public, and how much he enjoyed the fact that no one knew he was high. This was the ultimate goal for him, a way to win at life, to "maintain." That is, to enjoy a nice buzz while still taking care of the responsibilities of life.

Despite what you might assume, he still remembered most of his experiences with LSD fondly as well. He told me it really was like taking a "trip," without having to leave your room. He recalled many positive memories of taking acid with friends and listening to Pink Floyd's Animals for hours on end. I couldn't imagine what a psychedelic trip felt like, but I couldn't wait to find out. My dad's mistake, I told myself, was taking too much. As long as I kept the dosage reasonable, there was no reason I couldn't give it a try.

Within a span of a few months after becoming an atheist, I tried both marijuana and LSD, and loved them both. At the same time, however, I was struggling with feelings of guilt, and alienation from my parents. We were tight knit in our own way, though we were all expert at burying truths beneath the surface. Clearly, they knew something had changed in me, though I never talked about it and they never asked.

I joined the debate team in high school and became good friends with a Christian. Mostly, I thought, I enjoyed debating with him. When he invited me to come with him to a church camp the following summer, I agreed – only because I thought it would be fun to debate Christians for a week. But a couple of days later I converted, became "born again," and I was immediately "on fire for Jesus." I quit doing drugs completely. During my Junior Year in high school I grew my hair long and started wearing a large cross necklace. I earned a new nickname, which continued even into my Freshman year in college: Jesus.

In high school, my interest in computers faded and I became passionate about history. I had an excellent teacher who was skilled at keeping his students' attention by varying his approach from one day to the next. While covering a single time period, such as Ancient Greek Civilization, he would spend one class focused on architecture, another on battles and military tactics, and yet another on philosophy and literature. I had a hungry mind, and while I was interested in many subjects, I worried I would not be able to pick a single major when I went into college. History, I concluded, was a way for me to not have to choose.

I got a scholarship at a small liberal arts college near Austin, Texas, only a few hours from Dallas. This was close enough to home to make my parents feel comfortable, but far enough for me to find my independence. I couldn't wait to be on my own. And though I was still wearing my "Jesus" shirts and cross necklaces, my deepening interest in history and philosophy was gradually eroding my faith from within.

One of the first classes I signed up for in college was called "New Testament Perspectives." I was excited because I assumed it would deepen my appreciation for the Bible. What I was surprised to discover was that my professor had no belief whatsoever in the inerrancy of the Bible. As the semester wore on, my faith was being ground down by the discovery of more and more inexplicable contradictions between the gospels.

When I received the study guide for the final exam, one of the questions was "Compare and contrast the accounts of the resurrection as portrayed in the Synoptic Gospels." The Synoptic Gospels included Matthew, Mark and Luke, which were presumed to originate from a common source. John was not included because of its many radical differences and presumed alternate origin story. And so, good student that I was, I sat down to prepare for this exam question – taking notes as I reviewed the story in detail as it was portrayed in each gospel. By the time I stood up, the final nail in the coffin of my faith was all but driven in.

At the same time as the intellectual underpinnings of my faith were being weakened, a similar impact was taking place for me on the emotional side. One of my first acts as a Freshman at the university was to join the Christian club, "Cross Training." The truth was, however, I didn't fit in. I wasn't sure if it was my long hair and hippy fashion (pretty much everyone else was strait laced and "preppy") or if it was my more "Charismatic" non-denominational background, but whatever it was, I wasn't making friends.

One friendship I did make, however, was with a Lesbian woman named Amy who was in one of my philosophy classes. I am not sure why she even wanted to talk to me. After all, I made it quite clear to her that I believed homosexuality to be a sin. Perhaps she could sense that my "belief" was a reluctant, even shaky one. She and her partner would regularly play acoustic covers of the Indigo Girls at the campus coffee shop, the Korouva Milkbar. I had never heard these songs before, but I was struck by the power of the lyrics and the obvious love that was woven into them.

By the end of the semester, my faith came crashing down. I could not believe in the infallibility of the Bible any longer, nor could I believe that the love I felt in the music emanating from this Lesbian couple was anything other than the real thing. If God is Love, as I had always believed, how could these two people, who clearly loved each other, possibly be going to hell? How could hell exist at all?

I decided, again, to abandon my faith. But this time, the change was permanent. I did not become an atheist, exactly, I just admitted the one thing I had been taught to deny, dodge or bury my entire life – the fact of my own uncertainty. I vowed to search for the truth, but to never again claim for certain anything, any divine or metaphysical reality, that I did not, or could not, truly know.

By giving up my faith, I was in essence shedding my entire identity, one I had built over the last 3 years. Three years is not a long time, unless you're 19 years old. Teenagers, after all, develop identities rapidly and deeply. It is as though hitting puberty is an experience not unlike the one Elazar and Eve might have felt after first biting the forbidden fruit and becoming aware of their own nakedness. There is a need to clothe oneself in an identity, to set oneself apart from one's peers, to feel a sense of meaning and purpose in the world. Christianity had done that for me. Now that it was gone, who was I? I was overcome by a tremendous sense of anxiety, even agoraphobia.

When I shared the fact of my newfound agnosticism with my friend Jeff who lived across the hall, he asked "Does that mean you can drink now?" I shrugged. Truthfully, I was excited. Jeff always had a bottle or two of Evan Williams nearby. As far as I could tell he got drunk every night. He poured me a shot. I tried to drink it, and almost choked on it. He got me a cold Dr Pepper and then explained to me how to take a shot, which came down to this. Drink quickly, and don't breathe until you've swallowed.

Alcohol gave me a sense of ease and comfort I had never felt before. It wasn't long before I was drinking every night as well. Jeff was glad to have a drinking buddy. After a little while, I began to rely upon the feeling of relief, and could not understand why so many students only drank on weekends. I wanted that relief every day. Fortunately, I remained a driven student, and for the most part, continued making my classes, studying and completing my homework on time. I prided myself on making straight As, and my plan was to continue on to graduate school. Eventually, I hoped to become a history professor.

My sense of longing to be a part of something greater was still with me, but I didn't know where to find it. The second semester of my Sophomore year in college, I took a "Non-Western Philosophy" class, where I learned about Hinduism, Taoism and Buddhism. While these ideas were beginning to percolate, my friend Jeff invited me to take acid with him one weekend.

The experience was far more intense than any I had experienced in high school. I was having intense hallucinations, affecting all of my senses. Sights, sounds, tastes and smells intermingled into a liquid soup of sensations. My perception of time became substantially warped. Minutes felt like hours, and hours became minutes. It was difficult to say whether I was having fun. Mostly, I felt extremely uncomfortable in my body. I constantly searched to find a comfortable position to sit, to stand, to lie. It was a feeling of waking insomnia.

Halfway into the 8-hour trip, I was standing beside a bed when the feeling of discomfort became overwhelming. Exacerbated, I gave up, and collapsed onto the bed. Suddenly, all discomfort was gone. Also gone, however, was my body, my sense of self, my sense of time. I dissolved into what felt like a vast sea of emptiness and eternity and bliss. I witnessed what could have either been a massive hurricane, or a galaxy, spiraling around a black focal point which was the focus of my attention. Without words, I had the direct experience of knowing that "all is good," that there was, in essence, no distinction between good and evil, that everything is and was exactly as it should be now and forever. It was the classic mystical experience.

I would continue to chase after that experience for many years after that. Although I knew it was drug induced, it had felt more real to me than anything I had experienced while sober. Certainly, more real than any experience religion had given me. But no matter how hard I chased (I probably took LSD or other psychedelics a dozen times after this) I never had this type of experience again.

When I came home to my parents the summer after my Sophomore year, I brought with me the books from my "Non-Western Philosophy" class, and all the ideas that went along with them. Just like when I was 16, my parents and I reverted to the familiar dance of "don't ask, don't tell" regarding our differences in religious beliefs. Apparently, however, the discovery of my books on Eastern Philosophy was more than my dad could bear. He told me he wanted them out of his house. I didn't argue, but immediately began making plans to leave and go back to Georgetown.

That summer was a messy blur of drinking and drug use. I worked for a while as a waiter, but eventually stopped going to work. I began dealing marijuana and LSD (and dipping into my own supply). One night, while high on both, I decided to take a leave of absence that fall semester, get a credit card, and go backpacking through Europe.

This was the fall of 1999, when rumors and fears surrounding the "Y2K" computer bug abounded. The concern arose from the realization that old computer systems, especially the old COBOL systems like the ones my dad worked on, had been devised in the 1960s when evidently there was no expectation their work would live on for another 40 years. They shortened the "year" field in their databases to two digits (e.g., "69" instead of "1969") in order to save on disk space.

The question that was on many people's minds in the year 1999 was what would happen when the calendar rolled over to 2000? No one knew for sure, and in fact there was likely to be multiple impacts – the severity of which would vary from one system, or one organization to the next. But the uncertainty gave rise to many wild theories about the upcoming apocalypse which would happen at the stroke of midnight. Ordinarily my parents would be the first on the bandwagon for any end of the world predictions, but perhaps because my dad was on the Y2K team at his company and was putting in long hours to fix the bug in his own systems, the problem for him was more practical than conspiratorial.

Nonetheless, there was something symbolic about the changing of the millennium that was on many people's minds, and I recall discussing it in vagaries with multiple travelers I met in Europe that fall. I remember being drunk on multiple bottles of wine I had shared with a fellow traveler in Verona. He didn't speak English, and I didn't speak Italian, but we both knew a little Spanish. I asked him, "The year 2000, do you think it's all going to fall apart?"

He responded: "I wouldn't mind."

My journey through Europe was, in many ways, a rite of passage for me. It gave me my first experience of being fully self-reliant (never mind the fact that the trip was funded with a credit card I had no intention of paying back.) In a little over 2 months, I traveled through seven countries, though most of my time was spent in the Netherlands and Italy. I missed most of the important tourist spots of the places I visited. Historical landmarks and museums took a backseat to long conversations with backpackers from all over the world, with whom I shared beers and tokes of hash around campfires. I remember feeling I had discovered my tribe, those who had dropped out of mainstream society (if only temporarily) who were in search of a deeper meaning and purpose in their lives. We decried the evils of the world: wars, capitalism, the McDonaldization of the globe. Of course, we had no solution other than to laugh, complain and drink some more.

My flight back to Texas landed in Houston, and I had no specific plans for how to get back to Georgetown. I decided to hitchhike. After all, I still had everything I needed to survive in my backpack – tent, sleeping bag, a flashlight, my journal and even a small bottle of wine I had brought back from Spain. While I felt I had grown significantly throughout my time in Europe, I had one last thing to prove. Could I be just as adventurous and self-reliant here in the United States?

My journey went fairly well. It didn't take me long to get my first ride, by a middle-aged Hispanic woman, who told me she felt sorry for me because I looked so small. It wasn't exactly a boost to my ego, but I was thankful for the ride. She went out of her way to take me farther than her commute would ordinarily allow. She confessed this would likely make her late for work, but she hated her job anyway. What she really wanted to do, she said, was start her own catering company. As she dropped me off, I told her she should quit her job and do it.

After that, a short ride by a working-class guy in a truck who was jealous of my life and my evident freedom and opened up to me about difficulties in his marriage. As he dropped me off, I told him he shouldn't stay in a marriage; that made him unhappy.

In retrospect, it is clear to me how egotistical I was. At age 20, everything was so simple to me. I saw the vast majority of the adults around me as just "sheep" who were following the rules, never questioning whether a different life was possible. Ultimately, I thought I was smarter. I couldn't understand the complexities of life, particularly the impact having children has upon one's life choices. The idea of self-sacrifice, of staying in a job one disliked, or even a marriage, for the good of one's children, was beyond my comprehension.

Eventually night fell and it was clear I wasn't going to make it all the way back to Georgetown. I left the highway and followed a country road to a wooded area. I hiked off the road some distance and set up my little tent, which by this point I could put up in a matter of minutes. I drank my wine and wrote in my journal by candlelight until I became too tired and went to sleep.

I made it back to Georgetown by mid-afternoon the next day, feeling victorious. I visited the registrar's office and signed up for the next semester. I was ready to resume my studies and progress toward graduate school. I felt stronger after my Europe trip, but I deeply missed the tribe of nomads I had left behind.

I went back to my parents' house for around a couple of months before the next semester started. We had more or less reconciled after the tumultuous summer. Not that they accepted the abandonment of my faith, but at least it was a stalemate. There seemed to be an unspoken agreement to not discuss it.

One evening I was watching the evening news with my parents and there was a breaking story out of Seattle. A state of emergency had been declared. Tens of thousands of protesters had descended upon the city to protest a meeting of the WTO. Widespread, coordinated acts of civil disobedience in the streets had forced the meetings to be canceled. Now there were riots in the street led by masked young people who called themselves anarchists, members of the "Black Bloc." I was transfixed. Who were these people? Was this the tribe I had been looking for? How had I not seen this coming? I had so many questions, and my search for answers would dominate the next 5 years of my life.

Chapter 3

The world did not end at midnight on January 1, 2000. And so I returned to college in the spring, beginning my Junior year. It felt like a new chapter was beginning in my life. Instead of returning to the dorms, my friend Alan and I got an apartment off-campus. I felt wiser, more mature. But I was also on a mission. The images I had seen from Seattle signified something; I was sure about that. But what, I couldn't say.

The internet had not yet become the omniscient source of all truth it is today, but it was possible to find some information. The first thing I wanted to understand was, where did all of these people come from? How had I been completely unaware such a massive event was happening, and more importantly, how could I become aware for the next time? As I sat in the computer lab on my college campus, querying search engines like Yahoo, Excite, even Google, I began to realize the answers were beneath my fingertips. The protests in Seattle against the WTO were the first large-scale action in the internet age, and technology had played a key part in bringing people together for those three pivotal days in November.

Not that all of the organizing took place on the internet – far from it. The type of "decentralized direct action" which took place in Seattle those fateful days required dozens of hands-on workshops, planning session, even rehearsals. These were coordinated by what were called "affinity groups," who sent representatives to "spokescouncil meetings." The culmination that was the Seattle protest was, therefore, the result of both online communication and offline meetings all across the country.

Buzzwords like "decentralized direct" action, "affinity groups," and "spokescouncil meetings" more or less flew over my head at that time. I was still trying to figure out what had happened, before I could wonder about how it had happened. As far as I could tell, the events in Seattle were divided into three distinct types. The first were the marches. These are what most people think about when they hear the word "protest." Organized by large, established environmental groups and labor unions, these marches consisted of thousands of people carrying signs, meeting up at a pre-arranged location, and "marching" along an established route which had been agreed upon with the city, and for which a permit had been obtained.

The second were the "direct actions." Otherwise known as "civil disobedience." These involved many fewer individuals than the marches, though still numbering at least a few thousand. Through a clandestine network of communication I would eventually learn about, these people had agreed to divide up all of the major intersections in downtown Seattle surrounding the convention center where the WTO meetings were being held. They constructed large tubes out of metal, PVC, chains, locks and duct tape – into which they inserted and interlocked their arms. They formed enormous chains across intersections which could not easily be broken. Some stood in long or circular chains, others sat and clustered in large groups. Sitting was more vulnerable, but also more difficult to penetrate by police. The scale and the timing of these actions were so effective, these activists ultimately could take the credit for what should have been the most important headline of the day's events: the canceling of the WTO meetings.

The third type, the one that actually took the headlines, were the actions of the "Black Bloc" anarchists. While police were distracted by the marches and civil disobedience taking place in other parts of the city, the anarchists (operating through a similar but far more clandestine network of communication) gathered in Seattle's posh shopping district. Wearing black hoodies, their faces covered with black bandanas or balaclavas, and armed with hammers, slingshots and baseball bats, they meandered through the shopping district menacingly. As they passed stores such as Starbucks, Nike and Gap, several participants would emerge from the crowd and shatter the storefront windows. They then disappeared back into the anonymous mob.

Like most Americans at this time, I had no way of understanding who these people were or what motivated them. "Anarchy" was a word almost without meaning to me. If pressed, I could not tell you the difference between "anarchism" and "terrorism," "madness" or "chaos." Anarchists, I supposed, were people who wanted to destroy everything, foment chaos and confusion, and turn the world into a burning, terrifying wasteland. Unfortunately, the images from Seattle did not serve to challenge my assumptions – at least, not at first.

In my searches online, I came across something of a manifesto written by some of the participants in the Black Bloc, called the "N30 Black Bloc Communique," which sought to clarify the motivations and philosophical underpinnings of their actions.

"We contend that property destruction is not a violent activity unless it destroys lives or causes pain in the process," they wrote. "By this definition, private property – especially corporate private property – is itself infinitely more violent than any action taken against it."

In essence, their property destruction was an act of protest against an "inherently violent" system of corporate private property, epitomized by large, multinational corporations such as Nike or Starbucks, who used their power to enslave workers in the form of low wage factory jobs ("sweatshops"), and also to destroy the environment in their insatiable need for natural resources.

I was not immediately convinced, but I was certainly intrigued. The communique was well-written, articulate and confident. I could not deny that considerably more thought had gone into what they had done than I had assumed. They mentioned a writer named John Zerzan, to whom many journalists had connected them. "A lot of rumors have been circulating that we are followers of John Zerzan, an anarcho-primitivist author from Eugene who advocates property destruction. While some of us may appreciate his writings and analyses, he is in no sense our leader, directly, indirectly, philosophically or otherwise." I had never heard of John Zerzan, but even the denial stoked in me a deep curiosity I would continue to chase for many years.

My curiosity aside, I still could not identify with the anarchists, whom I considered to be antithetical to the movement I had been searching for since I first heard the Woodstock soundtrack. The marchers, on the other hand, did not inspire me enough. The nonviolent protesters engaging in civil disobedience, blocking intersections and effectively shutting down the meetings, were – as Goldilocks would say – "just right."

Admittedly, it took me a little while to move from the what and how questions to the one most people would consider most crucial: why. These questions, and various degrees of answers, would come in time. But the truth was there was something drawing me on a subconscious level to this new movement. I never doubted justice was on their side. I understood there were generally two issues at stake – workers' rights and the environments. While I had never thought too much about these issues in my life up to that point, it didn't take much for me to get on board. I decided immediately that large, global organizations like the WTO were evil, and I would figure out why along the way.

Late in the semester, there was an article in the Megaphone (our school newspaper) about four students from our university who had traveled to DC for protests against the IMF and World Bank, which were holding meetings there. The protesters had hoped to plan a repeat of Seattle and shut down the event. An estimated 20,000 protesters descended upon DC. Like Seattle, many thousands marched, fewer thousands linked arms and formed blockades in the street, and an even smaller number caught the headlines by participating in the Black Bloc.

I read everything I could get my hands on regarding the protests against the IMF/World Bank, which protesters had dubbed "A16" for April 16. (Likewise, the heaviest actions in Seattle, which took place in November of the previous year, were referred to as "N30." This naming convention for major "actions" would continue for years.) While the protests in Seattle were my first indication of an underground movement, the protests in DC made me realize this was likely to become a recurring phenomenon, and I needed to get on board.

Chapter 4

Based on my research online, the next "action" seemed to be in Philadelphia during the Republican National Convention July 31–August 3. I wanted to go, but certainly not by myself. I wrote an email to the author of the Megaphone article, Dean, who had also been one of the four participants in DC. I asked him if he was planning to go to Philadelphia that summer for the RNC protests. He responded an hour later saying he had not heard about the protests, but that he absolutely wanted to go.

I met up with Dean that weekend at the Korouva Milk Bar. He was 2 years younger than me, still a Freshman at the time. He was tall and slim, but muscular. He had dark hair and eyebrows, tan skin and angular features. There was an air of intensity and seriousness about him that I detected immediately. Though he had a decidedly goofy side about him, I would not learn about that until much later. Our first meeting was all business.

He gave me a more in-depth analysis of A16 and why, in his opinion, it had not been successful. Like me, he was fully on board with those engaging in nonviolent civil disobedience, particularly the blockades. He believed the goal of these "convergences" should be to physically prevent the meetings from taking place, not merely to march for miles in the heat while holding signs and repeating chants. But he also disagreed with the actions of the Black Bloc, whose menacing appearance and violent actions served mainly to undermine the objectives of the majority of the protesters who believed in nonviolence.

"Still," he conceded, "I have to admit it was pretty great to see them come to the rescue at one point. We were linked up across an intersection and a group of motorcycle police were heading toward us. All of a sudden, about a hundred or so anarchists came up a side street and started dragging dumpsters and newspaper stands into the street, blocking the police from reaching us. Then they ran the other way, and the police chased after them." I couldn't help but smile as I imagined this.

I hadn't had very much interaction with the police up to this point in my life, and honestly the idea of confronting them in street protests made me nervous. On the other hand, the way Dean described their interactions with police made them seem like obvious villains. They fired tear gas to clear the streets, pepper spray to break up blockades, batons to subdue the more aggressive protesters resisting arrest. I was, like everyone else, aware of the way police in the past had beaten protesters during the Civil Rights movement and anti-war protests of the 1960s. I had also heard my dad use the word "pigs" to describe them. But somehow, I thought those days were long behind us. Based on Dean's descriptions, they seemed to have picked up right where they left off.

"It's a police state," Dean said matter-of-factly. "I don't even think the police realize it themselves, but they are cogs in a larger machine. They are protecting the interests of the corporate elites. They are the ones who are really in charge."

We talked more about the "big picture" behind what was motivating the protests. It came down to this. The "elites" were essentially the capitalist class of ultra-wealthy individuals who used the mechanism of multinational corporations to circumvent any and all restrictions on their expansion of power and wealth. Organizations like the WTO existed solely to serve the interests of these corporations, knocking down what they termed "barriers to trade": especially environmental regulations and labor laws. The WTO made it possible for large corporations to clear-cut forests, dump their byproducts in the water and air, and build sweatshops where workers were paid ten cents an hour and forced to work long hours – all in the name of profit. PEOPLE BEFORE PROFIT became a rallying cry of the "anti-globalization" movement.

As for the two major political parties, the Republicans and

Democrats, it was the same story. The very same corporations contributed heavily to both parties, essentially a big game of roulette where they were betting on "red" and "black," and could not lose. Dean told me about the Green Party, which was also putting forth a presidential candidate, Ralph Nader. He believed the Green Party was the only ethical choice for the 2000 election. This analysis of the two-party system helped me make sense of my participation in the upcoming RNC protests, even though my decision had already been made.

Dean and I quickly became best friends, going to parties together and having political, philosophical conversations late into the night over beers and joints. We enjoyed a shared sense of being part of history, and the word "revolution" began to be thrown around. A real belief was growing within us that we were part of a turning point in world history, where all of the oppressed people in the world, supported by activists in high income countries like ourselves, would overthrow the global capitalist system and put in its place...we weren't exactly sure. We weren't communists, so the future worker paradise described by Marx was not something we could grasp. But we felt intrinsically that a new world where people lived in a cooperative, equitable society built in harmony with nature was somehow possible.

We learned that a group called the Campaign to End the Death Penalty from Austin, TX was sending a contingent to Philadelphia and was offering seats on a rented van for $50 apiece, so Dean and I signed up. The van would be picking us up in Dean's hometown of Waco, TX, about an hour north of Austin. I came to Waco a few days early to hang out with Dean. Early in the day before the van would pick us up that afternoon, Dean and I climbed up to a treehouse in his backyard. He and his brother had built it with their dad when they were kids. I was impressed with its size and stability. We sat cross-legged across from one another and said a prayer to the "universe," or the "Great Spirit," asking for guidance and direction for our journey. We sealed the agreement with a few tokes of marijuana from a handmade wooden pipe.

We shared a sense of spiritual purpose and direction in our lives, although neither of us subscribed to a strict religious view of any kind. I had shared with Dean the mystical experience I had on LSD, and he shared similar experiences with me. We had no particular beliefs but were especially open to Native-American spirituality. After all, Winona Duke, the Native-American environmental activist, was Ralph Nader's running mate.

We met up with the van just off the highway in Waco, Texas – the parking lot of Elite Cafe (famous for the fact that Elvis Presley once dined there). A motley group piled out of the van to stretch their legs as we loaded our belongings into the back. There was a young hippy couple with long dreadlocks, wearing free flowing light fabric clothes. There was an elderly lady traveling alone. There was another guy who just looked like Tom Cruise. And another guy with long black hair and thick glasses. He approached us.

"Hi, I'm Mike, with the ISO."

"Who?" I asked. He grimaced slightly. I felt like I had offended him.

"The International Socialist Organization. Haven't you seen our paper?" It was then that I realized he had a stack of newspapers in his hand. He handed me one.

"They're normally a dollar, but you can have this one for free."

I thanked him and looked at the paper. It was called the Socialist Worker. I supposed he was a communist. Am I a communist, I asked myself? I wasn't sure. I had certainly been exposed to Marxism in my classes. I remember being surprised the first time I read Marx for myself. Like most Americans, the name Karl Marx was synonymous with Fidel Castro, Saddam

Hussein or the Devil. But when I read his actual words, I found only a careful, thorough and meticulous thinker. I could not find fault with his analysis of the way in which the peasant class in Europe had been intentionally displaced and forced into the cities to become factory workers. Manipulation and inequality throughout history was a fact. There were winners and losers, and obviously the winners – the landowners, the factory owners, the wealthy and powerful – were well situated to pull the levers of the engine of society to ensure their power continued. I also knew that without Marx, workers would never have felt empowered to band together in labor unions and fight for their rights. It seemed to literally be the only reason conditions had improved for workers since the Industrial Revolution. It was Marx's vision for a future society where things got fuzzy for me, and in this way, I was certainly in good company. A society where the "workers" reigned supreme sounded well and good, but I also believed people would be people. I had also read Animal Farm, after all, and knew a little about what had happened in Soviet Russia.

I had plenty of time to ponder all of this during the very long drive to Philadelphia. We discussed Socialism, the Republicans, the Democrats, the Green Party, globalization, the Death Penalty, and finally grew sick of talking. There didn't seem to be any issue we could all agree upon, other than that we didn't like the status quo. Some of us believed a revolution was necessary, while others were still firmly committed to working within the current system.

It was nearly impossible to sleep. It was a 24-hour drive, but there were no stops. At one point, the van was winding through some mountain roads in Virginia and James Taylor was playing on the radio. It was dark outside, and a sense of calm tranquility filled the van as everyone became silent. I began to doze off, sweet melodies forming the shape of my dreams. Suddenly the driver switched on the CD, and the honey smooth James Taylor was at once replaced with a full-throated, screaming punk band. We were all fully awake again, and unhappier with the status quo than we had ever been before.

Dean and I were looking forward to getting to Philadelphia and saying goodbye to this group. It was a cheap ride to Philadelphia, but we would be returning via Greyhound. The Campaign to End the Death Penalty only planned to participate on the first day at the "Unify 2000" march and then return to Texas – before the convention even started. Dean and I felt this group were pretty lame, but it was a means to an end. We couldn't comprehend the need to get back to jobs and families. Not when the revolution was at stake.

We were meeting up with two other students from our university who were arriving in Philadelphia before us. There was Isaac. Isaac had been with Dean at A16. He was still a shadowy, intriguing figure to me at this time. The first time I saw him on campus, he was smoking cigarettes with some friends while engaged in what seemed to be a deep conversation. He had a dark blue Mohawk. His entire body seemed to be chiseled out of wood, with broad shoulders. He had an intense, intimidating gaze – soft blue eyes beneath a drooping brow. The first time I made eye contact with him, I immediately averted my gaze. I saw a black anarchy symbol tattooed on his vascular forearm. I was scared of him but wanted to know him. I wanted to be on his side. There was also Valerie, the complete opposite. She was in my class and was one of the first people I had met during my Freshman year in college. She had black hair curled in tight ringlets and porcelain skin. She wore glasses and beamed intelligence. She was a pre-med student. She had not come to Philadelphia to "fuck shit up," but to take a stand for mainstream liberal values.

When the van finally arrived in Philadelphia, we couldn't get out fast enough. Dean and I asked them to drop us off at the first major intersection downtown. We found a pay phone and called the number to "City Hostel" where we were staying with Isaac and Valerie. Dean inquired about whether our friends had arrived yet. "Uh, yeah, the guy with the anarchy tattoo? He's here," the receptionist replied dryly. We got directions and then headed to the nearest subway station.

By this point Dean and I had enough travel experience between us that learning the new subway system was not difficult. We purchased one-way tickets and hopped on the blue line. We both wore backpacks and felt dirty alongside the other passengers. I wondered if they knew we were protesters. This was my first taste of feeling like an invader in an unknown city, a feeling that was at first uncomfortable but would soon become addictive.

We exited at 2nd Street and walked about a block before arriving at City House Hostel. It was a narrow, 4-story red brick building nestled between shops on either side. We rang a little replica of the "liberty bell" and a few moments later were buzzed in. We walked into the lobby where Isaac and Valerie were waiting for us. We exchanged hugs.

"Are you guys ready?" Isaac asked.

We all smiled and nodded, making eye contact with one another – unsure of the meaning of the question, which felt especially weighty coming from Isaac. Based on what we knew about the last protest in DC, not to mention Seattle, there were certainly going to be some surprises in store. We just didn't know what, when or where. Still relatively new to the scene, Isaac and Dean knew a bit more than me, but not much. We heard there was a "convergence center" at the American Friends Center. Quakers. It was the first Quaker community in the United States. In my mind, I imagined the man in the pilgrim hat on a box of Quaker Oats. What did they have to do with any of this?

"I'm just here to protest," Valerie interjected. "I'm not planning to get into any trouble."

"We may not have a choice in the matter," Isaac suggested darkly.

"As long as we follow orders and follow the parade routes agreed upon with the city, we should be fine," Valerie asserted confidently.

We went around in circles about this for a little while. On the spectrum, Valerie seemed to be the closest to the "change the system from within" end. Isaac seemed intentionally cryptic in his language, but from what I was gathering, he held the opposite view. That is, the system cannot be reformed. It must be torn down completely and rebuilt from scratch. Revolution. Dean and I were still trying to gain our footing, but Isaac's narrative certainly seemed more intriguing.

After depositing our belongings in the men's common room (the hostel was divided by gender into large communal rooms with bunk beds), we began making our way back to the metro station. We were headed for the "Unify 2000" march, the first demonstration of the week. A permit had been granted by the city of Philadelphia (reluctantly) for an estimated 20,000 people.

We took the metro to 30th Street station, near where the march was set to begin. As soon as we exited the station, protesters were everywhere. There were plenty of young people wearing bandanas around their necks. Bandanas had become something of a symbol in and of themselves since Seattle. Black bandanas were worn by the anarchists to protect their identity, but bandanas of all colors were worn by other protesters as either a symbol of solidarity or a possible makeshift gas mask. The folk knowledge at this time was that a bandana soaked in apple cider vinegar could help neutralize the effects of tear gas. And red bandanas were sometimes worn in solidarity with the Zapatistas in Mexico, who on New Year's Day 1994 had led an uprising in the state of Chiapas, coinciding with the implementation of NAFTA, a precursor to the WTO. Of course, most of this was not known to me at the time. I tied a blue bandana around my neck, if nothing else, to fit in.

There were large puppets everywhere constructed of papier mâché, including an 80-foot monster called "Corpzilla." There were a group called "Billionaires for Bush (Or Gore)" who dressed in fancy suits and dresses, the men smoking cigars and the women drinking from martini glasses. They held a banner that read: "Because Inequality Isn't Growing Fast Enough." One moment I heard what sounded like a marching band and turned to get my first glimpse of the infamous "Black Bloc," a group of young people wearing all black, their faces covered in black bandanas and balaclavas. Their "anarchist marching band" followed behind a large black banner that read: "WHOEVER THEY VOTE FOR, WE ARE UNGOVERNABLE." I found their appearance to be at once frightening and electrifying.

The march itself got underway an hour or so later, and I found it to be something of an anti-climax. We chanted, we carried signs, we marched for what felt like a mile in the summer heat. Police were everywhere, wearing matching baby blue and cordoning all sides of the march on bicycles and horseback. They were certainly intimidating, but less so than the all-black "Darth Vader-esque" images I had seen in the footage from Seattle. Maybe that comes later, I thought.

The following day, Monday, was the actual start of the Republican National Convention. Valerie returned to school, as did the group from Austin we had arrived with. Those who remained did so mainly to find ways to participate in the disruption of the convention. The main event of the day was the Kensington Welfare Rights Union. Unlike the Unity 2000 march the day before, there was no permit for this event. There was a moment of uncertainty as the crowd swelled about whether we could be "permitted" to march at all. I wondered what would happen. There were thousands of people gathered in the hot sun, many black-masked anarchists included.

The police decided to grant us two lanes on the street. We

wound through downtown in a long, tight column, with police bordering both sides of the march every step of the way, not granting a single inch. I tried keeping up with the chants and songs around me. The overall message was that the poor were left behind by Republican politicians.

The march seemed to end in an empty parking lot, a seemingly greater anti-climax than the one I had experienced the day before. The protesters around me seemed to share in my disappointment, meandering aimlessly, signs drooping beneath their waists. Suddenly there was an announcement made from a megaphone from somewhere in the crowd. I could not hear who was speaking, or even what they said, but the directionless crowd began to reform a direction. I heard someone murmur that we were headed toward Franklin Park.

The police seemed slow to respond. Whereas moments before we had been corralled on all sides, now they seemed to have been left behind us. We marched only a few blocks before we turned a corner and I saw the convention center. A massive banner read: "Philadelphia welcomes you to the 2000 Republican National Convention." A fence surrounded the area, but other than that, nothing stood between us and the building. We came right up to the fence, and Isaac suddenly sprang into action. His face covered in a black bandana, he began pulling up the chain-link to create an opening. It was happening – we were going to get into the convention!

The only problem was that Isaac acted alone. Somehow the Black Bloc was nowhere to be seen. Other protesters watched him with amusement, but no one, not even me or Dean, stepped up to join him. It seemed like seconds later that a black police van appeared, and a phalanx of riot police emerged. They rushed to the fence and zeroed in on Isaac. "Step away from the fence!" an officer bellowed behind a plexiglass face shield. Isaac looked around him and just then observed what the rest of us had already seen – no one else shared his courage. He wisely backed away.

The energy of the crowd quickly diminished, and we became an aimless mob once again. We waited for a while, but it soon became clear the protesters were dispersing. Our spirits sinking, they were momentarily revived when we saw a pair of familiar faces: Haulden and Lucia, who had ridden on the van with us all the way from Austin. Although we had barely spoken the entire 20-hour slog, they now seemed like old friends. We exchanged warm smiles and big hugs.

"I thought you guys were headed back already!"

"Nah man," Haulden said, "We couldn't leave! Not after yesterday, that just pissed me off. Police herding us like cattle. I wish I had my machete, I'd whack one of those pigs in the back of their kneecaps. Shit's just getting started."

My eyes widened at his violent statements. At the same time, I was intrigued by it. Was he serious?

"I have to admit, this isn't quite what I was expected," I admitted cautiously.

"Don't worry, man, I've been talking to some people. Shit's really about to go down. Tomorrow, man, that's when it's really going down."

They invited us to join them as they headed back to the American Friends Center. Located on the corner of Cherry and 15th, this red brick building was set back from the road and was surrounded by a tall metal fence on all sides.

We walked through the front gate into a sizable courtyard. Protesters were everywhere, sitting and talking in the sun, sharing snacks, making signs, holding impromptu meetings. The entrance to the building had a sign that read "PLACE OF SANCTUARY." I was amazed by how safe I suddenly felt.

Inside, we nourished ourselves on hot tea and coffee and peanut butter and jelly sandwiches. I felt so good I began making conversation with one of the women who was working there, preparing sandwiches. I somehow found myself opening up to this woman, sharing intimate details of my own life.

"I was raised in an evangelical, fundamentalist Christian household. I honestly could not imagine any of the churches I went to opening their doors to protesters."

"The Quakers have always been on the side of social justice," she said. "Quakers were among the earliest to advocate for the abolition of slavery. They were heavily involved in the Underground Railroad. They fought for women's right to vote, and prison reform. We are not here to judge, but to help. To be a friend to the friendless."

Listening to her speak warmed something inside me. I realized how little I knew about the world, and despite my major in college, how little I knew about history.

Dean approached me with a sandwich still in his hand, his mouth half-full.

"Hey man, Haulden and Lucia are going over to the IMC if you want to come with. They said they've been volunteering there, and they could use some help."

"What is the IMC?"

"The Independent Media Center. IndyMedia."

I had heard of it. I was pretty sure I had come across the website during my online research. I didn't know what it was about, but of course I didn't have any other plans.

Haulden, Lucia, Dean, Isaac and I walked several blocks before reaching what appeared to be an abandoned building. There was a black sign outside with a logo displaying a lowercase "i" with radio waves emanating from the dot. Disheveled looking activists, many with bandanas tied around their necks, were entering and leaving the building – some holding cameras, others spiral notepads.

As we approached the entrance, a couple of crusty punks approached us. They were wearing all black, with numerous homemade patches covering their pants and hoodies. They read "Food Not Bombs," "Eat the Rich," and "People Before

Profits." The guy had plugs in his ear lobes about the diameter of a nickel, and the woman a barbel bisecting her septum. Their hair was wild, seemingly a random pattern of long and shaved sections. They were not physically intimidating by any means, but I still felt nervous in their presence.

They asked to see our badges. Haulden and Lucia had them, but the rest of us did not. Haulden told them he could "vouch" for us. I wondered what that meant. They instructed us to walk inside and go directly to the registration desk. Inside was a beehive of activity. There were signs everywhere talking about "Security Culture," listing "Do's" and "Don'ts." "DO ask for a warrant," "DON'T talk to police." "DO ask to speak to your lawyer." Also ubiquitous was a phone number for something called the "R2K Legal Collective." We began noticing many around us had this phone number written in sharpie on their forearms. The atmosphere in the building felt generally paranoid, as though they were expecting a raid at any moment. It was exhilarating.

An attractive young woman with blonde dreadlocks greeted us not too warmly at the registration desk. She was wearing a badge with the name "Firefly." Dean, thinking on his toes, informed her we were writers for our college newspaper, and that we would like to help in any way we could. This was close to true. He had written about his experience at A16 for the Megaphone, and I had written a couple of editorials myself, albeit unrelated to politics. Isaac kept quiet. I was not quite sure he was even enrolled at the moment (an uncertainty that would linger for years.) She seemed actually delighted to learn we were writers, and Dean's brief description of his experiences in DC seemed to convince her of our authenticity. We were issued "IMC" badges and directed to a computer station.

"Here we have spreadsheets of all of the actions taking place this week. The ones that have been highlighted are already being covered. There is contact info associated with each action, so you can call the number indicated to find more information. You can use this computer to write the article and submit it to be published on the Philly IndyMedia website. We also have a physical paper this week that we are distributing daily around the city. Let me know if you have questions!"

We thanked Firefly for her help, and each sat down at a computer to start reviewing the spreadsheets. I saw one for a "Mumia" action taking place the next day. Unlike some of the other events, there was no time or place listed. I picked up a phone next to the computer and dialed the number listed. A young woman answered.

"This line is not secure. Can I help you?" I was puzzled by the greeting, but I pressed on.

"Hi there, I am calling about the Mumia action." She sounded immediately perturbed.

"You'll have to come to the meeting tomorrow. Are you with an affinity group?" I wasn't sure what this meant.

"Um, I'm with the IMC." This did not help matters.

"If you are with IndyMedia then you should know the media is not permitted to be present at planning meetings. We will call in a tip just before the action occurs. Thank you!" Click.

This was not going well. I glanced over at Dean, who was still scanning his own spreadsheet. Isaac had left the computer and had apparently found the free coffee. He was drinking a cup while conversing with a couple of guys on the other side of the room. I wondered what they were talking about. I felt totally lost and out of my element.

Finally, my thoughts were interrupted by a man in the center of the room who called for everyone's attention. He was holding several bundles of a small newspaper which had the same "IndyMedia" logo I had seen outside the building printed on the front-page banner. He was looking for volunteers to make "drop offs" around the city. Dean and I immediately volunteered, happy to finally have a job. We were each handed a stack and a piece of paper listing local businesses and addresses. Suddenly rejuvenated, we headed out. Isaac stayed back to continue his conversation.

It was something like a scavenger hunt, navigating the still unfamiliar city, locating addresses and scratching them off after each drop off. We distributed papers to coffee shops, bookstores and even some restaurants. We were also allowed to hand out papers to anyone on the street who wanted one. It did not take me long to figure out that the better dressed a person, the less likely they were to accept a paper.

The big headline in the paper that day was a raid of a warehouse in West Philly where activists had been constructing puppets to be used in protests that week. Claiming the protesters were constructing weapons, police carried out a SWAT-style raid on the warehouse, arresting 75 activists and confiscating props and supplies. According to the article, this was a clear and obvious infringement on the activists' First Amendment rights, a suppression of free speech and a coordinated attempt to crush dissent. I was astonished. Despite my innate skepticism, I had still come to Philadelphia with a basic faith in the democratic system. It was surprising, to say the least, to learn that such an obvious violation of free speech could take place in this day and age. A raid like this couldn't possibly be an accident, the result of one or two "bad apples" in the police department. It must have been planned in advance, preceded by intelligence gathering, and approved at the highest levels of the city government – if not beyond.

The next day, after Dean, Isaac and I had breakfast at the American Friends Center, we got word about the time and place of the Mumia Action. I was still deeply curious about what was being planned after the mysterious phone conversation the day before, which felt like something out of a suspense movie. We went to the intersection that had been passed to us by word of mouth, at the appointed time, 1pm. There were a couple of dozen people milling about, but like us, they seemed to have no idea what was going on. After about an hour, nothing happened, and people began leaving. I began to worry that the protests were losing momentum. Had everyone just gone home?

Not knowing what to do, or where else to go, we began wandering back to the American Friends Center. As we got closer, we began to hear some commotion on 15th Street. We looked and saw a mass of black-clad anarchists marching toward us. They held large black banners spray-painted with white writing "SMASH THE STATE" and the anarchy symbol on either side. Others flew large black and red flags, which hung from strikingly sturdy wooden "poles" the approximate thickness of police batons. They shouted, chanted and drummed. Their faces were covered with black bandanas or balaclavas. My heart thumped with excitement. After a quick glance at one another, but without a word, Dean, Isaac and I gathered our belongings and rushed to join them.

The crowd quickly swelled to a few hundred. I began noticing helicopters overhead. I heard sirens in the distance, which grew louder. I saw a police car pull into the intersection ahead and come to a stop. Fear rose as a lump in my throat. The crowd swarmed around the police car. I saw someone pull a can of spray paint from his backpack and paint an anarchy symbol on the hood of the car. The next thing I heard was shattering glass as one of the "flag poles" was used to smash the rear windshield. The police officer in the driver's seat seemed to cower in fear as we continued our progress, completely unencumbered. I was either unwilling, or unable, to process the rightness or wrongness of what I had just witnessed. I just felt more powerful than I ever had in my entire life. The feeling was totally intoxicating.

It was the complete reversal of what I had experienced in the previous two marches. The police seemed utterly powerless to stop us. Each time a police car emerged, we simply went around. When a line of bicycle cops attempted to barricade the street, we poured through them. We wound through downtown Philadelphia like a raucous black snake. I saw protesters dragging newspaper stands throughout the street to stop the pursuit of the police behind us. At one point, I saw another protester grab a full, black trash bag off the sidewalk and tear it open, dumping the trash on the street. I felt a little confused about what the point of this could possibly be.

Eventually we made a full circle and arrived back on 15th Street where we had first joined the march. It was at this point I saw protesters emerging from seemingly all directions. Most of them, however, were not anarchists. A few were wearing bandanas, but most were not. They looked like college students, like me. They began linking arms and blockading the intersections. Now police were everywhere, mostly arriving on bicycles. They wore large bundles of zip ties on their belts. Systematically, they began arresting those who were blockading the streets. Large buses arrived and the protesters were loaded onto them. It seemed this had all been planned in advance. Some altercations broke out as some of the anarchists attempted to intervene in the arrests. The boldest of them were singled out and subdued by police. They too had their hands zip tied behind them and were loaded onto the bus.

There was a moment when I, too, considered joining the blockade. But why? The scene unfolding before me was similar to what I understood about Seattle only in the most superficial sense. In Seattle, the blockades were strategic and strong. Human bodies were linked together with elaborately constructed "lock boxes" that could only be dismantled with significant time and effort by the fire department. This had resulted in real, actual disruption. These "blockades," on the other hand, were flimsy and yielding. I watched as protesters joined the human chain, only to be pulled away and arrested seconds later. I supposed it was symbolic, but what exactly did it symbolize? Nobility, or stupidity?

Having avoided arrest (we learned over 400 had been arrested that day), Isaac and I regrouped at the hostel and recounted the day's events over a couple of cheap malt liquors. While I had considered myself to be mainly an observer, Isaac had gotten more physically involved.

"I unarrested a dude," he said anxiously as he took a drag from his cigarette.

"Unarrest?" I asked. "What does that mean?"

"What does it sound like? The police grabbed an anarchist and were starting to arrest him. For some reason, I didn't even think about it. I rushed forward and grabbed him, dragging him out of the police's hands and back into the crowd. Once we got back into the Black Bloc, the police were too scared to pursue us."

This was the whole point of the "Black Bloc," I began to understand. Safety in numbers. And the identical black garb and face masks were another kind of safety. One person could emerge from the crowd and smash a window, let's say, and then become immediately reabsorbed. The more identical each person dressed, the more difficult it would be for the police to single out the offender. Their only choice would be to arrest the entire crowd, which was usually quite difficult to achieve.

Dean arrived later, full of zeal. He was speaking quickly, telling us there was an all-night vigil happening at Franklin Park, which was just across the street from "Roundhouse," the police headquarters where the protesters were being held. He said the jailed protesters were being hogtied and beaten. I was astonished, just as I had been when I first learned of the puppet warehouse raid. Was this America? It was a question I was starting to feel silly for asking. Dean insisted we needed to go to the vigil. Although I was reluctant at first (a part of me preferred to stick with Isaac and drink malt liquor) I ultimately could not resist Dean's sense of urgency. Isaac, however, stayed back to do some writing. He was clearly shaken up by the day's experiences and needed some time to process.

We took the subway most of the distance, but Dean wanted to buy some bread, peanut butter and jelly so we could make sandwiches to contribute to the vigil. We stopped a few blocks before Franklin Park, near Chinatown, and found a grocery store. As we walked toward the park, I noticed rain clouds forming overhead. I wondered if the vigil would be canceled if it rained.

There were at least two, maybe three hundred people gathered in the park. There were tents set up, including one that was designated for food. We contributed our sandwich supplies, placing them among the piles of fruit, granola bars and bottles of water scattered inside. While I was in there, I grabbed a handful of trail mix for myself. I decided to explore the park.

There were no cops to be seen – not in the park, not even along the perimeter. This was yet another puzzling discovery. If we had been considered so dangerous during the day, attracting hundreds of police to cover even a few dozen of us on the streets, why were we being completely left alone at night? In any case, I loved the feeling of this small community that had emerged. There was something familiar about it. There was just so much activity. There were several circles of people talking. Others were engaged in setting up more tents or tarps. And in the middle of it all, a large drum circle. The sound was entrancing, tribal in its feel, not one but many overlapping beats, yet all working in harmony. Several girls in flowy skirts danced. It was a mix of drums and other percussive sounds I couldn't identify.

"Hey, could you lend me a hand?" A guy wearing a hoodie and brown Carharts was holding the corner of a large tarp and held a couple of wooden poles in his hand. I grabbed another corner, taking one of the poles from him. He also handed me some string. Along with a couple of other volunteers, not sharing any plan – or perhaps any experience – we somehow managed to set up a temporary upright structure to provide additional protection from the rain. Judging by the rumbling sounds in the distance, it might be coming any minute.

I wanted to join the drum circle, but of course I didn't have a drum. I had never actually seen a drum circle, much less participated in one. Still, the attraction was irresistible. I wandered my way closer to the center and sat down. It felt as though we were all seated around a campfire, but there was no fire – at least, none that was visible. I picked up a couple of rocks on the ground and attempted to strike them together in coordination with the larger rhythm around me. It was a pleasant sound, and to my surprise it actually seemed to fit with the multi-layered drum beat.

This continued for some time. The rhythm meandered, sometimes slowing, sometimes accelerating. There was no communication between the drummers, or rather, the music was the communication. I heard the sound of my two rocks striking together, which echoed through the trees in the park, but somehow echoed much deeper – against the walls in the deepest recesses of my mind. For the first time in my life, I had found what I had been looking for. I was no longer isolated; I was a part of something bigger.

My time around the drum circle was an emotional, peak experience of sorts. Here I was surrounded by complete strangers, and yet we were united by a common purpose, a common vision. For each of us, this vision had been cultivated in many different ways, throughout our lives. In moments of sadness, anger, fear and, most of all, isolation, we had longed for a community of people who shared a desire to fight together for a cause. We didn't know what cause. In a way, it could be any cause, as long as we truly believed we were on the side of justice.

We stayed there all night, neither Dean nor I sleeping at all.

The next day, the media arrived. It all began to feel a bit unreal. Most of us in the park refused interviews. Dean, however, somehow got caught up in a morning "shock jock" interview. Speaking over a cell phone, Dean heard every word he said being mocked by a crew of disk jockeys. As he passionately relayed the cause for which we had all gathered, everything from social justice, the corporate corruption of the political system, to the mistreatment of the jailed activists, he was answered by clown horns and noisemakers. He felt like he had become the laughingstock of Philadelphia's early morning commute.

If that wasn't bad enough, some of the other activists gathered in the park, who were similarly sleep deprived, witnessed his conversation on the cell phone. They somehow came to the conclusion that Dean was an undercover cop. He was confronted with this accusation, and Dean became unhinged. His first reaction was to bring his accuser to me. I didn't know what was happening at the time, but when Dean asked me: "Am I a cop!?" I just laughed and said no. The guy standing next to him with long dreadlocks was unconvinced.

The problem for Dean (which was really more of a problem for the activist scene as a whole, then and now) was that he didn't "look" the part. Everything from the way he dressed, to the way his hair was cut, seemed mainstream. He was also handsome, with almost movie star good looks. I was somewhere in the middle – not yet a total crusty punk, but alternative enough to pass with my unkempt goatee, gray T-shirt and corduroy bell bottoms. It fundamentally bothered me that this community, which I considered to be united by ideals, could fall victim to the most superficial of judgments – fashion. It was a pass to entry that was not only meaningless, but laughably easy to imitate.

Eventually this incident fizzled out, and Dean's accusers moved on. We had a rather uneventful day at the park, except for the fact that the police presence was steadily increasing. A few of the activists were released from jail after "citing out," meaning they had given their names and were released with an agreement to return for their court date. The majority, however, were practicing jail solidarity. This was the same strategy the jailed protesters had used successfully in Seattle, where all activists refused to give their names (and were careful to not have any identification in their possession at the time of their arrest) and all demanded a trial by jury. As it was explained to me, this strategy exploited a vulnerability in the criminal justice system. Prosecutors would ultimately prefer to release all protesters, even ones who had never given their names, rather than deal with the overwhelming workload of hundreds of individual trials by jury. The trade-off was that the protesters had to remain in "solidarity," being willing to remain in jail for days or even weeks, even if their actual "crime" would have merited no more than a small fine or community service.

Word spread that the American Friends Service Committee was holding a candlelight vigil at the park that evening, followed by a march back to the meeting house. Most of us figured this was simply a compromise they had made with the police, since there had been rumors spreading that the police were on the verge of forcibly evicting us. At dusk, dozens of members of the Quaker community arrived with bundles of small white candles they distributed among the rest of us. For the most part, the Quakers were very average looking people, mostly in their middle ages or older. I wondered if I had seen one of them on the street a couple of days before, whether I would have bothered to hand them a newspaper. I noticed their ability to move freely between social groups, chatting up a crowd of gutter punks one moment, the police the next, each interaction seeming to be as genuine as the next.

The weather was making a turn for the worse, storm clouds rumbling overhead. Lighters were passed around and we lit the candles. But soon it was raining. Many of us made an effort to keep the candles lit by guarding the flames with our hands, but the downpour only intensified. After my candle went out three or four times, I gave up. It felt like defeat, a feeling that was solidified by the sound of the police announcement on our bullhorn ordering us to leave the park. If it weren't for the presence of the Quakers, we might have resisted. There was something calming about their energy, something mature and deep. I considered the fact that this moment, for them, was only the tip of a long line of struggle dating back centuries. It was, for them, a marathon rather than a sprint.

We marched back several blocks to the meeting house, escorted by police on all sides. It was reminiscent of the Kensington Welfare Rights Union march days before. We had come full circle. The Quakers led the crowd with various songs of resistance dating back to the Civil Rights era, but I was too depressed to join in. Finally, we reached our destination, and hundreds of us filed into the American Friends Service center, and ultimately into the original meeting house. It was like a church, but with no altar or pulpit. The room was filled with church pews, the ones in the center flat, the others around the perimeter raised like sports bleachers. More pews were on a second level. All of them faced the center of the room.

As everyone settled into the room, some standing, others taking a seat on the pews, an older woman with gray hair pinned back into a bun asked for our attention.

"We want to remind you that this is a place of worship, so we ask all of you to respect our space. We realize the past few days have been rough, but we would like to offer our message of love. The police are not our enemy. We are all human beings, and we are all equally deserving of love. That is what we want to offer you tonight. We have prepared a hot meal for all of you in the next room. After you have eaten, you are all welcome to sleep here tonight."

While several groaned at the words "the police are not our enemy," the mention of hot food seemed to raise everyone's spirits. I ate two plates of spaghetti and garlic bread, and two full glasses of lemonade. Dean and I took them up on their offer to sleep in the meeting house. I curled up on one of the hard-wooden pews, wondering if I would be able to sleep. I didn't wonder long.

Chapter 5

The next day, Dean and I took a Greyhound bus back to Texas, a journey that lasted over 20 hours. We talked, slept, talked and slept some more. At the tail end of our experience in Philadelphia, we learned that another protest of similar size and scope was happening in a little over a week, on the other side of the country. The protests at the Democratic National Convention in Los Angeles.

While the majority of Americans, then and now, considered the Republicans and Democrats to be polar opposites on the political spectrum, it was commonly understood by those of us in the emerging "anti-globalization" movement that these two parties were really two sides of the same coin. This was the reasoning behind the "Billionaires for Bush (or Gore)" protesters we had seen in Philadelphia, who were now continuing on to Los Angeles. The same multinational corporations who were pushing for "trade liberalization" – the lowering of labor and environmental regulations in the pursuit of profit – were also lobbying both political parties. While the Republicans and Democrats made a big show of holding their own side of the "culture war" issues – abortion, taxes, immigration – the real agenda driving the global economy was the one neither side mentioned. Whoever won the election in 2000, the agenda of profits before people would inevitably prevail.

I returned to my summer job at the physical plant at the university, experiencing something akin to culture shock. My recent experiences in Philadelphia had been utter sensory overload. I had experienced joy, confusion, serenity and fear – all in a matter of a few days. What I had stepped into did not seem like a one-time event. It was an ongoing battle, a parallel narrative taking place alongside the mundane life I had been living. The protesters did not seem like ordinary people like me who had just taken a few days off work to participate in an event. They felt like a different type of people, a different tribe, who had committed their lives to this purpose. And now they were migrating across the country to Los Angeles. The urge to join them was nearly impossible to suppress.

I sat in the break room in the physical plant building sipping coffee as the news played on the TV. There was a breaking story that had just taken place in Los Angeles at the Apple Building. Some intrepid activists had scaled a nearby crane and dropped a massive banner displaying the "Corporate Flag of America." The flag looked just like the American flag, but in place of the white stars on the blue background were corporate logos. Nike, McDonalds, NBC, etc. The commentators mentioned the Democratic National Convention was only days away, and massive protests were expected. I decided then and there, with less than $100 in my bank account, that I was going.

I found a ride board online, and it only took me a few minutes to find a posting by a guy in Austin who was planning to travel to Los Angeles and was looking for passengers to share the expenses with. His name was Dale. I gave him a call and he was thrilled. He, too, was going to the protests.

Shortly after I let Isaac know about my plans, I got a call from Maggie, who had just recently returned from a summer study abroad program in Belize. Maggie was one of the other students from my school who had participated in the IMF/World Bank protests in DC several months before. She asked if she could join me. I contacted Dale and he confirmed he had one more space. In fact, there was a third rider who was on his way from Baton Rouge to meet up with us. This brought the cost for each person to only $50 for the entire trip. It was really happening.

Maggie met me at my apartment early Saturday morning, August 12, wearing a large backpack. She was short and sturdy. I heard she played for our school's soccer team. It made sense. At only about 5'1," she appeared to be pure muscle, someone

I would not want to tangle with. We introduced ourselves awkwardly and sat quietly for a moment. As though not sure what else to say, she pulled a gas mask from her backpack. "Isaac gave me this," she said nonchalantly. "It's kind of uncomfortable."

There was another knock at my door. I opened it to find a tall man, at least 6 feet tall, in his early 20s. He wore thick glasses, sported greasy black hair, no facial hair, and crooked teeth. He smiled widely. "You must be Aaron and Maggie," he said. "I'm Dale!"

If we were judging by appearances, Dale would not have been someone I would easily classify as being part of the "tribe" of anti-globalization activists. No beard, no dreadlocks, no cargo pants, no holes in his T-shirt. He seemed basically mainstream. It didn't matter, however, because he had a car, and he was driving us to Los Angeles.

We loaded our packs into the trunk of his 1990 Toyota Corolla. It was in pretty bad shape, inside and out, and I wondered quietly whether his car would make it the nearly 450 miles to Los Angeles. Our first stop, however, was the Greyhound bus station where our fourth and final passenger would be meeting us.

His name was Jeff, a student at Rutgers University. Apparently, his ride from Baton Rouge was only the most recent leg of a much longer journey. He too had been at the protests in Philadelphia. And like me, his decision to continue on to Los Angeles was made at the last moment. He had thick curly black hair and round, wire-rimmed glasses. We exchanged greetings and piled into the car. It was going to be a long, cramped ride, but I didn't care.

Finally, we got on the road. Dale began talking.

"I hope this time turns out better than Seattle did." He laughed awkwardly. I perked up.

"You were in Seattle?" By this time, all anyone had to do

was mention the name "Seattle," and it was understood the reference was being made to the protests against the WTO the previous November and December.

"Yeah." He laughed again, for no reason. "Things got pretty crazy. The police bashed me in the head with a nightstick. I had to get a metal plate put in my skull."

We weren't sure whether to believe him. Our skepticism only grew over the next 20 hours, as his stories became more and more elaborate. His tales of charging police lines, throwing rocks and unarresting activists didn't seem to match the person before us, who seemed frankly nerdy and awkward. Still, calling him out as a liar didn't seem a good strategy given our dependence upon him. We began ignoring him instead. Maggie and I watched the scenery pass out the window, and Jeff wrote diligently in his journal. Dale kept talking.

Hours passed with no obvious change in the scenery. West Texas seemed to extend forever. Finally, we passed into New Mexico, and began seeing small foothills. I asked Dale to play a Willie Nelson CD I had brought along. The music provided a much-needed break from Dale's endless talking. I asked Dale if he would like to smoke a joint, and of course he eagerly agreed. I lit the joint and took a deep toke, then passed it around the car. Maggie declined. Once we were finished, I leaned back in my seat and placed my face against the glass, watching the desert scenery pass. I was struck by the subtle colors intermingled with the dominant brown – I caught traces of violet, maroon, gray, even blue, cut into the sides of cliffs and mountains. Sagebrush stood out like hands reaching out of the sand. Willie Nelson's voice flowed like honey through the country rhythms that seemed to be the soundtrack custom tailored to fit the scenery before me. Eventually I fell asleep, my eyes closing as the sun slipped beneath the horizon.

I awoke to a somewhat less tranquil vibe in the car. Maggie and Jeff were already awake, their eyes wide. We were finally entering the Los Angeles area, and Dale's nervousness was palpable as the traffic thickened around him. He frantically changed lanes, seemingly at random, oftentimes losing his nerve halfway through and returning to his original lane. Cars honked at us, and I noticed drivers flipping us off out their windows. As we entered the city, Dale seemed startled by the sudden appearance of stoplights, running two or three red lights in a row. At this point, more concerned about our own lives than offending our driver, we were shouting at him. This seemed to make him even more nervous.

We eventually arrived safely at the "convergence center" near MacArthur Park. This was a previously abandoned four-story warehouse in a largely Latin American district just to the west of downtown Los Angeles, Pico-Union. It was immediately recognizable as we approached, with large handmade banners hanging from the windows, many of them in Spanish. *La lucha sigue* ("The Struggle Continues") and *El pueblo unido jamás será vencido* ("The People United Will Never Be Defeated"). We found a place to park on the street and the four of us approached the entrance. There was a note near the front door about a restraining order against the police which a judge had granted in advance of the protests, and another stating entry would not be granted without a warrant. I wondered how much comfort to take from these warnings.

Activists with their recognizable symbols of dreadlocks, bandanas and cargo pants streamed in and out of the convergence center. We apparently looked the part and were not scrutinized by anyone as we entered. The place was a beehive of activity. On the right was a meditation space, with a large oriental rug, candles, incense and charms scattered about a nonspecific altar. To our left was what appeared to be a commercial kitchen, filled with volunteers chopping carrots and potatoes, stirring large pots, and unloading crates of yet more vegetables of dubious origin. (I would later learn many of them were found on a recent "dumpster diving" expedition.) On this same floor, many large papier mâché puppets were under construction. I heard people talking about the Spiral-Q puppet factory that had been raided in Philadelphia only a week before.

Somehow Maggie, Jeff and I lost track of Dale, which was fine with us. We proceeded to the second floor where we heard the Direct Action Network, the same group that had facilitated the mass civil disobedience in Seattle, was holding workshops. Jeff, Maggie and I joined one. As we sat in a large circle along with about thirty other activists, everyone was asked to introduce themselves, preferably with an alias, and also provide the name of their "affinity group."

By this time, I knew what "affinity group" meant. It was essentially the name given to a small group of tight-knit activists who knew and trusted one another, were responsible for one another, and planned their own actions. It was one tactic in a larger strategy of "security culture" activists were partly drawing from history, partly making up as they went along. If the goal was for thousands of people to coordinate secret actions, which were frankly illegal (even nonviolent civil disobedience), in a decentralized manner, how exactly could this be accomplished? If the actions were kept secret, it implied a central core of people making the plans, so it could not be decentralized. On the other hand, if the plans were widely disseminated, they would no longer be a secret. The solution, therefore, was that "plans" would only be made by small affinity groups. Each affinity group would send a representative to a larger "spokescouncil" meeting, where their actions could be coordinated in an informal, and nonspecific manner.

Although we hadn't discussed it beforehand, Maggie, Jeff and I decided to form an affinity group on the spot. I suggested the name "Texan Insurrection," which many found hilarious. As for an alias, I gave "Blackbeard," the handle I had used during my hacking days back in middle school.

The workshop was led by two women, one in her early 20s like me, and another closer to her 40s. She went by the name Starhawk. She was wearing all black and had a pentagram around her neck. She introduced herself as a self-proclaimed witch. I would later learn she was a key figure in the organizing of the actions against the WTO in Seattle.

We rehearsed a number of scenarios we might encounter in the streets, undergoing various role-playing exercises. I practiced linking arms with other activists, while others playing police tried to divide us, physically and psychologically. Then I played the role of the police. We practiced "puppy piles," where we would pile on top of activists the police were trying to isolate. It was explained to us that the police would target members of vulnerable groups – gay people, or people of color – and we should take extra care to watch out for them and protect them.

We returned to the circle and Starhawk began talking about her experiences in jail in Seattle. We listened intently.

"The purpose of jail is to isolate you, both from your activist brothers and sisters, as well as from the earth, and your own humanity. We had to find ways to combat this. We would touch the concrete floor, reminding ourselves that this is the earth element. And to breathe in the air. We would give one another massages at every opportunity to remind ourselves of our humanity. By remaining connected to ourselves, to the earth and to one another, jail solidarity becomes possible, and we can win."

We concluded the workshop with 5 minutes of meditation, followed by a period of sharing. I didn't have anything to share. Maggie did. She poured out her heart to this group of strangers and broke into tears. She was immediately comforted with hugs and words of solidarity. This moment confirmed for me that what I had experienced in the park in Philadelphia had not been a fluke. This movement was real, this tribe was real. Something was happening, history was happening – and, at long last, I would get to be a part of it.

The first event of the week was a big one. In the weeks leading up to the Democratic National Convention, the city of Los Angeles planned to create a "protest zone" about a block away from the Staples Center, where the convention was being held. This would essentially be a large parking lot enclosed with concrete barriers and 10-foot-tall fencing, with only one opening in and out. From the perspective of the police, this would allow them ultimate security and control over the protests. From the perspective of activists, obviously, this represented an outrageous infringement on their constitutional rights to free speech and free assembly. After the plans were published in the Los Angeles Times, and court challenges followed, the "protest zone" was moved to the parking lot across the street from the Staples Center. Several different activist groups were granted permission to set up a stage, and each of them was given a time slot to use the stage along with its audio equipment. Many were still upset by the fact that there was a "protest zone" at all; however the close proximity to the Staples Center, mere yards from the front door, was considered by many to be worth the trade-off. After all, in Philadelphia we had only glimpsed the convention center once.

A final twist caught the city and police by surprise, when *Rage Against the Machine* offered to give a free concert, and all of the activist groups that had been granted permits to use the "protest zone" donated their time to the band. Rage were known for their incendiary, even revolutionary, music, which had sparked riots in other cities on normal days. This day, the first day of the Democratic National Convention, with thousands of protesters in town including anarchists ready to do battle, was not a normal day.

Maggie, Jeff and I gathered in Pershing Square in the early evening. Hundreds soon turned to thousands. By the time the march began in earnest, there were over ten thousand. The police presence was tight as we proceeded toward the Staples Center on Figueroa Street, and unlike Philadelphia, many of the police were dressed head to toe in full riot gear. They felt remarkably more menacing and frightening than the police in Philadelphia. More aggressive. Almost eager for a confrontation.

The march arrived at the large parking lot outside the Staples Center, merging with the large crowd that was already gathered there. It was an eclectic mix. Obviously not everyone was a protester. Many were just *Rage Against the Machine* fans, young locals who had come out to catch a free concert. But mixed with them were people like me who had come for something more. I was less interested in hearing the music than witnessing the effect the music would have on the crowd. And the police. I gazed across the parking lot toward the Staples Center. There was a large balcony where men in suits could be seen, presumably delegates at the convention. I considered them to be the enemy, and I assumed they were leering down at us with contempt. It never crossed my mind that some of them might be *Rage* fans, too.

I heard the sound system chirp as it came online. I heard a few notes as Tom Morello tuned his guitar. The crowd roared in anticipation. Finally, Zach de la Rocha took the mic and ignited the atmosphere with his emblematic cry, "C'mon!" With that call instantaneously followed by the drums and electric guitar, the unmistakable sound, the crowd exploded. Everyone around me was jumping up and down, singing along to the lyrics. During the song "Killing in the Name Of," perhaps their most famous, the well-known refrain "Fuck you, I won't do what you tell me" took on a visceral, embodied meaning. Ten thousand people sang along and raised their middle fingers to the delegates gathered on the balcony. I noticed some of them wave back weakly.

As I meandered throughout the crowd, I suddenly noticed a

very familiar mop of brown hair on the back of a young man's head. He turned around and I was taken back by the familiar face. "Haulden!" His eyes locked with mine and he grinned widely, almost maniacally. "Aaron!" He gave me a big hug.

"I can't believe you came," I said, still shocked.

"I couldn't not come, man! I mean..." his words trailed off as he gestured to the scene around us. It required no explanation. We were both driven by something bigger than ourselves, something we had searched for our whole lives, and having found it, were afraid to let slip from our grasps.

During *Rage Against the Machine*'s set, I noticed a situation was developing near the fence closest to the Staples Center. Riot police were just on the other side. Meanwhile, some Black Bloc anarchists had climbed the fence and were waving black flags. Other protesters were throwing projectiles over the fence at the police. I saw tear gas being fired at the crowd, and eventually the gas made its way toward me, causing stinging in my nose and throat. Many in the crowd started leaving at this time, but the obvious protesters were, of course, not going anywhere.

Rage did manage to finish their set, and they were followed by another well-known LA band, Ozomatli. While still political in their message, their music was much less incendiary in its sound – a fusion of jazz, funk and reggae. They only managed to play one or two songs, however, before they made an announcement.

"We've just got word that the LAPD is threatening to shut off our power if the two young men don't get off the fence in 5 minutes. Now, c'mon everybody, let's just cool off and have a good time. We gotta keep cool, so they can't shut us down!"

A part of me felt bad for the band, who seemed by all accounts to be a group of peace-loving musicians who would rather keep the music going than have the concert devolve into a riot. On the other hand, we had all just been chanting "Fuck you, I won't do what you tell me." Many of us weren't in the mood to follow the orders of the police. The crowd seemed to be as divided as I was, as many started yelling "get off the fence," while just as many screamed obscenities at the police and raised their middle fingers in the air. The two young men stayed on the fence, with black bandanas covering their faces, waving their anarchy flags high.

Five minutes later, as promised, the police cut all power to the stage, as well as all lights. It was jarring in its suddenness. It had been daylight when we first arrived at the Staples Center. I hadn't noticed it had gotten dark, but now suddenly it seemed pitch black. There was no longer any sound from the speakers, only the noise of the crowd all around me. Suddenly my senses came into focus, and I could smell the fear in the air. A moment later, I heard a brief squeal of feedback as a bullhorn was turned on, followed by another announcement by a serious man I could not see.

"Attention! I am Commander Grennan of the LAPD. I hereby declare this to be an unlawful assembly. If you remain in the area, regardless of your purpose in remaining, you will be in violation of Section 409. You have 15 minutes to disburse."

I had lost track of Haulden by this time, but Jeff was still nearby. I asked him what he wanted to do.

"I don't want to leave, man," he said, shrugging his shoulders as if to say: but I don't know what happens if I stay.

"Me either."

I spotted Maggie walking around with a garbage bag in her hands. I noticed a few others doing the same.

"Maggie," I shouted, getting her attention, "Jeff and I are staying!"

"I'm picking up trash," she said flatly, and continued about her business. I didn't understand her point. Maybe the police wouldn't smash her head in if she was doing something wholesome like picking up garbage?

Jeff and I wandered closer to the fence on the side of the

Staples Center. We decided to do what we had learned in our training back at the convergence center. We sat on the concrete, back-to-back, and linked arms. I imagined that whatever the police were planning to do, they would have a harder time doing it to a large mass of people engaging in nonviolent civil disobedience. The only problem was two people hardly constituted a "mass."

A few seconds later one guy joined us, and then another. However, I began to feel worried that momentum wasn't picking up fast enough. Swarms of people parted around us, many of them looking at us like we were insane. Suddenly, I noticed a change in everyone's faces as they turned and looked, and then started running. The police were coming.

Something possessed me at that moment. Watching the people run past me in a panic, I didn't see a moment of fear, I saw a lifetime of fear. In that moment, I knew that fear was what kept all of us making safe decisions, accepting the injustices of our society and our world. We were afraid to fight for a better world, because we feared the world we already had might get worse. For me, this moment symbolized every moment I had backed or kept silent, in the past or in the future. Almost maniacally, I shouted:

"This is fear! Can't you feel it? And if you run from it now, you'll be running from it your whole life!"

Time slowed as I continued shouting. I saw the people who were running toward me and swarming around me, suddenly making eye contact and slowing their pace as they listened. It was a strange statement, rather heavy handed, perhaps a bad line in a movie – but it worked. Suddenly another joined us, and then another. Before I knew it there were over a dozen of us sitting on the ground, arms locked at the elbows, seated in a large ring. We started chanting the famous chant from Seattle, "This is what democracy looks like!"

Moments later, I heard the sound of horse hooves on

the pavement and looked up to see a vision from my worst nightmares. The horses themselves seemed to be covered in armor, with guards and visors covering their noses and eyes. The men mounted on top of them, however, were much more frightening. They were wearing what appeared to be black military fatigues, helmets with face guards. Worst of all, they were wielding wooden nightsticks, 4 feet long, which were drawn. I gazed up at one of the men as he approached, with the nightstick raised above his head, and he shouted at me. He said, or I thought he said:

"How committed are you?"

I closed my eyes and ducked my head. I felt Jeff to my right and the stranger to my left squeeze their biceps tight, nearly crushing my elbows. Everything went dark. Suddenly I heard cracking, like the sound of a wooden stick finding skull, followed by screams, followed by mayhem all around me. Our circle broke and we all ran.

Naturally I ran toward the only entrance/exit in the "protest pit," with my back to the approaching police on horseback, and hundreds were running alongside me. Suddenly I heard shots fired. They weren't gunshots, but nearly as loud. I heard and saw people all around me being hit by rubber bullets. Looking ahead, I saw a line of fully outfitted riot police blocking our way, guns in hand, aimed directly at us. Panic rose in my chest.

Riot police in front of me, mounted police behind me and chain-link fence to the right, the only way to go was left. The entire crowd of us funneled in that direction, slowing to a walk as the increasing density of bodies made running impossible. I began to realize we were walking a gauntlet, with a row of police on horseback to our left, and a row of riot police to our right. We were completely subdued, but the riot police continued firing at us with rubber bullets, seemingly out of sport.

I expected they would try to arrest all of us, but they didn't. Eventually the gauntlet led to the exit of the protest pen and we were permitted to leave. Miraculously I managed to find Maggie and Jeff again in the aftermath. We were all unharmed. Moments later a van pulled up, a side door opened and a young girl inside called to us.

"Convergence center?"

We piled inside, where several other frazzled activists sat. No one spoke as we were shuttled back the several blocks to the convergence center where our adventure in Los Angeles had begun. Amazingly, the activists working in the kitchen had prepared an eggplant stew. I didn't realize how hungry I was until I took the first bite. It didn't matter if the vegetables had been "reclaimed" from a dumpster. It tasted like the best thing I had ever eaten.

Other activists were waiting to assist us in finding a place to stay for the night. A Quaker man had offered up his house, and about twenty of us were given a ride. His house, incidentally, was an American Friends Meeting House in South-Central LA. It was a lovely home, not large, with stucco walls and arches lining the front porch. With our latest arrival, there must have been fifty people staying there. One of them was Haulden. While glad to see me, he was clearly as shaken up as I was. Not yet ready to go to sleep, he and I walked a block away to the nearest gas station to buy beer. We brought back a case of cheap beer and found a place to sit on the back porch, where many others were gathered, drinking and smoking cigarettes.

A young man approached me and asked if he could have a beer. He was dressed in all black, with a black bandana still tied around his neck. He had patches pinned with safety pins on his tight black jeans as well as his cotton hoodie. They were handmade, screen-printed slogans such as "NO BORDERS, NO PRISONS," "NO GODS, NO MASTERS." There was an image on one of them of a man in a mask throwing a Molotov cocktail. And of course, there was the ever-present anarchy symbol, the circle-A. I realized this was one of them. I had so many questions. I figured he would talk to me in exchange for the beer. His name was Raven. I asked him, clumsily, if he was a Black Bloc anarchist.

"There's actually no such thing as a 'Black Bloc anarchist,'" he corrected me. But his tone was kind and instructive, not self-righteous. "The 'Black Bloc' is just a tactic. I am an anarchist, so of course the state sees me as an enemy. So, when I come together with other anarchists, we wear black and cover our faces to protect our identities and to protect one another." I took that as a yes. He continued, as he started rolling a cigarette. "The tactic dates back to the autonomen squatter movements in Germany in the 1980s. There were autonomous movements emerging around a variety of causes. Resistance against nuclear proliferation, pro-feminism, pro-gay movements, movements to defend immigrant communities. They were occupying abandoned buildings in West Berlin, near the Berlin Wall, building their own community. They faced heavy police repression and started wearing all black as a tactic to avoid identification by the police who would bring cameras to demonstrations. This tactic has since spread all over the world, but only recently here in the United States."

"So, what does it mean to be an anarchist? Do you really believe there should be no government? Wouldn't that just be chaos?"

"Chaos is what we have now. Sure, if you're white and privileged, this world works for you. But if you're brown and poor, you're at the mercy of the capitalist system. The majority of the world is suffering in the depths of poverty and oppression, working on plantations and sweatshops for pennies an hour. Just so people like us can buy cheap clothes and enjoy a high standard of living.

"To be an anarchist just means to be against all forms of oppression and coercion. We are against formal government, because it is just another example of a top-down structure predicated on violence. Racism, sexism, classism – these are not just side-effects of our system, they are embedded into the very fabric of our government. It is literally why it exists – to perpetuate the power structure of the elites who formed it, who maintain it, ultimately through the use of force and violence."

His words resonated with me in an especially powerful way that evening, with the images of police on horseback freshly imprinted on my brain. Watching this young man take draws from his hand-rolled cigarette, fresh back from a riot, squatting in an anonymous house somewhere in South-Central LA, while talking eloquently of political philosophy and the dream of a utopian future, I began to feel intoxicated by the beauty of the contrasts. In the media, people like Raven were cast as the worst of the worst, agents of chaos, violent and angry. But the person before me was neither violent nor angry. He was composed, thoughtful, even poetic in his style. He was willing to fight, sure, because he really believed the words he was saying.

That's when I felt a change happen inside me. I suddenly understood the magnitude of what we were up against. I heard the sound of a helicopter overhead, which for a moment cast its beam across the backyard where we were sitting. Of course, they knew we were here. Because we were a threat. Not a threat to a few plate glass windows in the shopping district, a threat to the whole system. All over the world, there were women and children slaving away in sweatshops and factories, or men engaging in backbreaking work in the fields, all so the rich could live ever more extravagant lives at their expense. Meanwhile, those of us in the "First World," the US and Europe, were kept comfortable, fat and docile, so we could be the managers of the system. It was an astonishing evil and injustice. And if that were true, if I really believed this to be the case, why wouldn't I fight? Why wouldn't I pour everything I had into the resistance? Nonviolence might be a lovely ideal, but it had one flaw – a faith in the ultimate goodness of the oppressors to see their own hypocrisy, to turn and change their ways. But the true oppressors, the rich and powerful global elites who played governments like pieces on a chessboard; how likely were they to change their ways?

After that night, I felt a deep and powerful urge to commit myself deeper to the cause. But how? This is what I was asking myself as I joined another march 2 days later, the third day of the convention. This one was actually taking place just around the corner from the convergence center, starting in MacArthur Park. The march was planning to end right at the front door of the infamous Ramparts Police Station. This particular police division was the most infamous within the already infamous LAPD. Ramparts was known for its "CRASH" anti-gang program (Community Resources Against Street Hoodlums). Stories abounded of officers framing suspects, dealing confiscated cocaine out of police lockers, even participation in robberies. The larger story was one of a racist police department terrorizing a vulnerable community of color, by labeling anyone causing trouble, even community activists, "gang members."

The mood at MacArthur Park was festive as I arrived; there was a display of many papier mâché puppets that had been constructed at the convergence center, as well as a large banner I had been admiring the night before. It was even more striking in the daylight. It was a portrait of the earth, anthropomorphized into a human face, whose expression was one of mourning. Electrical sockets were installed across her various continents, into which were plugged factories and skyscrapers. From the top of her forehead grew a large tree, perhaps the Tree of Life, around which people from all races were encircled, their hands joined. A Rastafarian man stood beside me, a djembe drum slung around his shoulder, admiring the artwork with me. He said, "Man, if people could just look at that and understand, we'd have no more work to do."

The crowd swelled from hundreds to thousands before the

march began. It was a hot day, and I felt the sweat soaking the blue bandana I wore over my head, not to mention the armpits of my simple gray cotton T-shirt. Having not had a shower all week, I must have smelled awful.

I was marching along with Maggie and Jeff. Haulden appeared moments later, videotaping the march, and once again wearing his IMC badge. He put his camera down for a moment and caught up with me. He began speaking to us in the closest thing to a whisper as he could manage, while still being heard above the noise of chanting and drums.

"Say, I hear there's gonna be a Civil Disobedience at the end of the march. Whoever wants to participate needs to move closer to the front."

I felt my heart rate rise with fear and excitement. This was my chance.

"What kind of Civil Disobedience?" I asked. "What are they planning?"

"I don't know, but I'm gonna be there when it happens." He grinned widely, patting his camcorder. And then he took off to continue videotaping and spreading the word.

Jeff, Maggie and I looked at each other, and without exchanging a word, the three of us began making our way to the front of the march. There we found others who had come for the same purpose. Sharpies were being passed from one person to the next, which were being used to write a phone number on their forearms. This was the number to the Midnight Special Legal Collective, the same group that had represented the protesters arrested in Seattle.

A card was being passed around with instructions to the protesters who were willing to engage in civil disobedience. Basically, it said to ensure we had no identification on us, to not give our real names, to answer no questions, to only ask to speak with our attorney, who could be reached at the phone number we should write on our arms.

I asked Maggie if she would take my wallet, but she said "No, I might be joining you." Jeff, too, seemed deep in contemplation. So instead, I found Haulden. I scribbled my address back in Georgetown on a piece of paper and asked him to please mail it to me. He agreed and gave me one last hug.

Finally, the march arrived at the front steps of the police station, where a large contingent of police were already gathered. This time they were dressed in their street uniforms, no riot gear or horses to be seen. There were various speeches given, cataloging the history of corruption and abuses for which this department was responsible. I could not hear most of what was being said, partly because of the acoustics, partly because of the heat and partly because of the buzz of inner dialog swarming in my mind.

Finally, the moment arrived. A handful of men and women made their way through the crowd and sat on the steps. More joined them. Maggie and I looked at Jeff questioningly.

"I can't get arrested," he said. "If this is something you two want to do, you have my full support. I will be waiting until you get out – however long it takes."

Maggie handed him her backpack and asked him to keep it for her at the convergence center. The two of us began making our way to the steps, fighting past reporters and photographers. We stepped out into the opening where we saw several activists sitting, most of them with their face covered. Maggie and I found a spot among them. More protesters joined us, until there were nearly forty of us in total, almost equally divided between men and women. As everyone was finding a spot, a drum was beating and someone was reading over the megaphone a list of names of those targeted, injured or killed by the LAPD.

It then became quiet. A high-ranking officer among the police, who stood at attention in their starched blues, took a megaphone and began speaking to us. He explained that by blocking the entrance to the police station we were preventing civil servants from carrying out their lawful duties. He cited a list of city ordinances we were violating, but I couldn't focus on what he was saying. I was looking at the other police who were staring us down, bundles of plastic zip ties hanging from their belt loops. They wrung their hands as if they couldn't wait to pounce on us. I was afraid.

The police, in a group of four or five, approached the protesters individually. Each person was given the opportunity to leave. If they refused, they were handcuffed and either escorted or carried into the police station. Maggie was gripping my hand.

"I think I'm going to leave," she whispered. "I'll wait until they come to talk to me and then I'll get up and leave."

"I might do the same," I said.

Finally, the police came to us, and spoke to Maggie first. She did not get up and leave like she said she would. In fact, she didn't stand up at all, so four officers grabbed her by her arms and legs and carried her inside.

I was next. I sat cross-legged and stared ahead as they read the list of charges to me. I never spoke a word. I felt an officer grab my arms and pull them behind me, meeting at the wrist. My hands were zip tied together. They asked me if I wanted to walk, but I kept quiet. Like Maggie, they picked me up by my arms and legs and carried me inside. Into the belly of the beast, I thought.

Chapter 6

Once inside, I agreed to walk on my own. Two police officers accompanied me through the station, hitting me with questions immediately. What's your name? Where are you from? Do you have a girlfriend? I did exactly as I had been instructed in training.

"I'm not going to answer any questions until I speak to my lawyer." I wanted the words to sound strong, but as they left my mouth, they seemed forced and uncertain.

"Ok, bud, we'll let you talk to your lawyer. You know, you guys really disappointed us. We were hoping this week was gonna be more like '92."

He was referring, of course, to the Los Angeles riots of 1992. They were sparked in response to the acquittal of four police officers who had been videotaped beating an unarmed black man. For six days, the city was consumed by riots. Stores were burned and looted. Sixty-three people died, thousands injured, and tens of thousands were arrested. I took his comment as a joke, one I considered to be in very poor taste.

As we continued down a hallway, I heard singing. I was led into a large room that resembled a basketball gymnasium. The protesters who had been arrested before me were sitting in two rows, back-to-back, handcuffed to metal chairs. It looked like a scary game of musical chairs. I was led to an empty chair and instructed to sit. One of my wrists, which was already bound to the other by a zip tie, was handcuffed to the chair behind me. The singing continued.

We have come too far,
We won't turn around
We'll flood the streets with justice
We are freedom bound

The police rolled their eyes and made jokes with each other. In my mind, I fluctuated between feeling silly, and feeling righteous. I concentrated on the latter. Like it or not, I was committed now. I had crossed a line, and there was no going back. I simply couldn't afford to question why I had made the decision I had made. I joined in the singing, imagining the Civil Rights protesters of the 1960s, marching alongside Martin Luther King. I imagined I was one of them.

As the police continued escorting more protesters into the gymnasium and handcuffing them to the empty chairs, some of the other arrestees began firing off questions and demands to the police.

One man with long brown hair and round rimmed glasses asked, "Where are you taking us?"

"To Twin Towers."

"Will we be processed individually or collectively?"

"Uh, one at a time."

"We will not allow you to separate us."

"Well, it's not really up to you."

I was surprised by the audacity of the other protesters, who spoke to the police with authority. I was honestly a little worried it would backfire on us. Whether we were kept together or separated really wasn't up to us. What good would it do to speak to the police as though we possessed some kind of power that was not evident to me as we sat handcuffed to metal chairs? More to the point, what good would it do to piss them off, almost daring them to put us through a sort of misery I assumed they were all too capable of inflicting? After all, didn't these police in particular have a track record? Wasn't that why we were here?

My assumption that we did not have power would be quickly dispelled. Once all of the arrests had been made, 37 in total, the police took us to the rear exit of the station and began loading us onto a small bus. When it became evident that we would not all fit on the same bus, the police radioed for a second bus. Some of the more seasoned activists jumped into action and began arguing with the police. They insisted "We would not be separated." Although the police dismissed them at first, reminding them they were not "calling the shots," the police eventually loaded us back off the small bus and a larger bus was brought in to accommodate all of us. I was frankly astonished by this. We were not exactly a scary bunch, however much I would have liked to believe that. Besides, we were handcuffed. I wondered if they really gave into our demand or if they decided independently that a single bus was more convenient for them.

We were taken to Los Angeles County Jail, otherwise known as "Twin Towers." During the bus ride we learned one another's names. Since the men were already separated from the women (the one separation we ultimately could not avoid) I mostly learned the men's names. There was "Grumpy," a short, stocky gay man in his late-40s/early 50s. "Bear," who couldn't have been more than 19 or 20, with messy blond hair and acne scars. "Sandino," a clean-cut man in his mid-20s with neatly trimmed black hair. "Samsara," a British man with long brown hair and round glasses. Sandino and Samsara were among the more vocal and assertive, and I remembered they were the ones who had already started making demands and engaging with the police. "Quixote," a tall, skinny Latino man. "Don Juan," an imposing figure of a man who could have played "Little John" in a Robin Hood movie. Once more, I gave the alias of "Blackbeard."

We entered Twin Towers in single file, and the process began. Each time we were asked our names, we responded John Doe or Jane Doe. Fingerprints were taken, and I noticed the words "FBI" on one of the computer screens. I assumed I was being added to the database. Some of the more veteran among us made comments about how they were probably already in there.

We were photographed and questioned again and again at different steps in the process. The fact that we were not giving our real names was causing considerable confusion among the staff working in the jail. When collecting my personal belongings, they asked where my wallet was. I told them I didn't have one, and they stared at me puzzled. The only thing of real value to me was my blue bandana, which I had worn with me throughout Europe the summer before. I was sad when they confiscated it, assuming I would probably never see it again.

As we were marched throughout the jail, it began to feel like I was descending deep into a maze. I doubted I could find my own way out, even if I was given the opportunity. We were taken to a shower room and told to strip. I remembered this scene from Shawshank Redemption. Our clothes were taken, and we were handed stacks containing a flimsy white towel, a pair of white boxers, blue canvas pants and a blue canvas shirt, as well as some black canvas slippers. After dressing, I caught a glimpse of myself in the mirror. I looked like an inmate.

Our next stop was a holding cell where we were handed bags of lunch. Inside there was a wheat bun, small packets of mayonnaise and mustard, a type of mystery meat in a baggie that looked like bologna but smelled like potted meat, a few sticks of celery, an apple, a cookie and a juice box. We sat around the room, sitting on metal benches, eating quietly. I noticed the guy sitting next to me with dreadlocks, who was constructing a celery sandwich. When he saw me watching, he explained.

"I'm vegan."

I felt sorry for him, and handed him my bag of celery, which he accepted gratefully.

Suddenly I heard Samsara speak, in a slightly panicked voice.

"Two of us are missing! Grumpy is one of them. Who is the other?"

We eventually realized the other was Don Juan. The fact that Grumpy was missing was particularly concerning, however, considering he was gay. This is exactly what we had been taught in workshops, that the vulnerable among us – gays and lesbians or people of color – would often be targeted by the authorities. Now it was happening, and I had to ask myself how brave I really was.

We set our lunches aside and gathered in a circle to discuss the situation. This immediately caught the attention of the guards, who began calling for support on their radios.

"What should we do?" Bear asked.

"Ok, guys, time to move out!" barked one of the guards.

"We have to lock down right now in this cell and demand to be reunited with our brothers," Samsara said with authority.

"Should we try to negotiate first?" I asked, a bit weakly.

"Why not," responded Amanita. "There's no reason we can't discuss this with the guards before taking action. Who knows, there might be a simple explanation."

"Hey, we said move it!"

"Ok, I'd like to make a proposal that we attempt to negotiate with the guards and lock down if they do not return our brothers to this room. Are there any concerns?" This was Sandino speaking, who was already emerging as the natural mediator and diplomat among us. Everyone nodded in agreement, exchanging glances of unexpressed fear.

"Sirs," Sandino said, finally addressing the guards. "Two of our brothers are missing. There were nineteen of us, and now we count seventeen."

The guards looked around, as though the two missing men might have been misplaced somewhere under the metal benches. They conferred together for a moment before responding.

"You'll meet up with them in the dorm. They're still in processing."

All of us responded instantaneously, converging together in the middle of the room and piling on top of one another, interlocking arms and legs. Those in the center of the "puppy pile" (the safer ones, I thought) wrapped their arms around the legs of the metal benches, which were fastened to the concrete floor.

"What is this shit?" I heard the guards murmur. And then I heard the crackle of the radio. "We need backup in here."

Within 10 seconds, the room filled with guards. I took particular note of one, who was about 6'2" and 200 pounds of solid muscle. He looked like a bodybuilder. His biceps threatened to rip the short sleeves of his beige uniform, wielding what looked like a paintball gun. I doubted it contained ordinary paintballs. He paced the room, his fingers twitching as though he couldn't wait to fire up on us, or even better, get his bare hands upon us. I felt true fear, which tasted like metal upon my tongue and throat.

"You guys have it all wrong," one of the guards hissed. "You're not calling the shots here. We are. We are in charge. You're gonna do what we say, or you'll regret it."

Another guard, who seemed older and possessing authority, stepped forward to address us in his best "good cop" voice.

"Now what seems to be the problem? You'll see the other two guys when you get to the dorms. They are just held up in processing, is all. It's totally normal. Nothing for you to worry about."

"Sirs, we refuse to move until they are brought back in here to join us," Sandino responded. The guard cleared his throat.

"I'm sorry, that's not how it works. Now I'm going to need all of you to stand up right now and obey our instructions, or we will be forced to use chemicals on you. Now what's it going to be?"

Chemicals. The sinister word rang in my head. I saw the bodybuilder retrieve a pair of latex gloves from his pocket and snap them on his hands. His hands looked huge and swollen, pink beneath the stretched translucent latex. Facing the police on the streets was one thing, with cameras and witnesses all around. But facing guards inside a completely enclosed concrete cell with no cameras or witnesses was a far more devastating prospect.

"We aren't moving," Sandino responded, without the slightest hint of hesitation in his voice. "We would rather be reunited with our brothers, so we can cooperate with you." It was a novel choice of words.

"There's no negotiation. You'll either cooperate with us now, and be reunited with your friends in the dorm, or we will use chemicals on you now and be forced to separate all of you."

I could not keep quiet any longer.

"Let's find a compromise." Samsara, from the bottom of the pile, shot me a fairly disgusted look, presumably disappointed by my traitorous weakness. However, it immediately became clear I was not the only one interested in finding a middle ground. After all, if we were all separated it was game over. And I did not doubt for one second the ability of the guards to accomplish just that.

"When exactly will we see our friends again," asked Amanita.

"After your showers. Thirty minutes at the most."

"Listen," I whispered to the group, with my back fully exposed to the guards. "There's absolutely no reason we can't do this again in 30 minutes, if we have to. But if they separate us all now, we won't even have that choice." Samsara, nestled securely in the core of the puppy pile, wasn't backing down.

"We're just supposed to believe him? He's lying. And if we let him get away with it now, it will just keep happening."

"So next time we don't give in! Let's just give him this one chance. Please!"

"Alright boys, we are about to get the chemicals. What's it going to be?"

"You must give us your word," Sandino responded, "that we will see our brothers again in 30 minutes."

The guard smirked, shrugged his shoulders and looked around at the other guards. I worried that Sandino had pushed it too far.

"Ok," he said. "I give you my word."

We separated and stood. The guards leered at us as we exited the room. To my surprise, Grumpy and Don Juan were reunited with us only moments later, as we made our way to the showers. They were completely unharmed, and it seemed what the guards said had been true – they were simply delayed in processing.

Finally, we were taken to Cellblock 1500. It was a large room with cinderblock walls, approximately the size of a gymnasium. The room could probably accommodate a hundred or more inmates but was instead filled with dozens of completely empty bunkbeds. There was an observation room, situated in such a way that the guards inside had a clear view of every corner of the room, even showers and toilets. There were four payphones directly beneath the viewing windows. The guards handed each of us a stack containing a pillow and a thin sheet. The large metal door was shut with a loud clang, and we were left alone.

I had no idea what time it was, nor any way to determine the time. However, I was physically and mentally exhausted. We all instinctively migrated to the furthest end of the room, as far away from the observation room as possible. I started making my bed. After placing my pillow and sheet upon the 3-inch-thick mattress, I was about to join them before Sandino piped up.

"Ok men, we need to have a meeting."

Nothing could sound less appealing in that moment, but obediently I joined the others in a circle on the concrete floor.

"I want to tell you all about the lawyer who will be representing us," Sandino began, in storyteller fashion. "Her name is Katya Komisaruk. As some of you know, I worked with her in Seattle. She was the brains behind the jail solidarity tactics that resulted in hundreds of jailed activists being released, and all charges dropped. But her story goes back much further than Seattle.

"In the 1980s she was part of an activist group called the 'Ploughshares.' The name comes from a passage in the Bible, something along the lines of 'and they will beat their swords into ploughshares.' They are still very active today. Many, but not all, of the Ploughshare activists are Christians. Recently there was a big story about a group of nuns who were arrested for destroying an F-16 with sledgehammers at an air show."

The image of this evoked laughter among several of us.

"Yeah, they're not playing around. Anyway, during this time Katya was doing some research on this facility in San Diego that contained a mainframe computer used to control a nuclear missile launch system. So, one night, she dressed in all black and snuck onto the base in the middle of the night and managed to get inside the room where the mainframe sat. She pulled out a hammer and smashed everything in sight."

"Damn," exclaimed Bear. "Did she get away with it?"

"Actually, 'getting away with it' was never part of her plan. Once she was done, she just waited for security guards to rush in and arrest her. Five minutes turned into 30, then an hour. She got so bored she pulled a flute out of her backpack and started playing to entertain herself. Finally, she realized no one was coming, so she decided to leave a note instead. She named the time and place of a press conference she would give the next day and signed her name. She was arrested the next day."

Woah. One of the guys whistled. It was an impressive story, a beautiful convergence of intelligence, commitment, courage and integrity. I had never heard anything like it.

"Did she go to prison?" I asked.

"Yes. She was sentenced to 6 years in federal prison, although she was released after 2 for good behavior. After that she went to Harvard Law School. Once she got her license to practice law, she started the Midnight Special Legal Collective, dedicated to defending activists like us, free of charge."

Sandino went on to discuss the details of jail solidarity and what we could expect moving forward. Tiredness began to get the better of me, and I only caught the highlights. Don't give your name, ever. Read the statement provided to you at your arraignment. We negotiate collectively, never individually. And be prepared to be here for the long haul. The seriousness of the situation was only gradually setting in, a heavy weight that began to tug at my eyelids, as though my eyelids might defend me from understanding the consequences of a decision I had made so impulsively. As soon as I could, I snuck away from the group, thin sheet and pillow in hand, found a bunk and curled up to go to sleep.

Chapter 7

"Chow time!"

I awoke at what seemed like four in the morning (although I had no way to mark the passage of time) to the bellowing of the guards and the clanging of their nightsticks on the metal of our bunks. We arose reluctantly, remembering where we were and the new military-style life we had suddenly committed ourselves to. We lined up and were herded like cattle at a rapid pace throughout the halls of the jail. We were taken to a cafeteria where we were served breakfast on metal trays. Scrambled eggs the texture of soft plastic, runny grits, a patty of strange smelling mystery meat, and a half-pint of milk. All of us activists sat at a table together and were not permitted to interact with the other inmates. I was one of the few people who actually ate all of my breakfast.

Our arraignment was later that morning. After showers, we spent most of the day in a small holding cell. When the time came, we were escorted to the outside of a courtroom, which we were not permitted to enter. Instead, we stood outside and watched the proceedings through the glass. It was a typical courtroom, with a judge's bench front and center, and the prosecution and defense council facing the judge on the right and the left. The gallery was packed with journalists and other activists who came to support us. I saw our lawyer, Katya Komisaruk, for the first time.

Katya was an attractive young woman in professional dress, with a short bowl cut that outlined her face, which bore an unrelenting, contagious smile. The moment came for her to give her opening statement before the arraignment, when we would each enter our plea. She addressed the courtroom with a confident authority that captured the attention of all in attendance.

"Your honor, my clients I am representing today are activists, not criminals. These young men and women committed nonviolent civil disobedience in the tradition of Mahatma Gandhi and Martin Luther King. They sacrificed their bodies in the pursuit of justice, and I ask your honor to serve them justice here by dropping all charges and releasing all these activists."

Katya had prepared small cards on which were printed the exact words each of us were asked to read when addressing the judge. When my turn came, I spoke through an opening in the plexiglass, trying to sound calm.

"Your honor, I am in solidarity with all of the activists here today. If released, I will not return for trial. I demand the right to collective bargaining. I plead not guilty and ask that all charges against us be dropped. I will not reveal my identity and I will not negotiate with the prosecutor individually. I demand my right to a speedy trial and a jury of my peers."

The crux of the jail solidarity strategy was to thwart all of the mechanisms of the criminal justice system that had been designed for efficiency and cost effectiveness. By declaring our unwillingness to return if released, we were forcing the county to keep us in jail. By refusing to negotiate with the prosecutor and demanding a trial by jury, we would be imposing the maximum possible strain on the court system. Also, in a strange twist that the prosecutor himself would point out, we were requesting individual trials by jury, even though we were demanding the right to negotiate collectively. Evidently, 39 speedy trials by jury was a tall order, even for a city the size of Los Angeles.

The lawyers and the judge had a tense exchange for the next several minutes, and while most of the discussion went over my head, I had the distinct sense the judge was siding with the prosecution on most every point. There was considerable doubt brewing in my mind about the wisdom or effectiveness of our strategy. It actually seemed a little crazy. How could we possibly get away with snaking our way through the court system without ever revealing our identities? It seemed more like a recipe for life in jail than a recipe for success. Still, I was committed at this point and felt I had little choice but to fall in line with the others.

Later that afternoon or evening, we were back in our cell block when we got word that the Jane Doe's had begun a hunger strike. We had a consensus meeting to decide whether or not we would join them.

"Consensus" decision-making was an integral part of the activist scene at this time, and of course was a major component of the organizing behind the WTO protests in Seattle. Supposedly the process could be traced back to the Quakers. The objective was an audacious one on its face. Rather than make decisions by a majority vote, the goal was to ensure that all decisions were made unanimously. Rather than looking at decisions as binary, black and white, the consensus process embraced the shades of gray in between, where compromises could be creatively forged. Of course, some level of common ground and shared values was a prerequisite. Assuming this was the case, however, the idea was that a decision could always be found that everyone would agree upon, assuming everyone was committed to the process and was willing to continue the discussion for as long as possible.

In practice, however, consensus process meetings could become quite long and tedious, and in some cases, it was hard to tell the difference between a "consensus" being reached versus the will of the most long-winded defeating those with less stamina or will to keep up the fight.

This particular question, however, whether or not to join the Jane Doe's in their hunger strike, was a fairly easy one to answer. We were all on board. If nothing else, we weren't going to let the women make us look bad. Most of us decided on an all-water fast, while a few opted to go on a juice fast. My feeling was that my body would probably perform better with just water, without the addition of the pure sugar water given to us in the juice boxes in our lunches. Sandino, who had emerged as our spokesperson due largely to his experience with the process, opted to continue eating. It was a good idea to keep at least one clear head in our group.

We demanded to see our attorney at every opportunity. Katya was finally allowed to visit us in our cell the next day. Unlike the day before in the courtroom, she was not smiling.

"Frankly, guys, it's not looking good. I have spent a lot of time speaking with the prosecutor. He is not sympathetic to the argument that this was civil disobedience. In his mind, this is a cut and dry case. You committed a crime, and therefore you must suffer consequences. However, I will continue to push on my end. In the meantime, I just need all of you to stay strong. Continue the hunger strike. Do not speak to anyone unless you have to. Do not reveal your identities, even to one another. They are surveilling you closely and anything you say can and will be held against you."

We continued the hunger strike for several days. We were harassed constantly by the guards, who would come into our cell block suddenly, ask us to line up, and then march us around the jail for seemingly no reason. We would then be returned to the cell block without an explanation. They were clearly trying to rattle us psychologically.

One day, during one of these marches, Grumpy fainted from fatigue and suffered a bloody nose. While he was not seriously hurt, the news of this incident seemed to spook the staff of the jail, and our treatment improved considerably. We were given extra blankets, even books, papers and pencils that we had been requesting since the first day. The marches around the jail came to an end. We weren't even required to attend the mess hall, as had been the case the first few days.

Eventually we learned we had become the top story on the local news. Tom Hayden, infamous member of the Chicago Seven during the trials that followed the protests after the Democratic National Convention in 1968, was personally petitioning for our release. Now he was a member of the California State Senate. We heard a rumor that he was attempting to pay us a visit, although this never materialized. The tide of public opinion seemed to be tilting in our favor. The press surrounding our hunger strike, in addition to the continuous pressure being applied by our lawyer, was enough to convince the prosecutor to come meet with us.

We had many meetings preparing for his visit, as we tried to decide how to make the best use of the opportunity. At this point I had been on hunger strike for 4 days. I was a small guy to begin with, normally around 130 pounds. While I did not have a scale to verify it, I felt like I had lost nearly ten pounds. My ribs were showing. I was totally lethargic and had a difficult time following the topics discussed at those meetings. Mostly I kept quiet.

The prosecutor arrived the following morning along with Katya. He was a Jewish man in his early 60s. He smiled kindly as he greeted each of us individually. He looked around awkwardly as though searching for a chair, when Sandino suggested helpfully that we all have a seat in a circle. He graciously accommodated.

We had made the decision that we would focus our attention upon relating our own stories, including our prior activist experience and our motivations behind participating in the act of civil disobedience. I myself learned a great deal about my "brothers" in the course of this conversation and was surprised by the diversity of our backgrounds. We had every variety of "activist" among us. Those who had come from activist families, as well as those, like me, who came from conservative or religious backgrounds. We had those for whom this action was just one in a long line of struggle in defense of the rights of the poor and the oppressed, as well as others, like me, who were just getting started.

The prosecutor seemed genuinely interested in our stories, asking questions along the way. Eventually, however, the subject turned toward our immediate situation. Here there seemed to be no room for compromise. The case, as he saw it, was clear. We had obstructed a public building. We had been given the opportunity to disburse but did not. We had committed a crime and must pay the consequences.

We said our goodbyes and he left with Katya. While it did not seem any progress had been made, the visit was, nonetheless, an enjoyable break from the monotony.

Early the next morning, Katya arrived unexpectedly, her face beaming. She had a stack of papers in her hand, and she began passing them out to each of us, saying nothing. My nutrient starved brain struggled to comprehend the legal jargon written on the page. Eventually she explained. All of our charges had been reduced to "disturbing the peace." Seven days in jail was more than enough punishment for this crime. We were all to be released the same day.

"What happened? Why did he change his mind?" Sandino asked.

"Well, after he spoke with all of you, he had a similar session with the women. No offense, but they were a lot tougher on him than you guys were. That meeting lasted about twice as long. They really broke down for him the concept of justice, the principle upon which his resistance was ultimately based. They kept focusing his attention off of themselves, and upon the community on which their action had been based. By the time we left, I could tell he was getting worn down.

"He was starving, and so I offered to take him to find some kosher food. It was almost ten o'clock at this point, so finding kosher food in LA at this time of night was no easy matter. But this gave us a long time to talk. I kept trying to think of a way to reach him, and suddenly I remembered a story from World War

II. There was a group called the "White Rose" which engaged in nonviolent civil disobedience against the Nazi regime. I compared this with the oppression of the Hispanic community in Los Angeles. I asked him whether those who had resisted the Nazi regime were criminals. Slowly I think he began to understand that sometimes justice is more complicated than a simple equation of legal codes and punishment. I don't know whether or not I took the comparison between the Nazis and the LAPD too far, but in the end, he conceded to reduce the charges. You're all going home today!"

It took a full day before we were finally processed out. It felt like a dream. Most of all, I wanted to see Maggie. In my delirium the only thing I had been able to write in the last week was a note to her, and I had no idea whether she had gotten it. Even though we barely knew each other, our shared decision to endure this experience made me feel a closeness to her. I wondered if she felt the same way.

Processing out was almost like the reverse experience of processing in. When we were processed in, our humanity was peeled away from us step by step, and we were treated worse and worse. Now our humanity was being gradually returned, and I even felt we were being treated better and better each step along the way. It began to feel real once our original clothes were returned to us. I put on my jeans, socks and shoes, gray T-shirt, noticing they did not smell particularly well. My bandana, as I expected, had been lost somewhere along the way. I felt self-conscious about my messy hair, then silently scolded myself for being so shallow.

Finally, we saw the women. At first, they appeared on the other side of a glass partition but moving in the same direction as us. Finally, we converged into a common room, and we all embraced and cheered. I saw Maggie. Our eyes met, and there was a sense of connection, a bond unlike any I had felt before. I had been raised as an only child, and yet she felt like a true sister to me. We held hands and exited the jail together.

My senses were immediately flooded. There was the sight of over a hundred activists gathered to greet us. They held signs. Banners were spread everywhere. Then there was the sound of their cheering. Then the feeling of the night air on my skin, and the vast expanse of space all around me – especially above. And finally, the smell of food. There was a well-known group called "Food Not Bombs" that had put together a huge feast to welcome us on our release.

As I approached the table, I saw a box of avocados. This was the one food that, for whatever reason, I had dreamed about the most in the past week. I picked up one and found it to be slightly soft. I peeled away the thick skin slowly, reveling in the moment and the feeling of my fingertips gently sinking into the avocado flesh. I took a bite, and the taste was like an electric shock. I ate the entire avocado, in a state of continuous euphoria, and then felt completely full.

A kind woman, middle-aged and stocky with plain, straight brown hair tied back in a ponytail, approached Maggie and I, and invited us to stay at her home that night. She was, of course, a Quaker – and had even legally changed her last name to Friend. We stayed at her home for a couple of days while we regained our strength, mentally and physically. And then, we hitchhiked home.

Chapter 8

I returned to my university that fall semester a changed person. We now had something of a crew. Dean, Isaac, Maggie and I were now bound by our common experiences, our first-hand confrontations against the police in major cities in the United States. We were, so to speak, radicalized. Any doubt we might have once had about the seriousness and severity of what we were up against had been dispelled. The enemy was global capitalism; the state was its agent and the police were the soldiers on the front lines. But a resistance was growing, perhaps even a revolution. We knew we could not simply wait for the next mass action. We had to find a way to keep the struggle going on our home turf.

Dean started a campus chapter of the National Organization for the Reform of Marijuana Laws, otherwise known as NORML. He had, in fact, stopped by the national office in DC when he had been there the previous April for the IMF/World Bank protests and met the founder, Keith Stroup. Dean had little trouble piquing the interest of our student body, and when he called the first meeting at the Korouva Milkbar on campus, over fifty people showed up. Dean tried hard to link the struggle for marijuana legalization with the larger struggle against global capitalism we had confronted on the streets of DC, Philadelphia and Los Angeles. But truth be told, most of the students were just interested in getting high.

One notable exception was a student named Elazar who worked at the Milkbar. He joined the first meeting, smoking cigarettes quietly in the corner and listening. He was Latino, but his long black beard made him look more like a Jihadist, and he was used to jokes about this being made at his expense. After the first meeting he approached Dean and I and asked us about our protest experiences. He asked us to keep him posted on any future actions.

The subsequent meetings gained just as much attention. We elected a board, with Dean becoming president, and Elazar becoming treasurer. About fifty students signed up to be members, and when Dean registered our group with the national office, it got their attention. There was to be a protest for Hemp Legalization in Austin, Texas that fall, and Keith Stroup wrote to Dean asking if our group would be participating. When Dean responded that we would, we were invited to a follow-up meeting at the Omni Hotel, where representatives from the University of Texas chapter would also be in attendance.

Approximately a dozen of us – including Elazar, Dean and I – carpooled to downtown Austin, which was only about a half-hour drive from our university. We met at the Capitol Building, a gorgeous pink granite building modeled after the Capitol Building in DC, which sat in the middle of Austin, surrounded by a vast lawn and trees on all sides. It was a beautiful day with clear blue skies. There were about two hundred people gathered, a far cry from the scale of protests in which I had participated the previous summer, but I was just excited to have something happening so close to home.

We marched to the Governor's Mansion, which was just around the corner. There we heard speeches from some residents of Tulia, Texas. In July the previous year, 10 percent of the African American population of the city was arrested on drug charges stemming from the testimony of a single undercover officer. These arrests were considered racially motivated. Some of those arrested were facing up to 90 years in prison on trumped up drug charges. Keith Stroup took center stage after this, and talked about the connection between marijuana laws, racism, the prison industrial complex and for-profit prisons. As I listened, links were being formed in my mind, as I envisioned a long chain of injustice that surrounded the whole world, imprisoning us all.

After the rally, Dean, Elazar and I had a few hours to kill before the meeting at the Omni, so we decided to grab a late lunch at Kerbey Lane. We ordered coffee and queso dip. Elazar asked a lot of questions about our experiences with mass actions. We related our tales with harrowing details. We were clearly excited by the romance of it all. We were already beginning to think of ourselves as revolutionaries. Elazar was a little more hesitant.

"I am not sure I would want to participate in something like that. I get what we're doing today. I like that it's local. But I'm not sure how much can really be accomplished by big protests in the street. It seems to me a real revolution has to take place on a grassroots level, building connections with communities. Especially communities of color."

"I get that," I said. "I agree that it totally needs to happen. But also, I think it's important to connect at these big events to see we aren't alone. I mean, what we are up against is so huge. Our resistance has to be even bigger."

"That makes sense," he conceded. "I guess you need both. I'm just not sure those big actions are for me. Maybe it's just because I don't want to get beaten up by the police or go to jail." We all chuckled. "I just see my place, my particular role in this revolution – if you can call it that – is working to build community. If we build more communities that aren't dependent on the state, maybe we don't have to fight them."

"That's a lovely idea, Elazar, but it won't work," Dean joined in with his characteristic boldness. Elazar was visibly offended by this remark, and Dean tried to recover. "Sorry, that's putting it too bluntly. What I mean is, it would be great in theory, but the elites aren't going to just stand by and let communities become autonomous. They need our labor, our energy, to keep going. I totally agree that we need self-organizing, autonomous communities, but with any degree of success is going to come an inevitable response of state oppression. And we have to be ready for that. That, I think, is what these mass actions are preparing us for."

"I get what you mean," Elazar replied cautiously. "This is all still pretty new to me, and I need to give it some thought. But I have to admit, I think what you guys have been doing is pretty cool. I do think we need a revolution. I'm sure we have some time to figure out what exactly it's going to look like."

After scarfing down hefty amounts of chips and queso and guzzling multiple cups of coffee, we took a bus downtown to the Omni Hotel. At this time, it was one of the tallest buildings in Austin. We walked into the posh lobby, feeling a bit out of place with our ratty clothes and backpacks. We stepped into an elevator along with a well-dressed couple who had clearly been drinking. They looked at us with obvious condescension before asking us our floor number.

"Penthouse Suite, please," replied Dean, wearing a shit-eating grin. The funny part was, he wasn't joking.

We reached the top floor of the hotel, leaving the couple behind several floors below, and stepped out to see another lobby area. There were a handful of other students about our age, which I assumed to be the representatives from the UT chapter. There were also a few older guys, including Keith Stroup, who were representing NORML nationally. We all introduced ourselves and sat down to begin the meeting.

The purpose of the meeting seemed mainly to encourage the work the college chapters had been doing, and to help us better understand the messaging NORML was trying to convey. It was very pragmatic, and most of the main points we knew already. Marijuana had not been directly linked to any deaths. It was non-toxic, non-addictive. By comparison, tobacco and alcohol were exponentially more dangerous. But a combination of tobacco, alcohol and even paper and plastic lobbies had conspired to keep marijuana (and its industrial counterpart, hemp) illegal. As students, we all felt privileged to be in the presence of what we considered to be wise men, who were at the heart of a countercultural movement that we felt certain was destined to succeed.

The meeting concluded unceremoniously with some handshakes and pats on the back. The men from NORML began heading back to their room on that floor. The students from UT began heading back to the elevator in the opposite direction, and Dean, Elazar and I followed behind. Suddenly we heard a "PSST!" and looked back over our shoulders. The three men from NORML were motioning us to follow them. They pointed specifically at the three of us. We glanced back at the UT students who had noticed we were being singled out. I will never forget the envious glares they shot us as we shrugged and turned back around to follow Keith Stroup and his crew to their hotel room.

I knew exactly what was going on, but I still couldn't believe it. We were invited into their suite and told to make ourselves at home. We set our backpacks aside and sat on one of the beds. One of the men pulled out a large Tupperware container and opened it. The smell of sweet pine immediately filled the room.

"Northern Lights," he said, with a glimmer in his eye.

From there began a chain of endless, perfectly rolled joints that circled the room. As soon as one joint was lit, the next one was being rolled. We listened to Keith pontificate upon the unfairness of marijuana laws, the persecution of the lawful citizens who chose to enjoy it recreationally, as we stared out the window of his penthouse suite. We tried to keep up, both with the conversation and the smoking, but after an hour or so we were failing at both. I was higher than I had ever been in my entire life, and as exhilarating as this experience was, I was ready to leave. Fortunately, Dean and Elazar felt the same way.

They collected their backpacks, and we said our goodbyes. We returned to the elevator and descended the dozen or so floors to the lobby, not saying a word. We exited the hotel and walked into the night. The city was alive with music, pedicabs, food and drinking. We walked for blocks without saying a word, until finally I broke the silence.

"Does anyone else think it's amazing we just smoked out with Keith Stroup?"

Dean and Elazar erupted with yeses and laughter and high fives. And no sooner did we begin our celebration than I suddenly felt all the blood leave my face.

"Shit! I left my backpack in their room!"

We returned to the hotel, but this time the hotel staff did not allow us to return to the penthouse suite. They phoned the room, but there was no answer. The next day, however, I returned to the hotel and the backpack was waiting for me at the front desk. It had been a stressful and embarrassing end to an otherwise badass experience.

Not long after the legalization rally, we learned of another event taking place in Austin in October. This time, however, the connection with the emerging anti-globalization movement was more direct. The Fortune 500 was holding a summit at the Four Seasons Hotel on October 13. The nickname of the action was "O13," linking it to the nomenclature of N30 in Seattle or A16 in DC. An announcement regarding the "Unwelcoming Party" was posted on the newly published Austin IndyMedia website.

Dean, Maggie, Isaac, Elazar and I drove to Austin together that Friday afternoon, the day of the protest. Several other members of NORML agreed to meet us there. The rally started in the early afternoon, with a march down Congress during rush hour. The timing was intentional, in order to disrupt "business as usual." A few hundred of us took up a lane and marched down to the Four Seasons Hotel. There we heard various speeches, and eventually the crowd dispersed without incident.

The "action" itself was very tame by the standards of the other protests I had attended the previous summer. Nonetheless, I was energized. It still had the same feel, the same familiar symbols. Many of the protesters covered their faces with bandanas. Dreadlocks abounded. There were even some wearing all black, although there was no "Black Bloc" to speak of. I saw a banner that read "Class War Now," which I didn't understand. Another that read "Viva Zapata!" I figured this had something to do with the speech by Vicente Fox, president of Mexico, who would be addressing the conference that evening, but I didn't fully understand the connection. What was clear to me, however, was that the seeds of revolution were right here in Austin, even if we weren't quite ready for a full-scale uprising.

Some Latino students from UT handed us a flyer announcing a "Student Encuentro" taking place at the Center for Mexican American Cultural Arts (CMACA). "Encuentro," according to the flyer, meant an "encounter, which celebrates the diversity of activists and opens a space for dialog." None of us had any plans and were eager to check it out.

The CMACA was a run-down metal building situated behind a neighborhood near I-10, just a few hundred yards from the Barton Creek Bike Trail. The center was buzzing with activity when we arrived. The first thing I noticed when we walked in was the delicious smell of Mexican food wafting in our direction, especially corn tortillas and tamales. The feeling was similar to the one I had felt at the convergence center in Los Angeles. Everyone was busy doing something. In one corner, activists sat in a corner deep in discussion. In another, crusty punks were painting papier mâché puppets. In yet another, food was being served. I was starving, so this was my first stop. I quickly learned all the food was vegetarian, which didn't bother me in the least.

That evening I met a number of the activists who were prominent in the Austin scene. There was Eric, who along with a few others had started up the Austin IndyMedia center. At this point IndyMedia centers were spreading like wildfire. There were at least 25 in the United States, and probably that same number across the world in Australia, Europe and Latin

America. There were Stacy and Scotty, who were in the process of starting an autonomous community on the east side. Then there was Nikita, a pretty, short girl with long curly black hair. She approached me and asked if we had met before.

We hadn't, but eventually we figured out why she recognized me. She had been the one to first organize the vigil outside the jail in Los Angeles. The entire time I was inside, she had been spreading the word, organizing food, making signs and building puppets. She had also been to Seattle and basically every mass action since. I had a crush on her immediately. We talked intently for the next hour, and I lost track of the rest of my crew. I didn't even notice the room was being set up for the movie screening until they made the announcement. Nikita and I found seats next to each other.

The movie was a documentary called This Is What Democracy Looks Like, which was a collaboration between a collective called "Big Noise Productions" and Seattle IndyMedia. It was a close-up account of the events which took place on those fateful days in Seattle the previous November/December. I had never seen anything like it. I knew it had been bad, but I had no idea just how bad. The police, dressed in full riot gear, terrorized nonviolent, defenseless activists. I gasped in astonishment at the scene of a riot cop literally soaking activists, who huddled together on the ground, with streams of pepper spray. He even lifted one of their bandanas in order to get a direct shot to the face.

It was horrifying, and yet inspiring to a point that it sent tingles through my entire body. The brutality of the police only raised the courage of the activists in stark relief. They never gave up or backed down and kept returning to the streets even after being beaten, shot with rubber bullets, sprayed and threatened with arrest. The documentary interspersed shots from the protests with speeches by political activists who provided background, placing the events of Seattle clearly in the context of a global struggle by the people against the dehumanizing, brutal forces of corporate capitalism. The message was clear, and utterly convincing: we were a part of history.

I remember being especially struck by the interviews with a young woman about my own age. Her name was "Warcry." She had dark hair and skin, and was possibly of Indian descent. She was dressed in all black, with a bandana tied around her neck. She was seated comfortably on a couch as she explained the political and philosophical underpinnings of the actions. It seemed she must have been one of the ones who participated in the most militant actions in Seattle, but of course this was never stated. When discussing the Black Bloc, she commented, "Well, of course, you have to respect a diversity of tactics." She was elegant, confident and articulate.

We all decided to go and get drinks afterwards, and Nikita joined us. We walked a few blocks down to 6th Street to a dingy pub called Lovejoys, popular with the punk crowd. Several others who had been at the protests earlier in the day, as well as the encuentro, were there. We ordered drinks and found a booth. For a while, we all chatted together, discussing the alarming amount of paramilitary gear the APD had worn at the protest that day – although they hadn't found reason to use it. We discussed the documentary we had seen, and Nikita shared some of her own terrifying memories from the WTO protests in Seattle. However, one story led to another, one city to the next. It seemed Nikita was completely nomadic, being carried away from one adventure to the next with few breaks in between. She spoke passionately, with a dreadful seriousness about the environmental destruction happening to our planet – the rivers and oceans, the tropical rainforest and the old growth forests of the Pacific Northwest. At first, everyone was listening intently, nodding in agreement. But eventually, fatigue set in for everyone else in my crew, who began breaking off into their own conversations and leaving the booth, until it was just she and I talking in the booth. Or, more accurately, she was doing the talking and I was doing the listening.

I was relieved when Isaac came back to the booth and told me one of the students from the encuentro had offered us all a place to stay at his house. As pretty as Nikita was, I was becoming exhausted. Everything had begun to seem so heavy, and I wanted a break. It turned out, however, that she didn't have a place to sleep that night either, and so she came with us. She continued talking the entire walk, seven or eight blocks, to the student's house.

It didn't take long, once we arrived there, to get settled in. He had a spare room, which Dean, Maggie, Isaac and Elazar quickly claimed, leaving Nikita and I alone in the living room. We sat on the couch, my eyes nearly closing involuntarily as she related her experiences of running supplies to the tree-sitters outside of Portland, until finally I kissed her.

Chapter 9

The night of the presidential election, November 7, I was ambivalent about the outcome. I had cast my vote for Ralph Nader, as had most of my closest friends. Many of our more moderate liberal friends, including Valerie, were frustrated by our decision. The common refrain we heard, even from our professors, was that Nader was "stealing away votes" from Al Gore. I resented this. Al Gore did not own my vote, so how could Ralph Nader "steal it?" My typical response was that the corporations owned both political parties. Whichever of the two candidates won was immaterial, because in either case corporate capitalism won. At least a vote for Nader would be making a statement.

Deep down, I certainly preferred Gore over Bush, although I never admitted it out loud. I was, after all, pro-Choice and anti-war. I was also pro-gay rights and strongly believed in the separation of church and state. Clearly none of these points would be advanced by a Bush administration. Also, having personally experienced the help my dad had received from the government after his accident, I was in favor of all social services – even though my emerging anarchist views were a little difficult to square against that. Ideally, I felt all social needs should be met by small, autonomous, self-organizing communities – but until that became possible, better to have some safety net than none at all.

For whatever reason, I assumed Gore would win the election. We had a party at my apartment, which I shared with three other roommates. We went through cases of Lone Star beers, interrupted by an occasional shot of Evan Williams. As the night wore on, however, I began feeling concerned at how close the results were as they were being reported. But then Al Gore was declared the predicted winner. Everyone cheered, and

I couldn't help but to join in the celebration.

About an hour later, however, the networks retracted their initial prediction, as Florida returned to the "undecided" column. The party became less festive. People began going home. I stayed up well past midnight, just staring at the TV. Beneath the pictures of the two candidates were the strange words "Too Close to Call." I went to sleep that night still not knowing who our next president would be.

To my shock, the answer still had not been resolved by the following morning. In fact, the question would drag on for weeks more. Bush was tentatively declared the winner on November 26, and Gore immediately contested the results. Finally, the issue was settled by the Supreme Court. Bush had won the national election narrowly according to the electoral college, even though Al Gore had received more than half a million more votes nationwide. My ambivalence transformed to rage.

I was, of course, not alone in this feeling. I began spending every spare moment on the IndyMedia websites, stopping in at the computer lab between classes to read and comment on articles. Protests against the inauguration in DC the following January began to be organized very quickly. The coalitions that had formed as a result of the anti-globalization movement now focused their attention on the "stolen election." Environmental groups, labor activists, women's rights groups as well as the International Socialist Organization joined together to call for a mass mobilization in DC on the day of the inauguration.

What caught my attention, however, was a post by a group that identified itself as the Barricada Collective:

A Call for a United Revolutionary Presence at The Presidential Inauguration

WE ALREADY KNOW WHO WON...CAPITALISM AND

THE RULING CLASS.

TAKE TO THE STREETS OF WASHINGTON AGAINST CAPITALISM, AGAINST THE STATE AND AGAINST THE DEATH MACHINE OF GLOBALIZATION. CLASS WAR NOW. FOR A CLASSLESS, STATELESS SOCIETY. SATURDAY, JANUARY 20, 2001. WASHINGTON DC 10 A.M.

I could hardly contain my excitement. This could be more than just a protest. This could truly be the turning point, the beginning of a real revolution. After all, at least half the country was at a boiling point. While the past year had laid the groundwork and built the coalitions, this could be the tipping point that radicalized millions. So much depended upon what actually happened in DC the day of the inauguration. The fuel was prepared, the kindling stacked. We just needed to light the match. I decided that I, for one, was willing to do whatever it took to make that happen.

I copied and pasted the link into an email which I immediately fired off to Isaac, Maggie, Dean and Elazar. As soon as I did so, however, I regretted it. What if my email was being monitored? I figured it was unlikely; however I wouldn't be surprised if I got a lecture from some of them about "security culture" for my impulsive decision. I printed out the announcement so we could discuss it in person.

Later that week we met at the Korouva Milkbar. The five of us sat on the back porch with hot cups of coffee to help keep us warm as we discussed. I had brought the printout with me, and it was passed around as we talked.

"So, are we, like, an affinity group?" Isaac asked, lighting a cigarette. I felt annoyed at his seeming apathy, but I shook it off.

"I think we should be. I mean, we all know and trust each other."

Isaac looked directly at me with his penetrating blue eyes.

"So, tell me, what are you ready to do? Are you ready to fight police? Are you ready to kill police?"

The directness of his question pushed me off balance. I couldn't help but fumble my words.

"I mean, no, not really. I mean, I would try to defend myself if I had to. I don't think I could kill anyone."

"So how exactly is this going to work? Let's say it sparks a revolution like you're saying. Let's say the whole city goes up in flames. You don't think there is going to be bloodshed?"

"Let's just take this one step at a time, Isaac," said Dean, laughing nervously. He was trying to defuse the situation.

"No! I really want to know! Is that what we are talking about here?"

"I am ready to kill, if I have to," interjected Maggie. I was somehow shocked, and not shocked at the same time. Maggie was still a mysterious person to me, full of secrets.

"You would kill a cop?"

"Not unless I had to!" She was laughing now, and this did manage to relieve the tension. "You know I'm an anarchist. I believe in revolution. I do believe it is going to come down to that one day. It's called Class War, after all. But there's no way in hell that's what's going to happen in DC."

"That's what I was thinking," said Elazar. "I mean, it might get a bit rowdy, but the revolution isn't happening on January 20th. Maybe not for a long time. And maybe not ever the way we are picturing it."

I felt deflated, perhaps even a little silly. Dean came to the rescue.

"To me, it's about the symbolism. We need to be there as a revolutionary presence, showing the rest of the country there is an alternative to this fake democracy. Maybe it will spark something, or maybe it will just plant another seed. But I feel like this moment is too important for us to stand by passively."

Everyone was quiet. Isaac stood up and paced for a few

moments on the porch, smoking intently. Finally, he wandered back to the table, and took a deep breath before speaking.

"Ok. I'm in."

"So am I," said Maggie.

Now all eyes were on Elazar. He looked at each of us and grinned.

"Not me. No thanks. I don't want to get beaten up by the police, and I don't want to go to jail. And as the only brown guy in the group, I'm sure I'd be the first one to go down. But I support you guys. If you get into any trouble, be sure to call me."

My next task was to figure out how to join the spokescouncil, expected to take place the night before the action. The details were not published online, but there was an email address. I used a new anonymous email account with RiseUp.net to contact them, keeping my inquiry brief and to the point. I signed my name as "Blackbeard." A response came quickly:

> Blackbeard,
>
> For security reasons we cannot disclose the time and location of the spokescouncil meeting to you until you have been vouched for by known members of our community.
>
> If you have worked with anyone in the anti-authoritarian/ anti-fascist community, please have them contact us at the phone number below. Once we have confirmed with them, we will reach out to you with details regarding the spokescouncil.
>
> Solidarity,
>
> The Barricada Collective

My initial reaction was total deflation. I didn't know a single person who had participated in a Black Bloc (at least not definitively) besides that guy Raven I had met in Los Angeles. But I had no way of contacting him. Even if I did, I doubted he would "vouch" for me. I racked my brain, trying to come up with someone I knew that they would also know. Of course, I didn't know who they were at all. I briefly considered Keith Stroup. No, I don't think a pot-smoking icon is quite what they have in mind. I was beginning to meet activists in Austin, but it was hard to say if any of them were prominent enough to be known outside of our small circle. I thought about the guys I had been in jail with in Los Angeles. I felt I was getting closer to a solution, and then it dawned on me: Katya Komisaruk! A "vouch" from her would be unquestionable, not only due to her work freeing hundreds of jailed activists in Los Angeles and Seattle, but also her own impressive history of direct action, which almost certainly overshadowed anything anyone in the "Barricada Collective" had done.

Would she do it? Only one way to find out. Since the Midnight Special Legal Collective had a website, she was not difficult to find. I decided I should call, rather than email, so I would not create an electronic paper trail linking her to whatever might go down in DC. Initially, I got her voicemail, so I left her a message explaining my intentions briefly without going into too much detail. She called me back an hour later. My heart was racing as I answered.

"Hi Katya. My name is Blackbeard. I am not sure if you remember me, but I was one of the activists in jail in Los Angeles."

She paused briefly.

"Oh yes, sure I remember. How are you?"

"I'm good! The reason I am calling is because I am going to DC for the inauguration to participate in an action, and they are asking if I know someone who could vouch for me. I was wondering if you could...do that for me?"

She laughed out loud.

"Are you serious? Vouch for you?" My mind was racing. I felt embarrassed. Was this something not usually done? This was all so new to me I had no idea what was considered normal.

"What is the name of the group?"

"The Barricada Collective."

"Hmm, I've never heard of them. They are in DC?"

"Yes, I think so." I didn't exactly want to tell her this was a "Black Bloc" collective.

"Well, I don't see why not. Give them my number and I'll vouch for you, Blackbeard." I could hear her smiling on the other end.

It worked. I got an email back from the Barricada Collective the next day, providing me with a phone number that I was instructed to call an hour before the meeting, which was going to take place at 6pm, January 19. I was to give the password "BAKUNIN." (Bakunin was a prominent nineteenth-century anarchist). Only then would I be given the location of the meeting. It was beginning to feel like I was living in a spy movie of some kind. Would I be one of the good guys or the bad guys in that movie? Only history would decide, which, as they say, is written by the victors.

I put a great deal of thought and effort into collecting everything I figured I would need on the day of the protest. I went to Walmart to gather supplies. First, I picked out a black hoodie, black cargo pants and a black bandana. Then I continued to the grocery section and found some apple cider vinegar and a small plastic bottle I figured I could keep in my pocket. Finally, I proceeded to the sporting goods section and picked out a small hunting knife. I stood in the aisle, thinking back to the intense exchange I had with Isaac at the Korouva Milkbar, his blue eyes staring into my soul.

No, I wasn't planning to stab anyone. Not a cop, not anyone. Rather, I figured I could use this knife, if necessary, to slash the tires of a police car. I thought of this more as a pragmatic plan, than a violent one. It could be an easy way to prevent a police car from pursuing the protest, possibly saving dozens from arrest.

It would also transform a threat into an ad hoc barricade. It made sense to me, so I added it to my shopping basket without giving it another thought.

Being broke college students, we needed to find the most economical way possible to get to the protests. There were a number of organizations that had chartered buses from Austin to DC, but of course, the Barricada Collective was not one of them. We ended up joining up with the International Action Committee, which had obtained the largest permit in DC that weekend and was organizing buses all over the country. The round trip would only cost about $50 each. The challenge, of course, was how to make it to the spokescouncil meeting in time.

We boarded the bus to find a diverse group of activists. There were some young college students like us, but also middle-aged and even older people. To my disappointment, some of them even held blue "Gore/Lieberman" signs in their seats. The last thing I wanted this protest to be was an opportunity for mainstream Democrats to complain about losing the election, even if it had been a particularly unjust defeat. I wanted people to see the bigger point, that the whole system was rigged, and that democracy was a sham. It was a long drive to DC, and while we did engage in some conversations about this – some of which got quite heated – we eventually decided to stick to ourselves and keep quiet.

We stopped for gas about an hour outside of DC. I had been watching the time nervously. It was now already about 5:30pm, and it seemed there was no way we were going to make the spokescouncil meeting. I stepped off the bus and found a payphone and called the number I had been given. A woman answered.

"Password please."

"BAKUNIN."

"The meeting will be taking place at a warehouse near Dupont Circle." She then proceeded to give me the address.

I explained we were unlikely to arrive in time for the meeting, due to our bus being behind schedule.

"No problem," she said. Just be at Franklin Square tomorrow morning at 9am sharp. Any actions you intend to participate in should be coordinated with your own affinity group. See you tomorrow, Blackbeard."

That evening we stayed with Dean's aunt and uncle who lived in downtown DC. They had also let Dean and his friends stay with them during the A16 protests. Dean's uncle was left-leaning himself, and very supportive of activism in general. They lived in a brownstone row house with a basement, and we were given the entire space to ourselves. By the time we settled in, arranging our sleeping bags on the floor, it was after midnight. I was utterly exhausted, but so excited about the next morning I lay awake for hours trying to imagine it in my mind.

Dean's alarm went off around 6am. I wasn't even sure I had slept. We each arose slowly, groaning and stretching on our sleeping bags. It hadn't been the most comfortable night's sleep. I found my backpack and took it into the small basement bathroom to change. I came out dressed in all black. Black boots, black cargo pants, black hoodie. A black bandana was stuffed into my pocket. Isaac whistled at me.

"Looking good, Señor Anarchista!"

As was often the case with Isaac, I wasn't sure if he was genuinely mocking me, or if it was just good-natured ribbing. It did seem there was some rift between us in terms of our understanding and approach to activism, although it was hard to define. Surely Isaac was an anarchist himself – after all, he had an anarchy symbol tattooed on his forearm. Once, when I asked him why he had the tattoo, he said: "Well, one day, if I ever find myself working in some soulless corporate job, I want to look down at my arm and see that tattoo and remember that I should quit." But Isaac never called himself an anarchist and would respond in cryptic ways if ever asked. Perhaps this was an expression of his own interpretation of anarchism, a rejection of all labels.

By this time, I did consider myself an anarchist and would gladly call myself that. I considered labels to be important. After all, aren't all words labels? Don't we need words to communicate with one another? I had begun reading some of the classic anarchist writings by nineteenth-century writers like Bakunin or Kropotkin, as well as more modern esoteric thinkers such as Hakim Bey or John Zerzan. In my way of thinking, it was vitally important that we communicate the political philosophy of anti-authoritarianism and mutual aid in no uncertain terms. My straightforward adoption of the "Black Bloc" dress code was just an extension of this same line of thinking.

Everyone else got dressed as well, in varying degrees of adherence to the Black Bloc style. But everyone brought bandanas to cover their faces. We had a brief discussion about whether or not to carry any identification, but agreed it was best not to. In case we were arrested, jail solidarity was our best bet of getting released without having to face charges.

We made a brief stop at a nearby coffee shop to get some coffee and scarf down some bagels, before continuing on to the metro. When we boarded the train, we saw many other protesters on board, carrying signs. Once again, we saw some annoying Gore/Lieberman signs, but also some from the National Organization for Women (NOW). There were some other young punks with dreadlocks and piercings, but I couldn't be sure if it was just fashion or if they were also headed the same place we were.

We got off the blue line at McPherson Square Station, which was just two blocks from Franklin Square. When we exited the metro, however, and out into the open street, it seemed to me two blocks might as well be two miles. There were police everywhere. There was a contingent of motorcycle police right across the street. Another block away, to our left, I could see a police van with police standing all around, suiting up in riot gear. I felt a knot of fear, mingled with excitement, tighten in my stomach. I was eager to join the protest but was terrified we might get picked off before we even got there.

We were, fortunately, not stopped by any police before we made it to the park. There were hundreds gathered, a sea of black-masked activists, waving black and red anarcho-syndicalist flags and bearing large banners, including an especially prominent one bearing the words CLASS WAR, which was the one mentioned specifically in the announcement. We could hear drums, whose beat matched the beating of my own heart, increasing in intensity. Without speaking, the four of us removed the bandanas from our pockets and covered our faces, tying them behind our necks. I raised the hood of my hoodie over my head. We entered the park and blended into the crowd.

Almost immediately, the crowd began moving and spilling onto 13th Street. Unlike the marches I had participated in previously, I found everyone sticking closely together in a dense mass. This was presumably for safety. The familiar chant began: Whose streets? Our streets! My adrenaline skyrocketed as I joined in, bellowing the words from the deepest depths of my diaphragm. It was freezing cold this morning, in the low 30s, but suddenly I felt warm and energized by the bodies around me and the bold, aggressive energy. I looked behind me and saw the police were already in pursuit, mostly on motorcycles. Some of them were now on the sidewalks. The knowledge that we had taken the streets without a permit, and there was seemingly nothing the police could do to stop it, was utterly intoxicating.

We made a left onto K street and passed in front of the Washington Post building. Several black-clad anarchists emerged from the crowd. One raced up to the building and spray-painted an anarchy symbol on the brown brick. Two others shattered the plate glass windows, presumably by hurling ball bearings too small to see. They then returned to our march, blending in imperceptibly. Someone began to chant *Fuck the Corporate Media!* and we all joined in, raising our middle fingers at the building.

If there had been any doubt about the intention of our gathering, or whether it might be considered lawful, those questions were now behind us. However, I was all in. I was completely in alignment with others in our movement who considered the media to be among the worst offenders in perpetuating injustice in our society, and the world at large. They were the ones who perpetuated the narratives put forward by the elites, the capitalists and the politicians who served their interests. They were the ones who diminished the size or significance of the anti-globalization protests, or often failed to report on them at all.

We made a right on 14th Street. There was a police cruiser in the middle of the street with its rear to us. We swarmed around it. Before I could think about using my knife, someone beat me to it. I heard a loud pop and saw one of its tires flatten, a large gash across it. Contemplating something like this from the safety of Walmart was one thing, but seeing it actually happen was another. We were causing real trouble, and I couldn't help but wonder with trepidation how this was going to end.

The plate glass windows of an army recruiting center were the next to get hit. There was now a strong police presence behind us, including motorcycles and police cruisers, as well as many on foot. We turned another block to find a line of riot police approximately a hundred yards ahead. Those in the lead made a quick turn into an alleyway, allowing us to avoid disaster. The effectiveness of this move was short-lived, however. When we emerged from the alleyway, now back on 14th and K, having come almost full circle, we found police on all sides of us, and more in the alleyway from which we had just come. Some did manage to escape by aggressively charging police lines before they had a chance to solidify. Maggie was among them. Isaac,

Dean and I, however, were among the hundreds who were now completely trapped.

"So, do we try to escape, or do we wait to get arrested?" Isaac asked.

I considered the situation. We were surrounded on all sides, but the police line was still sparse. Soon reinforcements would be arriving, and our entrapment strengthened.

"The longer we wait, the harder it will be," I concluded.

"Well, let's go," said Isaac. Again, his blue eyes penetrated mine, hypnotizing me in that moment as time began to slow. He took a few steps backward, toward the police line, and I followed. Then, he turned, and we both started to run. I aimed for an opening in the line where two police were separated by about 10 feet of daylight. They spotted me. They bent their knees slightly and put their arms out, trying to anticipate my direction. I was reminded of the times I had played football with my cousin in middle school. I saw one of them, a black man, widen his eyes and begin mouthing the words "No, no, no!"

No sooner had I entered the breach than I felt myself grabbed from behind and tackled to the ground. The officer was on top of me, and he punched me in the ribs. I was surprised at the fact that it didn't hurt, but still I was flooded with panic. The officer shouted at me: "Do not resist!" I didn't. I wondered if I would be unarrested. No help came.

I waited for the handcuffs or zip ties to be placed on my wrists, but I was simply kept on the ground as I heard the police conferring with one another. Eventually I heard someone, perhaps a commanding officer, say "Throw him back in." And so they did. I was raised to my feet, led back to the police lines and then thrown back into the encirclement with the other protesters.

I saw Isaac, who was red in the face, visibly shaken up. He had evidently suffered a similar outcome.

"Well, that didn't work," he said.

There was nothing to do now but accept our fates. As expected, more police arrived to reinforce their lines. Moments later, a bus arrived outside the cordon. I began to notice police distributing large bundles of white zip ties among themselves. It was looking pretty clear that I was heading to jail for the second time in less than six months.

Suddenly we began to hear chanting on the other side of the police line, coming from the direction of the inaugural parade. I saw signs for the NOW, the Justice Action Network, and yes – even some Gore/Lieberman campaign signs. It seemed word had gotten out about our impending doom, and a crowd of more than a thousand had come to the rescue. They were now putting pressure on the opposite side of the police lines. One thing I was learning very quickly – the police hate to be surrounded.

For five or ten tense minutes, it was unclear what was going to happen. Some of us within the encirclement began chanting "Whose streets? Our streets!" The protesters on the opposite side of the police line joined in unison. To my surprise, many of the police actually began to look nervous. I noticed there were a number of conversations taking place between the commanding officers. Suddenly, the police lines opened. We poured out of the encirclement and joined the second march. I was utterly euphoric.

What I didn't know at the time, due to the fact that we had missed the spokescouncil meeting the night before, was that there was a designated re-convergence at the Navy Memorial. As a result, we would miss some of the even more dramatic events of the day and would only learn about them later. For instance, after the Black Bloc reconvened, they managed to commandeer a construction wagon and use it to ram a Secret Service checkpoint, very nearly spilling into the parade route itself. This breach of security, in fact, resulted in the inaugural parade being halted. During the commotion, George W. Bush's limo was pelted with eggs and glass bottles.

At the Navy Memorial, a handful of anarchists climbed the platform where a flagpole stood, lowered the American flag and removed it. In its place, they raised a black and red anarcho-syndicalist flag. The police surrounded the platform, trapping one of the anarchists, who was left seemingly without escape. But, in a moment of boldness and quick thinking, he leapt over the police lines into the crowd of anarchists, crowd-surfing to freedom. This was all caught on video and was widely shared on the IndyMedia sites as an iconic moment of anarchist heroism. It was one of the few moments in which we actually appeared as heroic as we longed to be.

The rest of the day for Maggie, Isaac, Dean and I was decidedly less heroic. Unsure what else to do or where to go after narrowly escaping arrest, we proceeded to the parade route, stuffing our bandanas into our back pockets. Our adrenaline subsided, and the full force of the cold winter air punished our tired bodies. We watched with resignation as Bush's limo passed us, little American flags flanking the headlights. We booed loudly, and many others joined in. But there was nothing else we could do. The Bush era had begun.

Chapter 10

After returning to school for the 2001 Spring semester, I learned a recently hired sociology professor, David Redmon, had screened This is What Democracy Looks Like in one of his classes. I was excited by the idea that there might actually be support for what we were doing among the university faculty. I wrote him a brief email thanking him for showing the documentary to his students. It meant a lot to me, particularly after returning from the inauguration and seeing little mention of the protests in the major news media. The anarchists were described in the usual derogatory terms. Troublemakers. Hoodlums. I was so thankful some students at my university were getting to see the other side. If I was so touched and inspired by the film, maybe others would be too.

He wrote back, asking me more about my own experiences, which I gladly shared. It wasn't long before we decided to meet up for coffee at the Student Union building.

When I first saw David, I mistook him for another student. He seemed very young, about my own age although he must have been at least 26 or 27. He was about my own height and build, about 5'7," 130 pounds. He dressed casually and wore a brown newsboy cap. He was clean shaven with thick black-rimmed glasses.

David was brilliant. As I shared with him my experiences in the streets of Philadelphia, Los Angeles or DC, he related my observations to the theories of Michel Foucault or Jacques Lacan. As I described the problem of globalization as I understood it, the dominance of global corporate capitalism and the erasure of local culture and differences, he made off-hand references to the writings of Slavoj Žižek and Jean Baudrillard. I felt that David was in possession of some secret knowledge that could perhaps be part of the key to unlocking the great puzzle of our struggle: how to make a revolution actually happen.

Before long, David and I had become good friends. When there was a party on campus, I would invite him, and he would show up. We drank together and discussed revolution and cultural theory. Half the time I could barely keep up with what he was saying, but I enjoyed trying. He never made me feel like I was beneath his level of understanding, and in fact often praised my comments as being profound or insightful. He also expressed great interest in the protest actions I had participated in thus far. He asked me to let him know the next time an opportunity arose.

It didn't take long. As reports and first-hand accounts of the J20 Inauguration Day were still being added to IndyMedia, a posting for the next major action appeared. The "Summit of the Americas" was taking place in Quebec City in April, to continue negotiations for the Free Trade Area of the Americas (FTAA.) The FTAA was being described as "NAFTA on steroids." If these negotiations were successful, the trade agreement which previously covered only the United States, Canada and Mexico would be extended to include Central and South America. According to a statement formed by the 34 heads of state who would be gathering for the summit, the purpose of the FTAA was to spread wealth across the hemisphere through trade liberalization policies. In the minds of anti-globalization activists, however, this was just another step toward the elimination of all environmental and labor policies that had been hard won over the last century.

The call for a "Revolutionary Anti-Capitalist Offensive in Quebec" came soon after. The plans seemed even more secretive, nuanced and complex than anything I had seen before. There was not one, but three separate "blocs": green, yellow and red. While all were encouraged to wear black, the colors indicated the degree of risk the participants were willing to assume. Green meant, essentially, avoid arrest if at all possible. Yellow meant willingness to be arrested in a civil disobedience action – similar to the one I had participated in, in Los Angeles. Red meant willingness to not only get arrested, but to resist the police by any means necessary.

Similarly, the security of this event was on a level none of us had seen before. A massive security perimeter was being established in downtown Quebec City with a 2.4-mile chain-link fence enclosing the neighborhoods where the summit would be taking place. Proof of residency was required to come anywhere near the summit. Gas masks, bandanas or masks of any kind were banned for the week. This was to be the largest police deployment in Canadian history. Naturally, many activists in the United States were concerned about the likelihood of being able to cross the border into Canada.

Any hesitation I might have had about going to this protest instantly evaporated when I saw a post by none other than "Warcry" appear on the IndyMedia feed.

WE TALKED TO THE MOHAWKS!
NYC-DAN had a great meeting with the Mohawks of First Nations Tribes. They are definitely interested in taking CONTROL of the border on their reservation and allowing Americans thru. They are not into symbolic CD. They mean business! Now we just have to deal with the authorities en route TO the border and from the border TO Quebec. This is going to be a militant wild action. Ya Basta! and Black Bloc as well as Mohawks and others including some labor groups are going to converge on the little northern New York town of Cornwall on the 19th of April. We've agreed to be fairly open about planning this. Because the Mohawks have a history of armed resistance to State impositions on their Nation – the authorities will be hesitant to provoke such a dramatic confrontation. I think this is a great opportunity for Black Bloc and others of militant mind in the protest movement to

work with the Mohawks and LEARN some shit. We'll keep you posted via the NYC-IMC site or email me. The staging point for the Americans will be the Burlington Vermont convergence center open on the 16th of April. See www. vermontactionnetwork.org Stay tuned com-RADZ!!
Warcry

Other articles followed soon after. One featured a picture of a "Mohawk warrior" taken during the Oka Crisis in 1990. I gazed at the picture of the Native-American man wearing camouflage fatigues, his face completely covered in a black balaclava, a semi-automatic rifle in his hands. My imagination went wild. I pictured myself and hundreds of black-clad, masked anarchists making our way through the forest, accompanied by armed "Mohawk warriors" on all sides. They would guide us across the border in an act of overwhelming solidarity with our common cause against neo-liberalization, as an act of defiance against the border that cut through their land.

I read the remainder of the statement, which was put out by the Ontario Coalition Against Poverty (OCAP):

The US/Canadian border at Cornwall falls entirely within the Mohawk community of Akwesasne. Every day, in an affront to the sovereignty of the Mohawk Nation, US and Canadian authorities determine who crosses the border and who does not.

OCAP, in partnership with the traditional people of the Mohawk Nation, labor and community groups is organizing in solidarity with anti- globalization protesters en route to Quebec to open the border at Akwesasne.

It is, for the community of Akwesasne, both an assertion of sovereignty and an opportunity to expose the conditions Mohawk and Indian people generally live under. First Nations people are over-represented on the street, in the prisons and live crammed on tiny reserves often without running water or heat in the winter. As one Mohawk man said, "The state's not so worried about people crossing the border, but about non-natives coming into the community and seeing how we live."

OCAP is proud to stand side by side with Mohawk people, to open the border and grant safe passage to folks fighting the brutality of the globalization agenda.

I printed out the post in full color, making sure the image of the "Mohawk warrior" was clearly visible, and immediately went looking for Dean.

His reaction was similar to my own. He was absolutely thrilled with the prospect of the border crossing, perhaps even more so than the events in Quebec themselves. For us, working with the "Mohawk people," particularly in such a militant (possibly armed) action, would be incredibly affirming of the cause in which we were engaged. There was a moral authority to the "native" struggles that neither of us had direct access to. After all, our ancestors were the "oppressors." But if we had this chance to unite with native peoples in a common cause, it would be a kind of redemption. It would prove, definitively, that we were on the right side of history.

David, too, was immediately on board. Isaac and Maggie, however, were short on funds and decided to sit this one out. The three of us began meeting to make plans. David had a friend, Todd, who lived in Albany, NY, which was just a short drive to Burlington, VT – the site of the main convergence on the US side. In order to save time, we would fly to Albany. Todd agreed to loan us his vehicle once we arrived. At this time, I was not expecting to need the car to drive to the border. I was still anticipating a guerilla-style forest crossing through the mountains, dodging occasional fire from the Canadian border patrol.

Dean and I made it clear we were ready for action, and if all went as planned, we fully intended to be fighting riot police on the streets of Quebec City, and hopefully participating in the dismantling of large sections of the security perimeter. David was less committed, although he fully supported – as was the expression – "a diversity of tactics." This was the spirit of the times. Those on the left – who opposed capitalism, supported labor rights and environmental activism – were a broad spectrum. Some simply believed in reform, while others (like us) insisted "Revolution is the Solution." Some believed in pacifism, while others felt only violence could defeat violence. Despite the differences, however, there was an unspoken mutual support between these groups. This was why the moderate NOW or the Justice Action Network had pushed for the release of the Black Bloc in DC. And of course, had their groups been in any danger, we would have done the same. Certainly, there were criticisms of the anarchists among the various leftist groups, but there was also a sort of secret envy of their militancy and boldness. We were, for some, a guilty pleasure. Perhaps they enjoyed the fact that we disrupted the stereotype of the leftist as being weak or passive.

We arrived in Albany, NY late on Tuesday April 17. David's friend Todd picked us up at the airport in a dilapidated maroon Subaru. He was standing outside when we exited the airport, smiling big behind a pair of bifocals. He stood well over 6 feet tall, and by all accounts was thrilled to see us – even Dean and I, even though we had never met. "Are ya'll ready to fuck up some cops?" The contrast between the words he was speaking and the nerdiness of his appearance and tone was absolutely hilarious.

He took us back to his small apartment where he had prepared for us a lavish dinner of lobster ravioli. He, like David, was intimidatingly brilliant, and cited the works of dense postmodern philosophers with the ease most of us would have when discussing the weather. Also, like David, he was excited by our youth and militancy. It was as though we were acting out some drama they desperately craved but only experienced in theory. They too, were militants, but militant in their ideas. What they shared with us was the belief that the world that appeared on the surface, the world most of us consumed blindly, the world that was fed to us by popular culture and the corporate media, was not the ultimate reality. We stayed up late into the night discussing all of this, Dean and I struggling to keep up with the brilliance of their "theory," even as we were the subjects of continuous praise from David and Todd for the brilliance of our "action."

We woke up early and got on the road to Burlington, Todd gladly handing over the keys to his Subaru and wishing us luck. There was a lot that needed to happen over the next 48 hours if we hoped to end up in the streets of Quebec City in time for the "anti-capitalist convergence" on the Plaines d'Abraham. The first stop, of course, was the convergence center in Burlington, VT where we would meet with other activists in the US. Here the latest information about the border crossing and protests would be shared. Next was the meeting with the Akwesasne/ Mohawk community that evening. Here we expected to be let in on the more nitty-gritty details of the border crossing. Finally, we expected to cross the border itself on Thursday April 19. This would ensure we were in Quebec in time for the start of the protests at noon on Friday April 20.

It took nearly 3 hours, headed due north from Albany, before we reached Burlington. Soon, we were immersed in stunning views. Mount Mansfield became visible, and behind it, Lake Champlain, a huge body of blue water that extended all the way to Canada, our ultimate destination. For a moment I contemplated whether we might be able to cross on a boat, but decided it was far more interesting and exciting to cross with the Mohawk people from Akwesasne.

Soon we found the convergence center, complete with

the familiar sights and smells. Crusty anarchist punks were everywhere, replete with dreadlocks, patches and piercings. Outside, some of them were smashing television sets with baseball bats – presumably as a protest against mainstream media. The aggressive energy was an odd contrast with our quaint surroundings. Burlington was a lovely town populated by aging liberals, who passed by us in their cardigans and capris, averting their stares so as to avoid inadvertently becoming the target of these young men's rage.

Inside the convergence center, we found an information table covered with flyers and sign-up sheets for various volunteer activities. There was information about the FTAA protests in Quebec City, as well as the planned crossing in Cornwall. We also learned about various teach-in's taking place throughout the next few days at the University of Vermont. This, however, interested me less than the flyer for the "Ya Basta!" training taking place only an hour from now. The flyer explained the purpose of the workshop, which was to be a training in "practical, non-violent self-defense, inspired by the Tute Bianche (White Overalls) movement in Italy, as well as the struggle of the Zapatistas in Chiapas, Mexico." I shared this with Dean and David, who agreed we should check it out.

We took a flyer with us and headed back out in search of the address where the training was taking place. Not being familiar with the town, we quickly became lost. While walking down one street, a young woman caught my attention. She was walking in the opposite direction from us. She was a skinny punk dressed in all black, covered in patches. She had multiple piercings, in her ears as well as her nose. Her head was covered in platinum blonde dreadlocks. She smiled at me as she caught me noticing her, and instinctively I blushed and looked down as we passed each other. Suddenly I turned.

"Hey, are you looking for the Ya Basta! training?"

She stopped, approaching us.

"Yeah – what about you guys?"

"Yeah," I said. "I think we're lost."

She laughed.

"Me too. My name is Anna."

We shook hands and introduced ourselves. I couldn't help but continue to stare at her as we talked, and she also made eye contact with me several times, smiling each time. She was the epitome of everything I found attractive at this time in my life. Her radical appearance, the messaging on her patches (Go Vegan), even her odor – clearly, she didn't believe in deodorant – all turned me on. She was clearly a part of the Black Bloc. I felt far less "hardcore" by comparison and couldn't imagine why she would be interested in hanging out with us.

Nonetheless, she decided to accompany us as we continued searching for the training. Finally, after asking directions a few times, we found it. It was actually being held in an alleyway behind some other buildings. There were already a few dozen people there. Various materials of unknown purpose were stacked or scattered about. PVC pipe. Five-gallon paint buckets. Inner tubes. Yellow chemical suits. I felt like we were a part of something incredibly subversive, even clandestine. I visually surveyed the trees and the buildings surrounding us. I had an unshakable feeling we were being watched.

A tall handsome man raised his voice and introduced himself as Moose, from the New York City Ya Basta! Collective.

"Thank you everyone for coming. Before we get started, I wanted to share with you who we are and how we got started. We were originally inspired after seeing footage from the protests against the IMF in Prague last September. If you haven't seen it yet, I encourage you to head over to the Prague IndyMedia site and check out some videos.

"The protests there were some of the most militant we have ever seen. There was, of course, a massive Black Bloc, thousands strong, who confronted the police armed with clubs and shields, and also fought with Molotov cocktails and cobblestones.

"There was, however, another group that we had not seen before. They identified themselves as the Tute Bianche, or "White Overalls." They were a highly disciplined formation of individuals wearing thick padding, almost like football players, and white plastic chemical suits, and helmets. They described their tactic as radical self-defense. They came visibly prepared.

"The Tute Bianche came out of the Ya Basta Association, which was inspired by the Zapatista uprising in Chiapas which started on New Year's Day, 1994, the day NAFTA took effect. The Zapatistas, especially through their spokesperson Subcomandante Marcos, encourage the use of spectacle and humor in resistance movements. There is certainly some of that in the White Overalls strategy. There is something ridiculous about seeing protesters wearing so much padding and marching behind large banners backed with inner tubes. That ridiculousness is not unintentional, because it is, in fact, the capitalist state that is ridiculous. This form of resistance is designed to highlight this fact, and to make people think."

After this introduction, we began practicing formations. We awkwardly dressed in chemical suits and lined up in rows of eight. Those in the front held up a long banner which used inner tubes to provide structure. We locked arms and began practicing moving and turning in formation. It felt awkward, and actually quite silly. When some laughed, Moose reminded us that humor was, in fact, an integral part of our struggle, and in fact the anti-capitalist convergence in Quebec was also being referred to as a "Carnival Against Capitalism."

When we began practicing more confrontational situations, however, some of the humor began to evaporate. Now half of the participants pretended to be police, intent on breaking up the formation. The two sides collided like rugby players. Some, particularly the men who perhaps had some experience with physical sports, were becoming quite aggressive. Others, however, were visibly uncomfortable. At one point, a young woman was knocked to the ground. She broke down in tears and began shouting at the organizers.

"What is this machismo bullshit!? Is this how we are going to smash the state? By becoming just like them?"

Now everyone was uncomfortable. The practices stopped at this point, and we formed a large circle to begin discussing and processing the experience. Several other women began expounding on the argument that had just been made. They felt this type of tactic was, in and of itself, sexist. Others, of course, disagreed – including some women. They felt it was absolutely necessary to defend ourselves in the streets by any means necessary. After all, violence was not something we had chosen – it had been imposed upon us.

Eventually the discussion came to an end, though certainly no consensus had been reached. Personally, I was intrigued by the strategy. After all, this was ultimately no different than the Black Bloc. It was just more organized, better equipped. I was also interested in the connections with Italy and the Zapatistas in Mexico. I planned to explore these connections further.

Later that evening, some representatives from Akwesasne came to hold a meeting on the University of Vermont campus. We assumed this would be the opportunity to learn about the logistics for the border crossing. The best understanding we had, at this point, was that some activists from the "Warrior Society" had plans to take over the border crossing as an act of tribal sovereignty. They would then, of course, permit all activists planning to attend the protests in Quebec City to pass. This was good news, especially for the many anarchists in Burlington who had criminal records and would not be permitted to cross into Canada otherwise. It was also an exciting opportunity for militants of very different backgrounds to connect and work together.

Several Native Americans entered a large room where many,

mostly white, mostly crusty, "punk" anarchists had gathered. They began by offering a traditional blessing, and the mostly atheistic crowd played along. Finally, one of them, a man in his early 40s, plainly dressed, spoke to the crowd.

"We are here today to ask you, respectfully, to please not come."

I was shocked at what I was hearing, and I was clearly not the only one.

"The police have come to us. They have shown us videos of the protests in Prague. They have told you you have come to bring violence to our community. Please understand, we have suffered so much already."

The anger, frustration and disappointment in the room was palpable, but what could we do? Certainly, there was no way we could convince these Native-American elders that they ought to take up arms with us, take over the border and guide us across. But this is exactly what we thought they had intended to do. The situation was utterly confusing. How had we gotten such bad information? As the elders left the room, the anger began coming out. This was when I saw Warcry for the first time, the one from the documentary. The confident, radical intellectual. She rushed to the front of the room with her hands out, as if to say don't go! It felt like in that moment the anger began to spill out, and was directed at her, the one who had tricked us into this mess. Shouting began from all parts of the room. She begged for quiet, which after a few minutes was temporarily granted.

"These people who came tonight, they do not represent the Akwesasne people. They are not the ones we have been speaking with. These are part of the Traditionalists; they are not a part of the Warrior Society we have been working with. They still want us to come."

Suddenly, it hit me. Could it actually be that the Mohawks were not actually a monolithic people with complete agreement on political issues? Could it be that some of the Akwesasne people were radical militants, while others were not? Just like everyone else? I realized in that moment how naive I had been. One might even argue my simplistic thinking was a little racist as well. I certainly hadn't been the only one who suffered from this delusion.

Another long, drawn out spokescouncil meeting followed this meeting. Large sheets of butcher paper were taped to the walls and the agenda items were written in thick, black sharpie. Through the course of the discussion, we learned that what Warcry said was true – there was a contingent of the Mohawk people who were supportive of us. However, there were no plans at this time for any type of militant action, at least not by them. Instead, however, they had opened an invitation to hold a fish fry for us, where we could come to engage with their community. From there, there would be a caravan to the border. However, it was to be just an ordinary border crossing. In other words, IDs would be required, and each person attempting to cross would be evaluated on his/her own merits. There was, however, a suggestion that our numbers could possibly be enough to overwhelm the border. However, it was also mentioned that the Canadian police were expected to be in force on the other side of the border, waiting with buses. The odds were clearly stacked against us. Perhaps they always were, but now the "magic" of having support from the Mohawks was totally gone.

No one was happy about this change of events. David, Dean and I were incensed. Anna, who had now joined our crew, said little. I couldn't shake the realization that we could have just as easily purchased plane tickets directly to Quebec City and saved ourselves the trouble. Maybe we still would have been turned away, but surely our chances would have been better than they seemed now.

That evening we secured housing at a local Quaker's home.

He had a large library/study which was separate from the rest of his house, and we were basically given free rein. Anna came with us. To my great surprise, it was becoming clear to me that our attraction was mutual. We bought a case of Budweiser and stuffed the bottles into a mound of snow just outside to keep them cold. We stood outside drinking and venting about the day's events. After a while, we got out our sleeping bags and placed them along the floor. Anna placed hers right next to mine.

The next morning, we prepared for the caravan to Akwesasne. We had a discussion about what we should bring, and what we should ditch. David was the only one with a legit gas mask, which Todd had loaned him. We talked about leaving it behind, but we had nowhere to leave it and David wasn't sure Todd would be happy if he simply threw it away. Since we were keeping the gas mask, the most obvious signal of our intent, there didn't seem to be much point in getting rid of anything else either. So, the four of us, now, David, Dean, Anna and I, loaded into the vehicle with all our belongings and drove to the meeting spot in downtown Burlington.

Our spirits had fallen pretty low since the disappointing meeting with the Akwesasne "Tribal Council," but they rose again when we began to see dozens of vehicles parked in preparation for the caravan. There was a rented bus, about ten vans and dozens of cars including ourselves. There must have been hundreds of people. I saw Warcry decorating the bus with tinsel streamers. Other vehicles had anti-capitalism banners affixed to them. Everywhere I looked, black-clad anarchists, some of them with masks covering their faces, meandered between their vehicles, many of them having a smoke before the long drive. This was no small presence. It was a full-fledged automobile-based Black Bloc convergence.

The police were also, predictably, out in force. There were at least a dozen marked police vehicles, and an indeterminate number of unmarked vehicles. Some police were standing about with camcorders, filming our every movement. This was unnerving. The four of us took the cue from the others and covered our faces with bandanas.

A brief meeting was held a little after 10am. It was explained that the police would escort us out of town. Some walkie-talkies were distributed among several of the vehicles to serve as a communication system (this was still before the widespread availability of cellphones), but we weren't one of the lucky ones. We returned to our cars and waited for what felt like an eternity. Finally, the bus began moving. The vans followed behind. Then we, along with the other cars, formed the tail. Police on motorcycles flanked the sides of the caravan, essentially closing a lane of traffic. They stayed with us all the way to the border of the city. I reached my head out the window and saw the line of vehicles extending seemingly forever in both directions. I felt exhilarated. Maybe we did have the numbers to force our way across the border, after all.

The caravan proceeded very slowly for hours, first north, then west. I remembered the fish fry was scheduled to start at 1pm, but at that time we were only about halfway there due to the speed at which the caravan was moving. Our progress was further hampered by the occasional bathroom stops made along the way. We continued to see police filming us from the side of the road, our every movement being tracked. Our mood, which had been temporarily lifted by the size of the caravan, was beginning to sour again.

Our arrival in Akwesasne did nothing to help matters. Somehow, we had expected a large presence to greet us at the edge of the reservation, but there was no such thing. Eventually we made our way to what felt like an empty parking lot, with only a few dozen activists there waiting for us. The fish fry had been described as a huge community event, with families and children. Instead, there were only a handful of people who seemed like they might actually be from the community. Everyone piled out of the vehicles and joined a line where the fried fish was being served on Styrofoam plates. The fish was quite good.

After we ate, one of the activists from the community (who actually had a Mohawk) stood on one of the vans and gave an impassioned speech about the conditions on the reservations. He said the water was so impure that pregnant women risked miscarriage if they drank it. Another Latina activist followed, talking about the history of conquest in the Americas. Finally, another sang a song with a guitar. Everyone was trying, but the energy felt low. I personally felt like I could just lay on the ground and fall asleep. Finally, the time came to attempt to cross the border, and yet another collision between expectation and reality.

Again our energy rose as we began unfurling banners, masking up and linking arms. Again our energy fell as we realized the bridge we were crossing was over a mile long. The sun began to heat our hoodies and masks like hot plates. We gazed over the water at some kids who had been playing basketball on the reservation. They stopped to watch, their hands supporting their bodies as they leaned into the chain-link fence. I wondered how we appeared to them. Did we look like revolutionaries, like freedom fighters? A bunch of clowns? Did we look like anything at all? A while later I noticed they went back to their game, uninterested in the ultimate outcome. The tension, the suspense, was felt by ourselves alone.

Eventually the head of the march reached the border station. I could barely see the front. I saw a handful of activists, one of whom appeared to be Warcry, linking arms and approaching the guard station. Then they disappeared and I could no longer discern what was happening.

The rest of us just stood in the heat, waiting. Cigarettes were lit, masks were pulled up or off entirely, even though the police were still filming. Sure, we wanted to protect our identity, but on the other hand we were tired and hot. There was a general feeling of frustration and impatience in the air. None of us expected to get across, either legally or by force. We just waited, because there was nothing else to do.

Finally, word made it back to us. A decision had been made to turn around and attempt to cross somewhere else. We returned to our vehicles and the caravan re-assembled on the highway. The police presence seemed to increase. We were being tracked, filmed and followed. We drove for a few miles, the chain of vehicles stretching far ahead of us, until suddenly all the cars pulled over without explanation.

"What the hell is happening?" exclaimed David.

"I'm going to see if I can find out," I said. I got out of the vehicle and began walking along the cars to try to find out if there was a meeting happening. Before I got very far, again without explanation, everyone returned to their cars and the caravan resumed.

"This is madness," said Dean, as I got back into the car. "Whatever our chances of getting across the border, they are obviously way worse the longer we stay with this group."

"Should we try to cross by ourselves," asked David. "Somewhere far away from these people?"

Everyone emphatically agreed. As the caravan drove away, we stayed behind, studying a map in search of a place we could cross the border. The more remote, the better. We found a small highway, Highway 374, which was around 30 miles east of us, far away from the Akwesasne spectacle. It looked tiny on the map. Perhaps we could slip across without incident.

As we wound our way through the back roads of upstate New York, we tried to agree upon a strategy. On the one hand, we could simply be honest about our intentions – or, close to honest. There was no way we could admit we were planning to be a part of the most disruptive actions in Quebec City, such as the assault on the security perimeter. We could, however, say we were peaceful protesters planning to participate in the permitted marches. However, we felt this would doom us. We were confident the Canadian government would do everything in its power to keep the numbers down during the protests, and what could be easier than denying entry to protesters coming from the United States?

We decided, instead, to play on the fact that David was a professor. We came up with a hastily thrown together story about being students assisting him in filming a documentary about Canadian national parks.

Finally, the border station came into view, and we slowed our vehicle as we approached the gated lane. There was a small station in which a guard stood, similar to a toll booth.

"Good evening," he greeted us cordially. "May I please see some identification?"

David handed him his license, and the guard indicated he would need to see identification from each of us. Dean and I handed over our licenses, which we had fortunately decided to keep with us. It was then that we learned Anna had no identification whatsoever. This was clearly going to be a problem.

"What is your reason for entering Canada," he asked, starting to become suspicious.

"I'm a professor at Southwestern University," David said. "These are my students. We are coming to do research on a documentary regarding the Canadian national parks."

"Which national parks," he asked, raising an eyebrow. This was a question David was ready for. During the drive, we had found the park closest to Quebec City on our map.

"Parc National de la Jacques-Cartier," David replied, with the best French pronunciation he could muster.

"The park is closed for the season." David didn't miss a beat.

"We aren't planning to visit the actual park on this trip. We

135

are conducting interviews of academics, park officials."

"Are you sure you aren't coming to protest the FTAA in Quebec City?"

"What? No! What is that?"

The border official asked us to proceed ahead, make a U-turn and park. We were to then come inside for further questioning. We also must submit to a search of our vehicle. The gig was up. There was a moment when David considered gunning the vehicle straight into Canada but thought better of it.

The scene that followed would have been comical, had it not felt so tragic. They removed countless items from our vehicle which proved beyond a doubt we were coming to protest. Gas masks, flyers, printouts from the IndyMedia websites. We were brought into separate rooms for questioning. As far as I know, everyone stuck to the story we had prepared ahead of time, but it was no good.

"Are you coming to cause trouble in our country?" asked another border official, when we had all been brought back into the same room.

"No," Dean said. "We are peaceful protesters." At this point, none of us were surprised about him blowing our cover. We had been exposed anyway. The only shot we had was to be "honest" - or, at least, as close to honest as was possible.

"We are coming to protest the FTAA," I said. "We are sorry for lying, but we had been told you weren't allowing protesters to cross the border. Please let us through."

"You know, Canada also has freedom of speech. We would not prevent peaceful protesters from coming into our country. But we do not believe you are 'peaceful'. The fact that you have lied only confirms our suspicions."

We argued with the border officials for quite some time. David, especially, was relentless. We talked about the issues. We talked about how these free trade agreements favored rich countries at the expense of the poor, how they favored corporations and profit over environmental and labor regulations. We talked about how even the Canadian people could suffer. Suppose the FTAA were to decide the Canadian healthcare system was a "barrier to trade?"

For a split second, I thought we might have a chance, as they listened patiently. But finally, they said, "We are sorry, you will not be entering Canada today."

All that we got for our trouble was to be fingerprinted and documented in the Canadian system. The only one who avoided this was Anna, who, to our surprise, had absolutely no identification on her.

We tried to cross the border again the next day, this time attempting to be "honest" the first time. It was no good, however. The report of our first crossing was already logged in the computer system. We were told we were "banned."

Finally giving up on our attempts to cross into Canada, we returned to Burlington. It was April 20, otherwise known as "4-20." We learned there was a big event on the campus of the University of Vermont. We arrived to see, and smell, a gigantic cloud of marijuana smoke coming from the Academic Mall.

"Well, I guess this is our consolation prize," I said. "Let's go get high."

Chapter 11

I returned to school the following week, feeling defeated once again. Seeing the headlines from Quebec City not only on the IndyMedia feed, but in mainstream newspapers as well, was especially crushing. The front page of one paper displayed a dramatic scene of Black Bloc anarchists, wearing helmets and wielding sticks, battling riot police in hand-to-hand combat. A cloud of tear gas smoke surrounded them, and somewhere in the midst of them a red banner read "Ya Basta!" When I saw this, my stomach turned. I could have been there. I should have been there!

In one of my more reflective moments, I paused to question my motives. What did it mean, exactly, that the scene of a street battle filled me with regret for having been unable to participate in the fighting myself? I reminded myself that I had never even been in a regular fight before. Justice? I closed my eyes and tried to visualize the injustices I believed to be happening throughout the world. I imagined farmers displaced from their land in Chiapas, being forced to move into the cities. I imagined women and children working all night in sweatshops, their eyes nearly closing from exhaustion, only the threat of injury or punishment keeping them awake. I imagined ancient old growth forests being clear cut to make the paper I was holding. As I imagined all of this, I felt a dark cloud of anger, sadness and compassion swirl inside me. I opened my eyes to look again at the picture of the protests. Did this dark cloud have the power to become a storm that would motivate me to attack? I wasn't sure.

What I felt most of all, when I looked at this picture, was fear. There was a reason, after all, I had never been in an actual fight. It wasn't for lack of opportunity. Plenty of other boys had challenged me throughout my life, from elementary school into high school. I had been pushed and spat at. I had dirt kicked in my face. I had been insulted and openly mocked in front of my peers. Once, in middle school, a boy in the locker room had walked up and begun punching me in the chest for no reason whatsoever. My reaction, each and every time, had been the same. I simply took the abuse, never raising my voice or my fists to defend myself. Throughout this period, I considered myself a devoted Christian, and so I would remember the passage about "turning the other cheek." But beneath this flimsy excuse, I truly believed myself to be a coward.

Could it be that fear of my own cowardice was driving me toward these confrontations? Was I actually following in my father's footsteps, whose seemingly identical insecurities led him to that fateful decision to leap from the flight of stairs in order to conquer fear? I shuddered at the thought, tossing the paper aside. I did not wish to continue down this road of introspection any further.

In the meantime, there were other things to worry about, such as where I was going to live once the semester ended. Isaac, Maggie, Dean, Elazar and I began looking for a place together. We wanted someplace big, with land, where others could come and join us, where we could hold meetings and prepare for the next gathering. As luck would have it, we found just the place about 8 miles from the university down a two-lane country road. It was a farmhouse that sat on about 5 acres of land. The farmhouse itself had about three actual bedrooms, but we figured we could expand that to five by partitioning off half the living room and making use of the "mud room" in the back. In addition to this, there was a free-standing garage to the side of the house, a chicken coop behind the house, and another small shed. Finally, a good distance behind the farmhouse, next to the cornfields, stood a large red barn. All of the structures beside the house itself were in severe disrepair, but we were thrilled at the potential. It was a beautiful space, a large "century plant," (similar to an agave) at the entrance. Large pecan and oak trees lined the street and continued all the way to the barn. On a hot, sunny Texas day, with the sun shining, it felt like the perfect hippie utopia. Although, of course, we didn't consider ourselves to be hippies.

While the rent wasn't cheap, it became so after we began inviting others to join us. These included a few other students from the university, as well as two good friends of Isaac's, Bob and Erin.

Bob and Erin arrived one afternoon as we were moving in. Bob wore a perpetual, radiant smile. He had long brown hair and a long beard and stepped out of the car shirtless. His girlfriend, Erin, had short hair and pale skin, smiling less and looking a little bewildered. I would eventually learn of her struggles with mental illness, her constant rotation of different meds as well as cycles of refusing to take them.

Bob and Erin had brought a large green "circus tent" which they set up in the garage. They strung Christmas lights inside and out. Inside they placed a mattress and hung beautiful Indian tapestries on the side. They set up a little altar with Buddha statues. They also set up several fans to keep the tent reasonably cool during the day.

As for myself, I claimed the chicken coop. I spent the first weekend giving it a thorough cleaning. I moved a mattress and a small couch inside, hung a few posters on the wall (from past protests), and improvised a bookshelf using the studs along the wall. There were openings for windows, but no glass. In my mind I made plans to install glass as well as insulation, but never got around to it.

There were nine of us now living on the property, on three separate structures, which we considered to be a legit anarchist commune. All that was left now was to throw a party to celebrate. I purchased a half vial of LSD which came in a small eye dropper, as well as a roll of "Sweet Tarts." I went into the kitchen of the main house and placed a paper towel on the counter, and on the paper towel I placed dozens of pieces of candy evenly spaced in a grid pattern. I then placed a drop of acid on each one. Next to the paper towel I placed a jar, with a sign reading: "Candy. $5."

I took two for myself before the guests began to arrive. Within an hour, the candy was mostly depleted, and the jar honorifically stuffed with five-dollar bills. There must have been thirty people scattered about the property, although it was impossible to count. At one point there was a drum circle outside a firepit that had been dug beside the barn. There were some inside the house, listening to music. There were others communing in the circus tent. There was a wandering minstrel troupe somewhere in the corn field, the sound of a guitar meandering through the stalks. Gradually, all of us were drawn to the sound of the guitar, and in the end the entire party migrated to the depths of the cornfield. We were a wild tribe, separating and combining beneath the black Texas sky, with stars bright as fireflies and moving like them as well.

Of course, it was not all fun and games at the farmhouse. Having christened the place properly with a big bash, we immediately set out to make the farmhouse the functional anarchist commune we originally envisioned. Maggie started a garden, focusing on nutrient rich greens such as kale and collards. I decided to raise chickens, which of course could live in the chicken-wire enclosure attached to my room. I purchased a few baby chicks and some feed. How hard could it be? Dean, being more construction minded, focused on building a more elaborate fire pit, approximately 12 feet in diameter with two levels, one in which people could sit, and the deeper one in the middle for the fire. He also built an impressive staircase to the second level of the barn using spare lumber he found on the property.

Isaac took on the job of organizing the large number of documents we had all accumulated into something of a "library."

These included everything from papers on revolutionary theory to analysis of major protests and actions. Thanks to IndyMedia, anarchists from across the United States and even in Europe were sharing detailed notes about their own experiences and discussing strategies for street protests, as well as tactics for self-defense and improvised armor. These protests, in our minds, were not an end in themselves. They were simply preparation for something greater – a mass uprising we expected to happen in the coming years, a worldwide revolution against global capitalism. We expected these "street tactics" would one day evolve into urban guerilla warfare. It made sense, therefore, that it might be important to start maintaining our own library consisting mostly of printouts from the internet. After all, who could be sure how long the internet would last once the revolution began?

We began spending most of our weekends in Austin, after learning some friends of ours had started an intentional community there called, at first, the Warehouse – but eventually evolving into the Rhizome Collective. It was a large warehouse on Austin's east side, mostly decrepit and overgrown. The property was purchased by a guy named Scotty who had inherited a sizable sum of money after his mother passed away. He made it clear, however, that the property belonged to the collective. Slowly they worked together to carve out a living space in one part of the warehouse, art and workshop spaces in the rest. Another anarchist collective "Inside Books," which sent books to prisoners, set up a library and a workspace. Yet another, "Bikes Across Borders," which worked to repair old bicycles and bring them to struggling communities in Mexico, set up a bike shop. The warehouse was horseshoe-shaped, with an interior courtyard area which some began tilling up to make gardens. A fence was installed along the open side to provide privacy and a modicum of security against frequent police visits. The legal status of the property was questionable, but since it was, in fact, private property, we were mostly left alone.

Even though we personally missed the protests in Quebec City, the impact was felt worldwide. It had been the largest and most militant anti-capitalist convergence to date. The momentum surged into the next major action which took place in July in Genoa, Italy, at the meeting of the G8. If Quebec City seemed like an explosion, Genoa was an atomic bomb. We consumed the IndyMedia feeds ferociously as images and videos began to be shared. Tens of thousands participated in militant direct action, including both the Black Bloc and the White Overalls. The images were more reminiscent of urban warfare than any protest. Anarchists and communists, fully outfitted in improvised armor and helmets, battled police with sticks, stones or anything they had handy. In many of the scenes, it was clear the police were on the retreat. In the most dramatic instance of this, protesters had surrounded a police jeep in which one officer was trapped inside. A man we would come to know as Carlo Giuliani, wearing a black balaclava, was seen in one photograph standing outside the jeep with a fire extinguisher in his hands. In the next, he was lying on the street, blood pooling from a gunshot wound to the head.

Carlo Giuliani was the first official martyr of our movement, and we believed he would be the first of many. The accepted story in the media was that the police officer acted in self-defense, and the picture did seem to show that Carlo was prepared to hurl the fire extinguisher at the police officer inside the jeep. However, more pictures were widely shared across IndyMedia which seemed to show the opposite might have been the case – that the police officer had thrown the fire extinguisher at the protesters from inside the vehicle. But this was where I failed to follow the conspiracy theory. If Carlo picked up the fire extinguisher after that, what was he planning to do with it? To me, the entire argument was off base. This was the beginning of a revolution. Sure, Carlo was attacking the jeep, and sure the police defended themselves. This time a protester died, perhaps next time a police officer will die. In a few years, we may be used to death.

We spent hours poring through the hundreds of photos of the protest, which served to heighten our anticipation of the next mass action: the protests against the IMF/World Bank in September. Articles began to appear even in mainstream publication, suggesting the upcoming protests in Washington DC could be the largest ever seen in the United States since Seattle. The official estimate was 100,000 protesters, though other sources suggested there could be twice that many. As for the anti-capitalist convergence, over 10,000 were expected. This time there would be no border to stop us.

The events in Quebec City and Genoa seemed to foreshadow a climax in Washington DC. It even felt awkward to call it a protest. We were preparing for a war. In fact, everything felt so monumental, so pivotal, I decided to take a leave of absence from school. I felt the need to devote myself to the revolution full time for the next 6 months. Hopefully I would return to school in the spring, but then again, by that point, things could look very different.

We began working closely with other activists in Austin. Sometimes they came to our farm, and sometimes we met at the Rhizome Collective. We began constructing shields and armor. Baalam, a particularly charismatic character with a long history of street protest, even pre-dating Seattle, took the lead on the construction of the shields. He "reclaimed" some large, black construction barrels made of thick plastic and cut them in half using a circular saw. They were about 4 feet in height, enough to cover almost our entire bodies. On the inside he bolted nylon straps with which we could strap in our arms. They felt solid. On the outside we spray-painted a letter on each one. There were seven of them, and together they spelled ANARCHY.

We would meet in the corn fields, which had recently been

harvested, providing us with a wide-open space, and practiced formations. Marching forward was simple enough, but we had to be prepared to change directions quickly without leaving anyone exposed. We decided to add pins and loops on either side of the shields so they could be linked together.

We also improvised armor by cutting thick sheets of plastic and attaching more nylon straps with which they could be affixed to our arms or legs. One day we were working in the courtyard of the Rhizome Collective when the box cutter I was working with slipped and cut deeply into the knuckle of my left index finger. I immediately felt faint as I began to see blood pooling, which was so dark it was almost black. With no thought of going to the hospital, a dreadlocked girl by the name of Dragonfly took me into her care and administered a healthy dose of goldenseal to stop the bleeding, and a few drops of "rescue remedy" under my tongue. Eventually it healed, but the scar would be permanent.

With only a week before our departure, I went to the campus early one Tuesday morning to check my email. (As long as I still had a school ID, I had full access to all facilities, including the library and computer lab.) It was a little after 9am, and I saw a strange subject line from someone who had just emailed the entire students distribution list.

SECOND AIRPLANE CRASHED INTO WORLD TRADE CENTER BUILDING.

What was this about? The email itself was only a few sentences and didn't say much more than the subject line. I suddenly realized the TVs were on in the lobby outside the computer lab, so I followed the noise to see what was happening. Several students and a couple of professors were standing around staring at the TVs. On the screen I could see an image of the twin towers in New York City with huge plumes of smoke emanating somewhere near the top. Footage of the second plane colliding into the tower, seeming to merge with it, was played again and again.

As absurd as it might seem, my first thought was, "Did we do this?"

For so many months, my mind had been focused so much on disruption and destruction of the capitalist system that I somehow felt responsible. One of the professors who was standing near me, a staunch leftist who I knew very well, made a comment.

"Well, this is what we get for our fuckery."

To which I immediately retorted, firmly defensively, "This is not our fault."

"No, it's not." she quickly agreed.

It was years before I thought back on this exchange and realized we were talking about totally different things. She, of course, was referring to the leftist argument that was commonly made after September 11, that the terrorist attacks were a natural consequence of our foreign policy in the last few decades, particularly our unwavering support of Israel in the oppression of the Palestinian people. I would come to agree with this argument whole-heartedly. But in this moment, I was far from connecting these dots. I was simply overwhelmed with the magnitude of what was happening, and couldn't shake the damning question ringing in my mind: Isn't this what you wanted? It wasn't, of course. I never wanted anyone to die. Certainly not like this.

Minutes later, the breaking story in New York City was interrupted by another breaking story in Washington DC. A third plane had struck the Pentagon building. My stomach turned. Now the news was showing simultaneous footage of the Pentagon and the twin towers, gigantic plumes of smoke pouring out. No, this has nothing to do with me or my movement, I realized. Our country was under attack.

As far as I knew at the time, planes were going to continue crashing into important buildings. What would be next? The White House? The US Capitol Building? Whoever was doing this, were they only going to use planes, or were bombs next? The scale of what we were seeing was already so far beyond anything we could have imagined, there was no reason to believe we had yet seen the culmination of what had been planned.

A while later, I learned about the fourth plane that crashed in Pennsylvania, and the rumors that the passengers had fought back against the hijackers. Eventually it was made clear that this was a terrorist attack coordinated by Osama bin Laden, who it was believed was living in the caves of Afghanistan.

The cliche that 9/11 changed everything was unquestionably true in my experience. I called my dad that evening, unsure of what his reaction would be, but feeling dread, nonetheless.

"What do you think?" I asked, my voice a little shaky.

"I'm ready, it's time to go!"

"What do you mean?"

"The final battle. The Last Days. This is it. Jesus is coming back, and we've got to get ready to fight!"

"I don't believe in war, Dad."

"This isn't like Vietnam, Aaron. This is pure evil. We have to fight."

I hung up the phone. My dad was completely blinded by his religious beliefs. How many more felt the same way? What about our president? This was a horrific act, there was no question. But it was an act carried out by a specific network of people. It was not the fault of the ordinary people of Afghanistan, and yet, they were the ones who would pay the price if President Bush used this as a justification for war, which it seemed was exactly what he intended to do.

After speaking with my dad, I wandered outside. It was dark and clear, and the stars were out. I walked around the property, smoking a cigarette, feeling the cool air on my skin. I looked up at the stars. Since we were so far out in the country, I could see millions of them, as well as the cloudy streak of our galaxy, stars too far away and too dense to detect individually. Looking at the stars always made me feel small, but now, I felt smaller than ever. What was to become of our plans in DC? We were supposed to be there in 2 weeks. My mind wrestled with contradictions. We had every intention of causing the maximum possible disruption in Washington DC, and yet, now, a disruption far greater than anything we could have imagined had already taken place. So, what had that accomplished? A terrible loss of innocent life, for sure. But beyond that, the "system" was still in full operation and was now preparing for war. I realized, in that moment, that the world was far bigger than I understood. Throughout my experiences in the last year and a half, I thought we were making an impact. I thought we were moving the currents of history in some way, at least a little bit. Now, I realized, we were barely a drop in the ocean. We were like children who had been playing a game. Now, something real had happened, and it was time for us to take our toys and play in another room while the adults handled things. I felt simultaneously humbled, angry and confused.

A couple of days later, we learned that the IMF/World Bank meetings in DC had been postponed indefinitely. All of the largest organizers canceled the protests as well. The anti-capitalist convergence, on the other hand, was more split. Heated debates began to appear on the IndyMedia feeds. Many felt that we should not come to DC at all. Others felt that we could transform our protest into an anti-war march. Among those, some felt we should not wear masks. Others felt we should. And somewhere in the mix, the conspiracy theories emerged. Could it be this was all planned by our own government, for the very purpose of derailing the expected actions in DC? A part of me wanted to believe this, but another part of me knew this was absurd.

Of all the possible factions, I aligned myself with the most militant. Yes, we should still go to DC. Yes, we should protest any war in retaliation to the terrorist attacks, and hell yes, we should still wear masks. We couldn't allow an atmosphere of fear and paranoia to roll back the gains we had made as a movement. Our cause was still just. We couldn't go backward.

In the end, Isaac, Maggie, Dean and I decided to go, although we left the shields and armor behind. We loaded into Isaac's Jeep Cherokee and drove the entire 21 hours to DC, stopping for a couple of days to stay with Isaac's dad in Virginia.

It was clear early on that this time in DC was not going to be anything like the last. The "anti-capitalist convergence" was held at a park across the street from Union Station. While I was somewhat encouraged to see a few hundred anarchists gathered there in all black, with their familiar banners and black and red flags, it was immediately clear we were vastly outnumbered by riot police who had already surrounded the park on all sides. They were not preventing protesters from entering the park. However, as we walked between the police lines, it felt very much like we were walking into our own doom. One of the cops looked at us and spat on the ground as we passed. "Fucking traitors," I heard him mumble.

I meandered about the crowd as we waited for the march to begin. Suddenly, I saw a familiar face.

"Jeff!"

He turned to look at me, not recognizing me, obviously due to the fact that I had a bandana covering my face. I lowered it.

"It's Aaron, we went to LA together!" He smiled.

"Of course, I remember," he said, as he gave me a hug.

"Things feel pretty tense," I observed.

"Yeah. It's a difficult time."

"You're not wearing a mask?"

"No. I just don't think it's the right time. Everyone is scared right now. I don't want people to feel like we are a threat. Not after everything they've been through."

This made me feel uncomfortable. After all, I had never worn a mask in the first place in order to make people feel like I was a threat. Not ordinary people anyway. As for the police, I hoped we were seen as a threat. I wanted to be a threat to the state, to capitalism, to injustice. Also, there was the matter of protecting our identity, as revolutionaries. I looked around and saw, indeed, there were a number of police with camcorders. I put my mask back on.

"Ok, brother. Stay safe out there."

The march began a few moments later. Everything felt different from what I had experienced before. As we stepped into the street, we were immediately swallowed by riot police on all sides. The usual chants began (Whose streets? Our streets!) but felt hollow. They were clearly their streets.

As we wound our way through the city, in a mobile enclosure which felt like a cage, I struggled with a mix of emotions. I wanted to feel powerful, revolutionary. I wanted to believe that the attack this city had just experienced less than 2 weeks ago had nothing to do with the importance or imminence of a global revolution against capitalism and injustice. And yet I couldn't help but feel some pangs of guilt. I wondered about the difference between Jeff and me. There was a thought, a feeling I could not shake. The fact that I simply liked this. I enjoyed putting on the costume of the Black Bloc, I enjoyed feeling tough, marching alongside this intimidating mass of people. I enjoyed the feeling of the bandana covering my face, my black hoodie covering my head, my black cargo pants and black combat boots. Sure, there was a part of me that genuinely believed our cause was just. But how much of it was nothing more than a kind of psychological salt that made a deeper, more selfish motivation palatable?

Isaac, Maggie, Dean and I were relegated to the rear of the march. Soon we saw, and smelled, clouds of tear gas up ahead. It became clear that wherever we thought we were headed, we were, in fact, going wherever the police wanted us to go. In the end, we met up with a large anti-war march, and the police directed us into the more peaceful march as one might direct a water hose into a pond. We were diluted, and eventually, disintegrated.

Chapter 12

Since I had taken a leave of absence in the fall of 2001, there was no reason I needed to return to Texas after the protests in DC. Instead, I accepted an invitation from David to come join him in Gettysburg, PA where he had just started a teaching position. Knowing my background with computers, he was hoping I could help him edit a documentary he had started working on.

David's PhD dissertation had been a sociological study about Mardi Gras. He was interested in the rituals of exchange between beads and sexual acts which took place on Bourbon Street in New Orleans. He wondered what could compel otherwise ordinary people, who presumably would normally be horrified at the prospect of engaging in sexual acts with random strangers for money, to suddenly be completely fine with it as long as plastic beads were exchanged. I got a glimpse of David's final draft of the dissertation when we were in Todd's apartment in Albany. I tried reading some of it, but the density of the writing and his layering of deep cultural theory into his observations made my head hurt.

As David became interested and eventually involved in the anti-globalization movement, he gradually shifted his focus more toward the beads themselves. Where did they come from? He often noticed small white tags with the words "Made in China" littering the streets in New Orleans. The same summer I was practicing medieval style formations in the corn fields of Texas, David traveled to the Tai Kuen Bead Factory in Fuzhou, China. The owner of the factory assumed David was merely interested in learning about his innovative methods for achieving maximum efficiency in the production of beads. ("We have a chalkboard here that shows how many pounds we produce every day.") David was given nearly unrestricted access to film the factory and interview the workers.

He returned with this footage and planned to incorporate it along with the hundreds of hours of footage he had already taken from Mardi Gras into a documentary film he wanted to call "Mardi Gras: Made in China." He floated the idea throughout the academic community and was invited to present the pilot to a committee at Yale, for possible funding. Having no prior experience with editing software, David asked if I'd be willing to help.

We spent hours in a crowded storage room at the library of Gettysburg College combing through his footage and figuring out the basics of Final Cut Pro – splicing, transitions, titles, audio layering. I became immersed in the process of shaping a narrative from the many hours of disconnected footage. A moment in the factory, with the loud sounds of machinery overwhelming the quiet voice of the worker, would suddenly spark a memory for David of another interview in the streets of New Orleans. He would rifle through the tapes in his bag, studying the handwritten notes, until finally popping one into his camcorder. Once he found what he was looking for, we would put the tape in another machine that digitized the footage onto a hard drive. Then we imported it into the software. It was a time-consuming process and took us months to piece together a more or less coherent 30-minute pilot.

In between editing, we discussed philosophy and politics. I observed that the factory in China reminded me of the huge factories I had read about in England in the nineteenth century, the very ones that had led Karl Marx to develop his theory of history and his belief in an eventual communist revolution.

"We tend to think of factories as a thing of the past, something that we as a society have evolved beyond. But really, nothing has changed. The factories are now just on the other side of the ocean."

David was fascinated by this observation, and he suggested he interview me for the documentary. I agreed, on the condition that I do so anonymously. One evening we found a secluded patio area behind a coffee shop in town. I was wearing full Black Bloc garb, complete with a black bandana. I expounded upon these observations, borrowing everything I had learned in my history classes, as well as my readings on anarchist theory. David included these clips in the original pilot, and I was identified only as "Blackbeard."

During this time, the events of September 11 weighed heavily on our minds, as well as the war we knew was coming. There was no question of if, only when, and who would be our target. It was now common knowledge that the terrorist attacks against New York City and Washington DC had been masterminded, not by any state or government, but by a clandestine network known as Al Qaeda. Some country, however, was destined to pay the price.

One afternoon we learned that the bombing of Afghanistan had begun. David and I jumped in the car and drove straight to Washington DC, which was only a few hours from Gettysburg. We arrived at the White House to find a few dozen people already gathered. We were among the first to protest the war, but we wouldn't be the last.

I began to worry about the fragmentation of our message. As anti-capitalists, our previous protests against globalization and inequality had seemed clear and coherent, at least to us. But the attacks on September 11 had, in a sense, opened a new ideological front that could not be ignored. What was the anarchist analysis of Islamic-inspired terrorism? It seemed simplest to assert this attack was simply an expected consequence of the United States' unwavering military support of Israel, which was responsible for apartheid-style repression of the Palestinian people. After all, the Palestinian cause was specifically named by Al Qaeda as a justification for their attacks. Getting behind this argument, however, came with risks. Did this mean we also affirmed the righteousness of the attacks? We knew we could not, nor would we ever, align ourselves politically with the terrorists. On the other hand, clearly distinguishing ourselves from them was easier said than done.

Not long after the protest in front of the White House, David and I learned of another mass action happening in Canada, this time in Toronto. OCAP was calling for a "day of rage" against war and poverty. We decided to go. I looked forward to the opportunity to converge again with my "tribe," and to be able to do so outside the immediate context of US politics was a bonus. We were only vaguely familiar with the causes advanced by OCAP, as they were largely local issues. We did understand, however, that they were an extremely militant, anti-capitalist group, which had already gained something of a reputation in Toronto.

When David and I arrived at the border, we wondered if our recent trouble with Canadian border crossings would come back to haunt us. Fortunately, it did not – but probably only because information did not travel as quickly at that time. Our luck, however, did not last long. I navigated using directions provided by "MapQuest" until we arrived at a park deep in the city. There were hundreds gathered already, although it was so early, the sun had not yet come up. Before we had a chance to find a parking spot, we saw flashing lights behind us and realized we were being pulled over.

The police officer approached the vehicle and David rolled down his window. Confrontational by nature, David immediately began demanding why he had been stopped. The officer claimed it was because of a broken taillight. David suggested it was probably because we were coming to protest. This provoked the officer to demand what we intended to do in his city. David's retort about "free speech" landed a bit hollow, considering we were no longer in our own country.

The exchange became so heated I worried we would end up in jail before the protests even began. In the end, however, they impounded David's vehicle but let us go free. We would have to claim it later in the day and pay a fine. David was irate. I was just happy to still be able to participate in the protest.

The march began on schedule, the crowd immediately taking the streets and heading for the financial district. Like most other protests I had participated in up to this point, the crowd was mixed. However, despite this diversity, the vibe was decidedly militant from the start. Several masked protesters dragged newspaper stands into the street, forming a blockade against the police who pursued us from behind. Another protester climbed to the top of a hotel veranda, seizing an American flag and setting it on fire, much to the glee of the other protesters.

In the end, the protest was fairly unremarkable – another game of cat and mouse between the protesters and the police that spanned the course of several hours. It was becoming a familiar routine. Thoughts arose in my mind, wondering if and how these street dramas were affecting the actual policies we were protesting. I suppressed them as best as I was able.

Chapter 13

I returned to Texas and began preparations to return to school for the 2002 Spring Semester. Rather than returning to the chicken coop, I simply occupied an interior room of the house which was situated between the kitchen and the living room. Although I was excited to be taking classes again, my mind was still largely preoccupied with global politics. The war in Afghanistan was raging on, and now the Bush administration was preparing for an invasion of Iraq.

One Monday morning, all the students received a surprising email from the president of the university announcing that the Kappa Alpha fraternity, which had been suspended for 5 years the previous spring, would be returning to campus the following semester. This was an unexpected reversal of a decision that had been widely praised the year before. The campus-wide email used by students erupted in protest, and I quickly joined in.

I was no fan of the fraternities in general. In fact, during my Freshman year I had briefly become the most famous – or notorious, depending on your point of view – student on campus after writing a "letter to the editor" of our school newspaper comparing fraternities to gangs. After all, I opined, what is the difference between scratching Greek letters into the walls of bathroom stalls, as compared with almost the exact same behavior I saw from gangs at my high school? And weren't the many alcohol-soaked parties they threw on a weekly basis no less illegal than the activity gang members were known for?

It wasn't necessarily the most thought-out argument. In truth, I probably was partly motivated by a feeling of being left out and unpopular, a dynamic I had hoped I had left behind during my awkward high school years. Thought out or not, I had certainly struck a chord. The next issue of the paper was dominated by responses to my letter, some supporting me, others denouncing me. I made friends, and enemies. I received calls from strangers, either thanking me for my letter, or threatening to kick my ass.

For those who were skeptical of the "Greek" presence on campus, however, the fraternity that had the worst reputation was by far the "Kappa Alphas." They were the "southern pride" fraternity, the "Sacred Order of General Lee," often seen wearing confederate flags on their party T-shirts. Rumors of scandal were rife, although particulars were difficult to nail down. For example, I heard they held a Halloween party in which several members wore blackface, or Confederacy uniforms. I was not sure if this happened at our school, or somewhere else. If nothing else, it seemed the members of Kappa Alpha were at least comfortable with the associations between their fraternity and the antebellum south.

As it happened, the president of our university, Jake Schrum, was himself a former member of Kappa Alpha, and it didn't take an incredibly conspiratorial mind to come to the conclusion that he might have caved to pressure from his fellow alumni. This, of course, was a connection I highlighted strongly in my own email to the student body.

The controversy surrounding the expedited reinstatement of the Kappa Alpha fraternity on campus coincided with a general feminist awakening taking place on campus, as well as within myself. I had begun attending weekly meetings of the "Feminist Voices" student group, held at the Korouva Milkbar every Tuesday night. I realized that "feminism" was not just for women. After all, had I not also been victimized by societal norms around masculinity? I was frequently bullied in elementary and middle school. I was called a "faggot" or a "girl" because I was not particularly tough or athletic, and my voice was high. When I first saw footage of a Led Zeppelin concert when I was 16, I witnessed in Robert Plant a totally different ideal – one in which a man could be sexy, indeed desired by women, while not embodying the typical masculine ideal. In fact, he seemed neither masculine nor feminine, but something in between. As I dove deeper into feminist theory, I found further permission to explore this "non-binary" ideal within myself.

It did not take long before I caught the attention of the president of "Feminist Voices." Her name was Mira. She was short, with thick red hair, white skin and a labret piercing on her chin. She was extremely passionate, serious and intense. She was, in fact, generally intimidating to most people. However, I soon began to experience a softer side to her. At parties, she began approaching me and asking me about the protests I had been involved in. She asked me about anarchism. She listened intently, nodding her head and moving closer to me with every encounter. I began to feel attracted to her, and it did not take long before this fact was mutually recognized.

When she and I began dating, we fell in love with the idea that we were bringing together two activist communities – the more punk "anarchist" community with the more intellectual "feminist" community. We were excited by the realization that we had much in common and began studying subsets of anarchist/feminist theory such as "eco-feminism," or "anarcho-feminism." If anarchism was ultimately about resistance to all forms of coercion and oppression, surely the patriarchy was a significant target of resistance. And we also recognized that the same forces that subjugated women were subjugating the environment. Everything was connected. That spring, which I remember as being full of sunny days and blue skies, was an exciting period of activism, theory and love.

Mira and I began organizing a concerted resistance to the reinstatement of the Kappa Alpha fraternity, which began with a march from the Korouva Milkbar to the President's Mansion on the opposite side of campus. The back porch of the coffee shop was packed with at least fifty students. We listened as multiple women spoke about their personal experience of sexual assault at the fraternity houses. I felt a lump of rage forming in my chest, and as I felt my heart beating, I matched this beat on my djembe drum which I had brought to lead the march. I stepped off the porch and everyone followed. We snaked across campus, to the sound of my drum and chants borrowed from the anti-globalization movement.

This is what democracy looks like!

We soon arrived at the President's Mansion. It was a large limestone building which overlooked the golf course at the eastern edge of campus. The sun was beginning to set. The crowd gathered about 50 feet from the front door, continuing our chants, but feeling unsure what to do next. I saw someone inside the house peek out of one of the curtains.

Several of us huddled together to come to a decision about how to proceed from here. We decided that three women should be elected as spokespeople to approach the door and ask to speak to Jake Schrum personally. Mira was among the three that were chosen. The rest of us sat down on the lawn, becoming quiet as the three women held hands and walked toward the front door. Before they could arrive, Jake Schrum walked outside and came to meet them.

They were too far away for us to hear, so we all sat silently as they discussed. I could see Mira's head bobbing as she spoke intensely. She was never one to hold back how she really felt. I did not envy Jake's position. After several minutes, Jake returned to his home and the three women returned. Mira gave the report.

"While he respects our feelings, he basically said nothing is going to change. He is working on a process by which the Kappa Alphas can be reconciled and learn from their mistakes, and he isn't going to put any timeline on that process."

"In other words, they're going to be back by the fall," I replied angrily.

"Pretty much," she said.

While there was a general feeling of discouragement, most of us knew that this was only the first step of many that would be required to make a real impact. Activism only works when it is consistent, persistent and disruptive. You have to push things to a point where those with the power to change things know they cannot avoid making those changes. It's not about convincing anyone. It's about leverage.

So, we continued to push. We continued writing campus-wide emails. We started chalk campaigns, covering the sidewalks of campus with colorful, sometimes profane messages. Admittedly, these were happy days for me. Everything was exciting. I was enjoying my classes, which themselves were full of feminist theory. I was reading John Zerzan, learning about anarcho-primitivism or "green anarchy" – the belief that the problem is deeper than capitalism, that civilization itself must be totally dismantled. I was spending time with Mira, discussing theory, planning our next action and smoking pot any place we could find some privacy. She always had the best pot.

As the semester was nearing the end, we knew our window of opportunity was closing. We would have to do something big, or risk losing the momentum of our campaign forever. We hatched a plan.

The first week of May, we planned a "walk-out." All students would be invited to walk out of class at 10:30am and meet in the middle of campus, on the Academic Mall. There would then be a march to the president's office to demand that the Kappa Alphas remain suspended for 4 more years, as originally announced. All of this information was disseminated publicly with campus-wide emails and flyers. What was not communicated, however, was that at the same time as the walk-out, three of us – me, Elazar and Paul – would occupy the president's office. We would refuse to leave until he agreed to our demands. Mira would lead the march to just outside the office, bringing attention – and support – to our sit-in.

The three of us, who all lived at the farmhouse, sat on the

front porch the morning of the action, smoking cigarettes and drinking coffee. It was already hot, even though it was only 9am, and the birds and grasshoppers were chirping loudly – a noise that was only occasionally interrupted by the grumbling engine of a passing truck on the highway in front of our house.

"I can't get arrested," Elazar stated plainly. I hesitated, unsure of how to respond.

"Neither can I," Paul agreed. This is my last semester. I can't risk not graduating."

In fact, this was the last semester of college for both Elazar and Paul. It was "almost" my last semester. As it turned out, I was one credit short – I would need to take a physical education course during the summer to meet the requirements for graduation. Perhaps this one technicality gave me a little more courage, or perhaps I just didn't have enough sense to fully comprehend or worry about the consequences.

"Well, I'm willing to get arrested," I said. "But here's the thing. They aren't just going to arrest us. We will get at least one warning. I know how these things go. What matters is not whether we're actually willing to get arrested, but whether they think we're willing to get arrested. We can't give them any reason to doubt that. Because that's our leverage. I'm telling you – they aren't going to want to arrest us. It will look bad. It will make the news. It will draw more attention to what's been happening, and it will be obvious to everyone that Jake Schrum is in the wrong."

"That makes sense," Elazar conceded, taking another drag from his hand-rolled cigarette.

"Ok, so we act hard core – at first," Paul said. "But when the time comes, Elazar and I will comply with the orders to leave."

"Yes, but it is important that you wait until you are threatened with arrest. They are going to tell us to leave, but until the time comes where they're actually bringing out the handcuffs, you have to be strong. Make them think nothing will scare you."

Elazar and Paul agreed, albeit a bit hesitantly. I hoped I was right, for their sake.

We drove to campus and parked near the administration building, known as "Cullen," which housed the president's office. The three of us walked inside the front door of the over 100-year-old building, composed of large, blackened limestone bricks. The old wooden floor creaked beneath us as we approached the president's office on our left. We walked through the open doorway, into an atrium where the president's secretary sat at a desk. The president's actual office was through another door behind her.

"Can I help you?" the secretary asked, smiling, clearly suspecting nothing.

"Is President Schrum here," I asked.

"No, he's actually out of town for a conference today."

We were not expecting this. I felt my stomach drop. Then Paul walked past the secretary's desk and put his hand on the doorknob of the president's office.

"Is this op--" I heard him ask, but before he could finish the question, he turned the handle and the door opened. The secretary jumped out of her seat.

"You can't go in there!"

Before she could do anything, Elazar and I followed behind Paul and we found ourselves standing in the middle of the president's office, which was surprisingly small. It was circular, situated in a tower on the southeast corner of the building.

"We are going to occupy this office until President Schrum comes to speak with us about the early reinstatement of the Kappa Alpha fraternity," Paul said, with surprising authority.

The three of us placed our backs against one another, locking our arms and forming a triangle, and then sat in the middle of the room. The secretary looked at us wide eyed, and then left the room to call the campus police. We could hear her in the other room frantically explaining the situation.

"Three students just broke into President Schrum's office and said they won't leave until he meets with them. Can you please..." she paused. "Do something? Ok, thank you."

The secretary never entered the office again, this whole situation clearly not a part of her job description. She sat back at her desk and returned to her paperwork and emails, ignoring us.

The three of us sat quietly for a few minutes. Soon, the chief of campus police arrived. Her name was Chief Brown. She was a fairly short, stocky woman with short hair and no-nonsense brown eyes. We had no idea what to expect but were certainly not expecting the first question she had to say to us. She crouched next to us.

"What are your demands?"

We had prepared a list of demands but had no idea they would be provided upon request. There were no threats of arrest, no orders to disburse, simply: "What do you want?"

There had been many discussions among the organizers about what our demands would be. As is often the case, there was considerable debate, sometimes heated – and in the end, a compromise was reached which disappointed many. The most extreme voices wanted all fraternities to be dismantled completely. Others simply wanted Schrum to return to his original decision to keep the Kappa Alpha suspension in place for 4 more years. But what was finally agreed upon was the demand that a council be formed among the student protesters, with which Schrum would agree to meet and negotiate a process for reinstating the Kappa Alpha order, on a timeline mutually agreed upon. We wanted a seat at the table. We wanted democracy.

We communicated this as best we could to Chief Brown, who said she would do what she could. As we were talking, we began hearing chants of a large crowd coming nearer, and soon the windows were filled with the faces of the students who had walked out of class. They were waving signs, pounding drums, chanting and smiling at us. I felt a tingle rushing up my spine as I saw Mira's face staring at me, as she mouthed the words "Te Amo."

Before leaving the office, Chief Brown said, almost in a whisper: "I appreciate what you're doing. I just want you to know I am not going to arrest you."

We were floored by this. The last thing we were expecting was support from the campus police. Perhaps, we reasoned, she knew more about why the Kappa Alphas were suspended than we did.

Soon we began receiving visitors, first professors – such as the known radical Eric Selbin who taught Latin American politics. This semester I was doing an independent study with him on "anarchism." We had met a few times to discuss, but the conversations always devolved into sharing tales of our own protest experiences – his dating to the 60s and 70s, mine very recent. However, nothing more specific had ever materialized. When he walked into the office, he said simply: "I can't think of a better capstone project for a study of anarchism than what you are doing here today." We all laughed.

He handed me a note his daughter had written, addressed to "those who were and are in the president's office."

Soon students began visiting. The secretary simply sat at her desk, head down, ignoring everything happening around her. I felt proud of what we had accomplished. This was certainly what Hakim Bey must have meant when he described the creation of "temporary autonomous zones," where people take the power. We had taken a space which represented top-down hierarchical authority and opened it up for everyone. What began as a tense, scary action by a few of us, had opened up into a carnival for all to enjoy.

We remained in the office well after the building had closed and the staff had gone home for the day, with the campus police providing security. Finally, we got word from President Jake Schrum that he was willing to negotiate with a group of students of our choosing the following evening. We had won – at least this battle.

Chapter 14

Ultimately, we knew we had done nothing more than slow the process down. It was May, after all, and most of the leaders of the movement – me included – would not be back in the fall semester. The momentum we had created might no longer exist after the summer break. We assured the younger students we would continue to provide support however we could. It was clear, however, that our minds and attention were drifting toward our future plans – a future that at the moment seemed boundless and full of infinite possibilities.

In the final days of the semester, everything was unraveling in a way that felt both sad and sweet. Mira and I were proud of the work we had done and were acutely aware of the fact that we had become leaders and role models to several younger classmates. Now, we were graduating, and leaving it all behind. Also, the lease was up at the farmhouse. I moved out, packing my meager belongings into a couple of boxes and stowing them in the back of Isaac's jeep while he and Maggie scouted out a new place to live. I then helped Mira pack up her own belongings at the house she lived at with several others across the street from campus.

Mira and I passed a pipe back and forth to one another as we packed and listened to reggae music. We were in our own world, figuratively as well as literally, considering everyone else in the house had moved out already. Once we were done, Mira realized something.

"Wait, where are we supposed to stay tonight?"

We had been so busy making plans that neither of us realized we had nowhere to go. The house was empty, and her bed had already been moved into storage. The farmhouse was similarly vacated, and while Isaac and Maggie had found a place closer to town, the lease was not yet signed. Mira and I laughed at our predicament, while simultaneously relishing the sense of freedom of being homeless, at least for one night. Bob Marley's "No Woman, No Cry" playing on her radio seemed oddly fitting to the moment.

> *Then we would cook cornmeal porridge, I seh*
> *Of which I'll share with you*
> *My feet is my only carriage*
> *And so I've got to push on through*

The only place to lie down in the house was a small loveseat which stood alone in the living room, surrounded by sealed up cardboard boxes. We laid on the couch together in an attempt to sleep, laughing as we found it too small to hold both of us, and I kept slipping off onto the ground. Finally, probably because we were so exhausted, we managed to fall asleep. The morning came in what felt like an instant, the light coming in the curtainless windows, her weight still upon me. It was a feeling of closeness I had never known before.

The new house Isaac and Maggie had found was on Olive Street, so we began referring to it as the "Olive House" and the name stuck. When the time came to discuss living arrangements, I agreed to take the worst room in the house – considering I would not likely be living there beyond the summer. I had agreed to travel to Boston in the fall, after I completed my PE credit, to continue helping David Redmon on his documentary. The reason it was the worst room in the house was because it adjoined the only bathroom – meaning everyone who lived there (at least six of us to start) would pass through my bedroom anytime they needed to use it.

I came up with a clever idea that I was not quite certain I could pull off. I would build a loft in the room so that I would always be guaranteed privacy. I made some measurements, took a trip to the lumber store and purchased everything I figured I would need. Not more than 3 or 4 hours later, my vision was achieved. I had a nice stable loft which sat in one corner of the room, with about 3 feet of clearance below the ceiling. I placed a mattress on top and surrounded it with a curtain. I placed a lamp inside, and it was actually quite cozy – a private space for Mira and I to enjoy throughout the summer.

As it turned out, Mira got a room in Austin, so we took turns visiting each other's spaces, though in truth I spent most of my time with her. It worked out well, because I ended up taking my PE course, "Martial Arts Conditioning," at Austin Community College 2 days per week. I spent many hours on the road between Austin and Georgetown that summer, playing a Bob Marley CD on repeat so many times I memorized all of the lyrics.

While I was planning for my move to Boston, Mira was making her own plans to spend the "semester" (even though we no longer had to think in terms of semesters, after 16 years it's a tough habit to break) in Honduras. Before she and I started dating, she spent a semester there studying abroad, and had connected with a family there. She was eager to return and spend more time volunteering, soaking in the culture and improving her Spanish.

Meanwhile, our relationship was becoming more serious, and we wanted to move to Eugene, Oregon together. We had been spending more time discussing the "anarcho-primitivist" ideas of John Zerzan, who lived in Eugene. We discussed the possibility of joining the "tree-sitters," who put their bodies on the line to save the old growth trees from destruction. We wanted to connect with a more progressive, radical community – and to learn who we might become in the process.

We thought the time apart would do us good, to spend some time discovering ourselves, before reuniting in December and making the move early the next year. Or, at least, I told myself it was "we" who were making this decision. In truth, I probably would have preferred to stay with her. I had fallen deeply in

love – or, at least as deeply as my 23-year-old mind knew how
to fall. The closer the time came for us to go our separate ways,
the more uncertain I felt.

When it was time to go to Boston, I took my usual mode of
transport – a Greyhound bus. I had become used to these long
trips, having taken so many of them to various protests around
the country the last few years. The trips gave me plenty of time
to think, write and read. I had just finished the first draft of
my novel, Miles Peak, which focused mainly on the semester
I had taken off after my Sophomore year to travel through
Europe – as well as my first two protests at the Republican
and Democratic national conventions. Now I was working on
something new, which did not yet have a focus. So far, it was
just random observations – about society and the alienation I
was seeing around me. I was noticing more and more people
had cell phones. It bothered me that people seemed to spend
so much time on them, ignoring everyone around them. If we
were to overthrow capitalism, I thought, it was crucial that we
be able to communicate with one another. Ironically, this device
which was invented to enhance communication seemed to only
be destroying it.

When I arrived at the bus station in downtown Boston, I
took a city bus to Sommerville where David lived with his wife,
Kathleen. Not having a cell phone myself, I had to rely upon
directions I had written in my journal, as well as a stop at a
payphone to get clarification. I came to an alleyway, walked
up a flight of metal stairs, and knocked on what seemed to be
a back door. David opened the door, smiling behind his black
square glasses, and gave me a big hug.

Kathleen stood behind him, smiling politely – but I could
immediately tell she was less enthusiastic about my arrival. By
this point, I was pretty crusty, with terrible blond dreads tied
back with a bandana, black jeans with hand-sewn patches and
a typical black hoodie. Kathleen, on the other hand, was very

nicely dressed, wearing a cross necklace. She was a Christian woman from the Dominican Republic who had married a college professor, wanted children and a stable life, and was not particularly excited about his descent into radicalism and the friends (like me) that he was making.

While I had sensed some tension between Kathleen and I during the time I had spent with them in Gettysburg, it seemed this time she tried less hard to mask the awkwardness. I did my best to stay out of her way. I was given a small guest bedroom to sleep in. She asked me immediately about my plans to get a job and a place of my own. This was not quite what I had expected, considering I had come because I thought David would be paying me to help him with the documentary. But I agreed to start looking for a job.

Depression hit almost immediately after arriving. The combination of missing Mira and the cold reception from Kathleen made me feel lost and afraid. What was I even doing here? I walked down to the nearest gas station and bought a small bottle of Southern Comfort. I'm not sure why I chose this, considering I found the taste totally disgusting. Perhaps it reminded me of the last time I had drunk it, trying to drown my sorrows after a rough breakup. I snuck it into my room at David and Kathleen's house and sipped it straight as I read through the job ads of a small quarterly I had picked up while I was out.

A small voice in my head wondered if my sudden desire for alcohol was a bad thing. Why was I hiding it? Perhaps this was the first situation in a long time in which I felt I would be judged for drinking at an inopportune time. At the farmhouse, I felt no such judgment, as we all felt free to crack open a beer at any time of the day, even right after breakfast. It had become a daily lubricant, smoothing out the ups and downs of my life. Something to celebrate a small victory, inspire the next plans, to relax me, to ease moments of heartbreak. But now, looking at this small bottle in my hand, juxtaposed next to the job ads in the local weekly, in a strange room in a strange city, something felt different.

I found a job canvassing for the Sierra Club, and I thought this sounded like a decent way to combine my desire to save the environment with my practical need to make money. I took a subway downtown and found a small nondescript building where the orientation was taking place. The trainers were all wearing matching shirts, tucked into khakis, and were unnervingly upbeat. It felt like a pep rally, and the fact that they were trying so hard to keep things positive made me nervous about the reality of what I had walked into.

The job was this. We were each given a clip board containing dozens of sign-up sheets. Each day, we would be dropped off in one of the various wealthy neighborhoods in the Boston area. We would then split off, each of us taking several blocks, and we would go door to door. We were required to follow a precise script – the goal being to sign up as many people as possible for a $100 membership to the Sierra Club. Each week, if we sold over 50 memberships, we would earn 10 percent of sales. Otherwise, we would earn only minimum wage.

I found this to be the most depressing, grueling work imaginable. Reading from a script made me feel completely phony. I felt totally disconnected from the words I had memorized. When people asked how exactly this membership would help the environment, I struggled with the desire to provide an honest answer (to which I had none) versus simply reciting what I had been told to say. One day I decided to completely go "off script," and actually had more success. But soon, this impromptu approach began to feel draining in its own right, and I returned to the script.

On the last day of the week, I realized I was close to hitting the 50 mark. In the last hour of the shift, I had only to sell one more subscription. Suddenly, it began to rain. With no umbrella or raincoat, I was quickly soaked to the bone. I was running out of time. I did some math in my head and realized I would actually earn more money if I paid for the last subscription myself. I knocked on one final door and took a radical approach.

A middle-aged man with wire rim glasses and a gray beard answered the door. He reminded me of a college professor.

"Excuse me, sir. I am with the Sierra Club. I have to sell 50 subscriptions, and I am one short. You are my last house, and if I don't sell you a subscription, I will only make minimum wage this week. So, if you don't want to buy a subscription, I will pay for it myself. It is $100."

I couldn't imagine how anyone could refuse this logical request, but he did, closing the door without a word – a slight look of fear in his eyes. I must have seemed genuinely insane, a young white man with dreadlocks soaked to the bone, offering to buy a stranger a $100 subscription to the Sierra Club.

I wrote his address on the clipboard, made up a name and stuffed $100 cash into the envelope.

And so, it was that I made my quota my first week on the job, which also was my last week on the job.

It was a good thing I earned some cash, because David was unable – I assume due to pressure from Kathleen – to pay me much to help him with the documentary. Still, we did get to do some editing together – which was in the same small guest room/office where I slept. The documentary had come a long way since I had worked on it. It had become cleaner, more focused, with better transitions. David talked about entering it for Sundance, and I was beginning to believe it might actually be possible.

Still, the tension between David, Kathleen and I was becoming intolerable. In secret, David apologized for Kathleen's behavior, and confessed they were having major marital difficulties. In the same breath, he suggested it might be better if I found another place to live. He introduced me to a student of his at Emerson College who was studying film making. His name was Rolando, an international student from Venezuela, who just happened to be looking for a roommate.

Rolando and I took to one another immediately. He was one of the few people I had met whose apparent passion and radicalism overshadowed my own. While I generally found myself needing to hold back in conversations with people, finding ways to sugar-coat my belief that the entire "system" should be destroyed by any means necessary, with Rolando I instead struggled to keep up. I had recently read Che Guevara's Guerilla Warfare, and I decided if Che had been reincarnated in the present day, he would be someone like Rolando. While there was an undeniable physical resemblance, with their matching black beards, brown skin and shoulder-length, wild black hair, the stronger similarity was in their shared sense of ultimate sacrifice to the revolutionary cause.

Rolando was an ardent supporter of Hugo Chávez. We met only about 6 months after the CIA-backed coup attempt in Caracas, which failed to unseat Chávez's socialist government. As an anarchist, I was skeptical at first of what Rolando called the "Bolivarian revolution," since it involved state power. On the other hand, learning about the CIA's involvement in attempting to overthrow Chávez, I was quite confident that anything the CIA was against, I was probably for. Eventually, Rolando won me over.

Rolando and I shared a room in a two-bedroom apartment. The total rent was $1500 per month, an astonishing amount to me at the time, but Rolando and I were only responsible for $375 each, which was manageable. The other room was occupied by another student who came from a wealthy family in Columbia. She did not share Rolando's radical views, but she tolerated him and generally the three of us got along amicably.

On a personal level, this was both an exciting and confusing time. I had come to Boston for what I thought was a clear purpose – to assist David with his documentary. This, obviously, was out the window, and I would very quickly need to find a way to support myself. The $500 I had earned from the Sierra Club was barely enough to cover my first month's rent, with little to spare. The remaining $125 was all the money I had in the world.

The secondary purpose was to give Mira and I space to learn more about ourselves before reuniting around Christmas time and start preparing for our move to Eugene. I wasn't sure if I was learning anything about myself, but I missed her so much it hurt. I wrote her long, poetic emails. I would then check my email as often as possible, desperate for a response. The responses, given the fact that she was in Guatemala with only occasional access to an internet cafe, were often long awaited. But then, one day, they would be there. My heart leapt with excitement when I saw her name highlighted in bold in my inbox. Her responses were always sweet, composed lovingly with her own poetic style. I would feel better, for a moment. Then I would write a response, and the cycle began anew.

Fortunately, Rolando and I lived in an interesting borough of Boston – Allston – which provided ample opportunity for distractions as well as job prospects. One block from our apartment was Harvard Avenue, a bustling retail district with stores and restaurants representing probably a dozen different countries. I walked up and down this street, stopping in at every business to inquire about employment opportunities. After being turned down countless times, I walked into a thrift store with very low expectations. I approached the counter, and there was a muscular blond man at the counter.

"Do you have any job openings," I asked, almost robotically at this point.

The man paused a moment and stared at me.

"Maybe," he replied, in what I immediately recognized as an Australian accent. "When could you start?"

"Immediately," I replied, suddenly much more enthusiastically. I just wanted a job, and I wasn't at all worried that working at a thrift store wasn't necessarily a dream come true for a recent college graduate.

I gave him my information, which mostly consisted of my name and email address. I still did not own a cellphone, and for now, email was the only way I could be reached. He promised to get in touch with me.

I decided this was good enough for the day and started walking back to the apartment. Along the way, I passed a liquor store, and thought about buying some alcohol. Just the day before I had decided to take a break from drinking for a while. The problem was, I wasn't sure exactly how long "a while" was. I felt a craving that surprised me. My mouth watered at the thought of whiskey, but it felt deeper than a craving for a certain flavor. Whatever it was, it was more than I could resist, and I walked inside.

I think this could be a problem, I thought.

One day, I knew, I'd have to face it. But that day was not today.

Chapter 15

I got the job at the thrift store and settled into my new life in Boston. The job itself turned out to be much more enjoyable than I expected. Most of the time I spent trying to arrange the thousands of items in the store in some orderly fashion. I was given almost total freedom in this regard. I started with the book section, dividing fiction from non-fiction, science fiction from fantasy, self-help books from poetry. I spent so much time doing this, eventually Chris asked me to move on to another part of the store. I switched my focus to dinnerware, separating bowls from plates, serving utensils from eating utensils. And then on to clothing. I took surprising pleasure in the act of imposing order on chaos. I was helping people find what they were looking for, even if they didn't know they were looking for it.

I worked part time, but it was enough to cover my rent as well as food, so I was content. I also had plenty of time to explore the city. I found that, in terms of food, I was able to stretch my limited funds far by taking weekly visits to the farmers' market. I purchased mainly fish, fresh fruit and vegetables. One day I came across a stall selling fresh cranberries. They were so red and shiny; I was hypnotized by them. I bought a pound of them, having no idea what I would do with them.

I gradually became involved in the local activist scene. This started with a visit to the Lucy Parsons Center, an anarchist bookstore. I spent a few minutes browsing the books, but the main thing I was interested in was the community bulletin board. I learned about a group called BAAM, which stood for "Boston Anti-Authoritarian Movement." They had posted a flyer advertising their next "business meeting." There was a date and time, but no location. I would have to email them for that. So, as soon as I got back to our apartment, I sat down at my laptop and sent an email asking for the location. I signed my name "Blackbeard." The response came the next day.

DEAR BLACKBEARD,
THANK YOU FOR YOUR INTEREST IN BAAM.
CAN YOU PLEASE TELL US HOW YOU BECAME AN ANARCHIST?
SINCERELY,
BAAM

Obviously this was a test. I was determined not to disappoint. I wrote a long email summarizing the evolution of my belief system, starting with my travels in Europe, witnessing the protests in Seattle in 1999, and my own involvement in various protests around the country. In describing my own belief system, I focused on what I considered to be the most important points. I was opposed to oppression and coercion in any form. I believed in cooperative relationships and mutual aid. I was against all of the "isms": racism, classism, sexism and – most importantly – capitalism.

Although I knew it was taking a risk, I decided to divulge my interest as well in a sect of anarchism popular out West among the tree-sitters: "Green Anarchy," which was closely related to, or possibly synonymous with, John Zerzan's "anarcho-primitivism." I had recently finished reading *Future Primitive* and was fascinated by the thesis that our "problem" was actually deeper than capitalism but could be expanded to include civilization itself. The inventions of agriculture and language, generally considered to be unambiguously good, were actually the origins of the separation of humans from the natural world. The idea resonated closely with the one presented by Daniel Quinn in his novel *Ishmael*, which I had read around the time of my travels through Europe.

While traditional anarchist philosophy, whose origins

were similar to those of communism, arose as a reaction to the inequalities and injustices introduced (or possibly just magnified) by the Industrial Revolution, "Green Anarchy" dug deeper into the problem of "humanity" which seemed to be thousands of years old. The Roman Empire, for example, had no concept of capitalism – and yet, did it not perpetuate its own fair share of injustice and oppression? Digging deeper yet, why was it that we as human beings were the only animals on the planet who do not feel we belonged? At bottom, I did not feel I belonged in this world. Green Anarchy gave voice to this deeper longing.

The risk of describing this in my response to BAAM was the fact that many "traditional" anarchists, usually described as "anarcho-syndicalists," did not consider green anarchists to be comrades in the same cause. The critique of civilization itself was considered by many to be counter-productive – reactionary even – the dirtiest of words among self-proclaimed "revolutionaries." And so, while anarcho-syndicalists focused on organizing in the streets, anarcho-primitivists spent much of their time protecting old growth trees from logging companies, or freeing animals from factory farms.

What I wrote was short for an autobiography/manifesto, but quite long for an email. I decided if they invited me into their group, we must be kindred spirits after all. I hit SEND and closed the browser window, glimpsing the green and black "green anarchy" flag on my desktop background before shutting my laptop and going to the kitchen to cook dinner.

The response came later that evening from a guy named Sam. His email was thoughtful and welcoming. He told me BAAM was not dogmatic in its views on anarchism, and that anyone working to undermine the capitalist system was welcome to join – even if that included "deeper" ambitions. He gave me directions to their next meeting and invited me to join. It was, incidentally, in Allston – not far from where I lived. He also mentioned a party afterwards.

The meeting was held in a two-story Lucian house near the intersection of Brighton Avenue and Cambridge Street. When I entered, it looked, felt and smelled like every anarchist abode I had visited in Austin. Mismatched furniture, the smell of incense and gently rotting compost from the kitchen, rolling tobacco on the coffee table in the living room, artwork and sculptures with no coherent theme, and posters of various actions and protests in the Boston area over the past few years. I was greeted at the door by Sam, who introduced me to several others. There was a guy with dreadlocks and a knitted cap, another with a shaved head and patches sewn to his black hoodie and tight jeans. A woman with short hair, horn-rimmed glasses and several piercings. Hippie, punk, radical feminist. A typical and representative sample of those who generally filled the ranks of anarchists at this time.

The main topic of discussion was the ongoing janitors' strike. The janitors' union in Boston had been on strike for a month at this time. While their demands were very mainstream – better wages, benefits and more full-time positions – the Service Employees International Union (SEIU) had launched a campaign "Justice for Janitors" that was actively recruiting help from student groups and others who had been involved in the anti-globalization movement. A concern was raised by the "punk" about whether the motives of the SEIU were truly radical, or whether they were recruiting other groups opportunistically.

"There is nothing anti-capitalist about SEIU," he said. "At the end of the day, they believe in reform, not revolution. Are we wasting our time by getting involved? I feel like they just want bodies in the street, and they have made specific demands that we not engage in any type of confrontation with the police."

Sam vehemently disagreed. "I'm not sure if you've noticed, but most people aren't anarchists. So how are they going to become anarchists? If we sit out actions like this, just waiting for the next anti-globalization or anti-war protest to throw rocks at the police, then the only thing people will know about anarchists is what the media tells them. We have to get out there and show we support any and all movements for justice and equality, even if they do not yet support our long-term objectives."

This was debated for some time. The issue of misogyny within the ranks of SEIU leadership was discussed. In addition, it was pointed out that SEIU operated in a top-down hierarchical structure, fundamentally at odds with anarchist principles. As a newcomer, I remained quiet throughout the discussion, until Sam specifically asked my thoughts.

"I tend to agree with Sam," I began, nervously clearing my throat. "The world we are fighting for will not be achieved overnight. We believe in dismantling all forms of oppression and injustice. Clearly the working conditions for the janitors in the city of Boston are unjust and oppressive, so if we can help dismantle that, we will make some progress – however small – to our ultimate vision. And we will create allies in the process. If we support the janitors, perhaps more of them will become interested in the anarchist vision."

There were general nods of agreement, and I felt some relief that I was gaining their trust. This was sometimes a difficult task, since the topic of infiltrators and undercover agents was always top of mind when a new person entered an affinity group. In my experience, however, these sorts of bad actors were easy to spot. They didn't look right, or dress right, and certainly did not know how to "talk the talk." There was a certain sincerity present in genuine revolutionaries that was difficult to imitate.

The other topic of discussion was participation in an upcoming anti-war rally on the Boston Commons. The Senate had just approved a resolution authorizing the use of military force against Iraq. This happened, we noted, with the support of top Democrats such as Hillary Clinton and Diane Feinstein. If I had been even remotely skeptical, after the Republican and

Democratic national committee protests in 2000, that the two political parties were merely two heads to the same beast, the escalation of military violence and imperialism since September 11 hammered the point home. George W. Bush was now invading a second nation, and in this case the connection between its inhabitants and the attacks in 2001 was even more spurious. For all of these reasons, and more, there wasn't anything to debate about our participation, as part of the Black Bloc, in the upcoming protest.

The meeting ended on a positive note, quite possibly because we knew we were going to see some action soon. I was particularly encouraged by the sense that I had been accepted into the group. I was eager to learn more about the east coast anarchist scene.

We left the house and walked a few blocks to the party. It was dark now, and given that this was mid-October, the leaves were changing and it was getting cooler, especially at night. Two of us lit cigarettes. As we walked, Sam asked me more about my experiences. I told him about the various protests I had been in, my experience on hunger strike in jail and my near arrest in DC protesting George W. Bush's inauguration. I spoke passionately about my belief in revolution, which was becoming stronger every day. I had begun reading more in-depth texts about the revolutionary movements of the late 60s, most recently Worker-Student Action Committees, which described the events of the Paris riots in 1968 which seemed to be on the verge of sparking a second French Revolution. In particular, it explained the detailed strategies of those who sought to seize upon the revolutionary moment. Propaganda, as well as street tactics. I told Sam how influenced I was becoming by the "situationists," as they were called, and I was very much interested in finding ways to create more "situations."

The conversation, unfortunately, fell apart once we entered the party. It was a smoky three-story row house. Most of the people there were from the Allston punk scene, identifiable by their black patches, tattoos and spikes. The punk scene was essentially where the "Black Bloc" style came from. While most punks were at least sympathetic to anarchism, they certainly were not all involved in the protest actions. Likewise, not all those who participated in the Black Blocs were punks. There was, nonetheless, a close affinity.

We were led to the kitchen and shown the keg and the plastic cups. We each filled a cup and chatted awhile in the kitchen before the group inevitably dispersed into various other conversations with others at the party. Since I was the only person who did not know anyone, I ended up spending a lot of time by myself. I became very drunk, and eventually stumbled out and walked the approximately seven blocks home.

The protest took place the next Saturday. I took a train downtown, leaning against a rail wearing black jeans, a black hoodie and a black bandana stuffed into my back pocket. I wondered whether anyone on the train noticed my outfit or connected it with the protest happening that afternoon. If they did, I had no way of knowing, but really it was highly unlikely. Most protests at this time got very little press, before or after. Some people were dimly aware of the anarchists, or the events in Seattle, but in my own experience most people were totally oblivious. This reality was particularly frustrating for those of us wishing to foment a global revolution.

Nonetheless, when I stepped off a train about a block from the Boston Commons, I could already hear the crowd that was gathering. When I cleared the block, I saw hundreds of people gathered in the middle of the vast green lawn. It was an astonishingly beautiful day, with blue sky interrupted by only occasionally puffy white clouds. And the trees lining the Commons were splashed with colors ranging from yellow to orange to the deepest reds. I felt my heart thump with excitement as I pulled the bandana from my back pocket and tied it across my face.

I found the BAAM banner after wading for a few moments through the crowd, and I recognized some, but not all, of the faces. Sam, who was quite large, was easy to spot. We were all dressed more or less identically, although some opted for black "balaclavas" rather than the bandanas. Both were face coverings adopted by the Zapatistas, and it was my understanding that this tactic was borrowed from them. As such, wearing masks served multiple purposes. It was a statement of solidarity with the Zapatistas. It was a practical strategy for avoiding identification by the police, who were increasingly bringing camcorders to protests. It was a political statement. We are here as individuals. We are here, as one, in solidarity with one another and with all movements fighting for justice across the world.

The first thing that I noticed, when the march began, was that the Boston Black Bloc (at least, the one assembled on this day) was both militant and cohesive. I got the feeling, as I joined a row of linked arms behind a "FIGHT THE RICH NOT THEIR WARS" banner, that most of the people in this group knew each other and had been working together for some time. This had not always been my experience. Particularly when joining a national or international convergence, most of those who joined the Black Bloc were strangers to one another. The idea was to come as affinity groups, rather than individuals, and to independently plan actions. Not only was this seen as anarchist in nature, and thus aligned with the principles we espoused, but it served some practical purposes as well. First, it isolated the influence of provocateurs. Had the philosophy been more leadership oriented, then undercover agents could easily take on that role and lead us into actions designed to get us arrested. The idea, therefore, was to support the actions of any other affinity group, while still requiring personal accountability and small circles of trust to be established by the participants themselves.

Since this was largely a local protest, the entire bloc – of which I estimated there to be about fifty participants – was most likely composed of individuals who had worked with one another many times in the past. Not just protests, of course, but other anarchist activities such as Food Not Bombs, which served the homeless using scavenged or "dumpster-dived" food. Or critical mass, in which the streets were taken over by dozens or more cyclists. Or any number of "benefit parties" which were the staple of anarchist social life. Unlike my experiences in Austin, however, I found this group to be highly disciplined and focused. We marched in orderly rows, shouting slogans in unison, while numerous anarcho-syndicalist flags were wielded among our ranks. The sticks upon which the flags were affixed were very thick and solid, approximately the same thickness as a police nightstick. I knew, of course, they were double use. Flag sticks now, weapons later. As was the pole used to hold the banner by the row in front of me, which could later be used to charge police lines.

The crowd began moving out of the park and onto Tremont Street. The Black Bloc made its way determinedly to the front of the march, and the other anti-war protesters, holding NO WAR signs rather than anarchy flags, politely stepped aside and smiled at us. This was an interesting experience, one that I was becoming accustomed to. Although the media enjoyed playing up the divisions "among the protesters," at least since Seattle, in my own experience I hardly ever witnessed such conflict. I always felt the anarchists' presence was welcomed. It wasn't just a feeling, of course. I myself had been on "the other" side during my first protest in Philadelphia. I had come as a straightforward liberal protester, with no particular ideology or ambitions. Had you asked me, at that time, whether I approved of violence as a form of protest, I would have said no. And yet, there was something magnetic about the anarchists when I first saw them. I was somehow able to not agree with them, and yet still admire them.

I suppose our presence at the head of the march helped the other protesters feel more powerful. The stereotype of the liberal is a self-righteous weakling. Full of convictions yet unwilling to throw a punch to defend them. This certainly was not the image one held of anarchists. We were here with the "peace protesters," and we were as adamantly against war as they were, and yet we weren't going to take any shit from the police. It felt good to play this role, and yet I had serious doubts about whether I was truly as courageous as I acted. I wondered about the others as well; however it was far more tempting to look at their faces and project a strength that I was not sure I had myself.

The original plans by the organizers were to make one giant loop around the Boston Commons, and then to return to the grass for music and speakers. The Black Bloc had different plans. I learned through whispers that as the protest approached the intersection of Beacon and Arlington, we were going to attempt to divert the march north toward 28 and take the highway.

As we marched, the police presence was noticeable but not overwhelming. There were certainly no riot police, but there were bicycle police lining both sides of the march. This made me nervous, as I was reminded of the incredible number of bicycle police that had been employed at the RNC protests in Philly. The police could, within seconds, dismount their bicycles, stand behind them, and use them as battering rams to corral protesters. And, obviously, they could move and deploy much more quickly than riot police. The good news was that they appeared calm, apparently unaware of any plans we were hatching.

I counted my breath as we approached the intersection, searching for courage. The bicycle police had formed a perforated line in a crescent shape across the intersection – guiding us in the direction the march was supposed to go, but by no means a fortified barrier. I heard someone in the row in front of me count down slowly. Five...Four...Three...Two... One! The row in front of me made a sharp turn 45 degrees to the right. I felt my own row turning in unison, the insides of my elbows straining against those of my neighbors on either side. I looked ahead and saw the eyes of the policemen widen in response. There was little time for them to respond. Some of them seemed unsure what to do, but two of them converged and began walking toward us, their bikes held sideways as I had seen in Philadelphia. The pole upon which the banner was suspended turned slightly, and as we reached the police it was used to divide them. Meanwhile, others who had the flags affixed to thick poles used them to defend our left flank. We pushed past the police line with relative ease, and I looked behind us to see that much of the march was following.

Before we could make it another block, however, police on motorcycles and a few squad cars had already blocked the next street. Our front line collided with them briefly but were pushed back by several large police officers wielding batons. This was ever our dilemma. The police, on average, were simply always larger than anarchists. I heard someone say that while we were in high school smoking pot or writing poetry, the people who became police were on the football field. Physically, we were no match. Our only hope lay in numbers, or speed.

Once our forward progress was halted, and we had lost the element of surprise, there was no realistic chance of continuing on. Many in our group screamed at the police and were joined by many in the larger protest. Our own forcefulness was, of course, justified. The police response, however, the mild shoving they had done with their bikes or nightsticks, was not. I found myself not joining in the verbal barrage against the police. The way I saw it, they were doing their thing, we were doing ours. While I despised outright police brutality as much as anyone, I did not hate police in general. I was often of the quiet opinion that if our "revolution" ever had a chance of succeeding, we might actually do best to try to win them to our side.

Since the police did not take any additional action to feed our energy, the march eventually resumed its originally planned course. We ended on the Boston Commons and listened to speakers. After a while, myself and others got bored. We gradually filed away, returning to our lives.

Chapter 16

November arrived, and with it, my birthday. I was entering my third month in Boston, and something resembling a normal life was coming together. I saw David and Kathleen rarely, I suspected because my arrival had brought to the surface something in their relationship that they were still working through. Rolando and I had become inseparable friends, sometimes talking late into the night about the Bolivarian revolution in Venezuela, and the extent to which it did, or did not, align with anarchist objectives. I was making friends at BAAM and getting involved politically. Even my job was going well. I had become good friends with the owner of the thrift store, a middle-aged Chinese woman whose husband was a physics professor at Harvard. When she found out I knew a bit about computers, she pulled me from the store and hired me to help her with her taxes. Truthfully, I probably spent no more time on her taxes than I did just riding around in the car with her as she chatted incessantly. We were becoming friends, and to my astonishment, she offered to give me my own store – a second thrift store in Brookline. She told me I could sell whatever I wanted. I suggested books.

"Books?" she looked at me with puzzlement, as if I might as well have said lizards. Then she shrugged. "Ok, then."

I told her I would have to think it over, because I had a girlfriend in Texas and we had been talking about moving to Eugene, Oregon. As I said those words to her, they felt strange. I felt like I was describing something I knew was not going to happen. But why would I think that? Sure, the correspondence with Mira had slowed in recent weeks, but that's just because we had both been busy. The plan, all along, had been for us to have a few months apart, and then get back together and move to Oregon early the next year, January or February of 2003. So why did I suddenly feel uncertain whether this was actually going to happen?

A survival instinct kicked in, and I told the owner that it was possible we might not move to Oregon together. That I appreciated her generous offer and would get back to her as soon as possible.

I needed to find out. What? I needed to find out if we were really moving to Oregon. No, more than that. I needed to know if she felt the same way about me as I felt about her. I didn't care about Oregon. I cared about her. And if that was the way she felt about me, then this offer to run my own store in Boston was totally meaningless. But, if she didn't, then I had to consider my own future. As painful as it was to consider, I had to admit the possibility that it might be better to let her go and begin a new life, rather than hold on to another that would never last.

I expressed these questions as best as I was able in an email. Talking on the phone took too much planning, and I felt I couldn't wait that long. I posed the dilemma to her as delicately as I possibly could and asked her to please tell me honestly how she felt.

The response I received from her could not have been more perfect had I written it myself. She expressed, without reservation, that she loved me, and she wanted us to be in each other's lives more than anything. She also acknowledged the gravity of the offer I had received and congratulated me on it sincerely. And then she expressed a kind unwillingness to hold me back from any opportunity I wanted to pursue. That, as much as it would break her heart to lose me, she would rather let me go than hold me back in any way.

I was elated, and I responded immediately with gleeful enthusiasm.

"I choose you, mi amor. You are where I want to be. And I want us, together, to go to Eugene. I've had enough of this Red anarchism. I'm ready for the Green!"

This email was quickly followed by a second one I wrote to

the owner of the thrift store, letting her know I unfortunately had to decline her offer.

I grabbed my pipe and ran up the three flights of stairs in the apartment building until I reached the metal ladder that led to the top. I followed the ladder on to the roof, and there I smoked a bowl of high-grade bud while staring at the full moon over the city, feeling as though my life was finally complete.

My birthday party, then, was also a farewell party. Surprisingly, I was going to have quite the turnout. David and Kathleen were coming, which I felt both excited and awkward about. Some of my friends from BAAM were stopping by. And, most exciting of all, my friend Valerie was in town for a medical conference and also would be coming. I told everyone I would cook for them. I went to the farmers' market and purchased a large filet of salmon as well as a handful of shark steaks. I bought kale, green beans and potatoes. And I bought another bag of fresh cranberries, along with oranges, excited to try the cranberry sauce recipe I had found.

Valerie arrived first, which worked out well because we were able to catch up a bit while I cooked in the kitchen. I asked her about the conference, and she gave me a long explanation I barely followed. It probably didn't help that I was high. Liver research, or something. This didn't surprise me, of course. Valerie had told me she was pre-med our first week of college, and she hadn't wavered since. I wondered what it felt like to have such an orderly life.

The one area where my life felt most disorderly, or at least threatened disorder, was the one involving alcohol. When I cracked open my own beer (a Yuengling Black and Tan) and offered one to Valerie (she declined) I already knew there was no telling how much I was going to drink. This was not a depressing fact to me, however. Quite the opposite, I was excited. The feeling of pot, mixed with alcohol, mixed with the good old-fashioned dopamine response of having my friends all together, made me giddy. I was outgoing, extroverted, the life of the party – everything I considered myself not to be in normal, waking, sober life.

It was awkward when David and Kathleen arrived, as expected, but my buzz smoothed out the edges, at least for my own experience. The food was delicious, and I got particular compliments on the cranberry sauce. It feels like Thanksgiving, someone said.

Before he and Kathleen left, David pulled me aside.

"Hey, man," he said, his eyes wide with apparent nervousness.

"Yeah, what's up?"

"I just want to say how sorry I am about everything that happened. You were supposed to come stay with us, and you and I were going to work on the documentary together, like in the old days. But Kathleen and I just have a lot of stuff we are trying to work out. It's not your fault. I'm just so sorry I left you in a kind of stranded position."

"It all worked out," I said, smiling, and hugged him. Truthfully, I had absolutely no grudge against him. I knew he was in a rough spot with his wife. In fact, if I had been smarter, I might have thought twice about accepting his offer in the first place. It was, admittedly, rough in the beginning. But I couldn't have been happier about how everything had turned out.

A few weeks later, I said my last goodbyes to all of my friends in Boston. Rolando accompanied me to the bus station.

"I'm going to miss you, my friend," said Rolando. We were both bundled up against the snow that was now falling everywhere. He smiled beneath his sparse black beard, which was like a forest against his brown skin. His eyes were kind behind his thick black glasses, and I thought again, surely this is what Che looked like, talked like, felt like.

"Te extrañaré también, mi amigo," I responded in my best Spanish.

But Rolando almost always spoke to me in English.

"You have to come visit me in Venezuela, man. You have to."

His words had the exact opposite effect on me as the words I had spoken to my boss about moving to Eugene weeks early. In this case, I knew it would happen.

I gave Rolando a big hug, and then boarded the bus bound for Texas.

When I finally made it back to the Olive House after a grueling, multi-day bus ride, I learned the loft I built was no longer available. During the time I had been gone, we had acquired three new roommates and things had been shuffled around. Fortunately, there was another room available. While it technically should have been considered an upgrade, considering it had a door and did not contain the only bathroom in the house, a part of me was sad to lose the little "safe space" I had created.

I didn't give it much thought, however. It was temporary. Two months tops and Mira and I would be moving to Eugene.

As I owned very little, it took me very little time to settle in. Mira arrived a few days later. I was sitting on the front porch smoking a hand-rolled cigarette when she drove up in her red Volvo. When we made eye contact, my heart skipped a few beats. I dropped the cigarette in the ashtray and hurried to greet her. She stepped out of her car and I noticed she had a septum piercing. Also, her thick red hair had started forming into dreadlocks. She was getting ready for Oregon.

"You like it?" she asked sweetly.

I gave her a big, long kiss for an answer.

We embraced for several minutes and feeling her body against mine was like being home again. I helped her bring her suitcase to my room. We smoked a bowl of delicious bud a friend had sent her from Amsterdam, and then we made love. Afterward, I lay in bed and watched her walk across the room naked. The contrast of her beautiful body against the peeling paint on the door frame reminded me of a moment from a

Henry Miller novel.

"Can I keep you?" I asked.

"No," she responded curtly. My stomach dropped. I felt I had said something wrong. "But you can hang out with me for a while!" And then she came to my side and gave me another kiss.

I sank into my head as she returned to putting on her clothes. Of course, I knew, that was a stupid thing to ask. It was possessive, patriarchal even. I had just been so caught up in the moment, the words simply spilled out. But what did she mean, for a while? Were these words just as careless as my own, or did they have a deeper meaning?

The words reminded me of a central fact of our relationship that I spent most of my time ignoring. We were not monogamous. Mira had made it clear that she did not believe in monogamy, and so our relationship for the past year had been, technically, an open one. What made the situation confusing, however, was that neither of us had actually been with another person since we started dating. And so, rather than it being a complicated arrangement that I might eventually get used to, it remained just a foreboding possibility that might arrive at any moment. Truthfully, I had no desire to be with anyone else. "We" agreed to be polyamorous in the same way "we" agreed it would be best if we were apart for the last 3 months. Meaning, she decided, and I pretended to agree.

For some unknown reason, I thought this might be a good time to bring up something else I had been thinking about our relationship.

"Have you ever thought about having children?"

She very nearly dropped the shirt she was about to put on. She looked at me, eyes widened with what appeared to be a mix of shock and horror. I saw her begin to grasp for words, or possibly gasp for air.

I wanted to save her. "I mean, not right now, of course," I said, looking down. "One day."

The words did not seem to register. Time widened between us as I awaited the words that were coming, one way or the other.

"I'm just...I'm not prepared for something like that," she said finally.

"Yeah," I said, waving my hand, as though to wipe away everything I had said in the last 5 minutes. "I just meant, one day."

"My heart is not prepared..."

"Forget about it," I said. "I just meant, well, you know I love you and one day it might be something we could talk about."

There was nothing to be done but change the subject and move on. So, when she offered me another hit off the blown glass pipe sitting on the nightstand, I accepted it gratefully.

During my absence, the residents of the Olive House had invented a new activity that was not only practical but included a political impact as well. Most people would call it "shoplifting." Maggie called it "appropriation." I called it "hyper-boycotting." Whatever its name, I adopted the practice whole-heartedly. We would never steal from local businesses, of course, but only from large corporations. Or businesses whose owners were racist or guilty of some other -ism. I figured the local HEB down the road fit one or both of these criteria, so I began making regular "appropriation runs" to pick up beer, vegetables, bread, toothpaste or anything else we might need. Most of us would simply fill up a shopping basket and head for the nearest exit. I, on the other hand, developed a more audacious strategy that I personally declared brilliant. I would fill up an entire grocery cart, pass by the checkout lane on one end of the store, and then purposefully walk in front of all other checkout lanes. I called the technique "obvious invisibility." My theory was that, by making a point of being seen by virtually everyone who worked the checkout lanes, they would collectively and silently assume there was no way I could actually be stealing in plain sight.

Who would be that stupid? I got away with this several times without incident.

On New Year's Eve, we decided to throw a party at the Olive House, and I offered to get us stocked up on groceries. My new housemate Nick, a musician with anarchist sympathies, offered to accompany me. He, too, had been practicing the art of hyper-boycotting, and we figured we'd probably need two carts of groceries to feed the huge amount of people we were expecting. On the way to the store, I was chatty with excitement. I told him about the party we had thrown at the farmhouse exactly one year prior. Dean had dug a gigantic firepit with two levels so people could literally sit inside the pit, with the fire contained in a deeper circle in the center. Maggie had decorated the upper loft of the barn with an elaborate chalk mural representing the four elements – a source of endless fascination for the numerous people tripping on LSD that night. I estimated we had over a hundred people at that party, which we had planned weeks in advance.

Tonight was different, however, because this time we had decided to throw a party literally on the same day. I was giddy with a sense of the unknown, which I expounded upon to Nick the entire drive to the grocery store.

"I feel like something special, something big is going to happen tonight, man. I don't know what it is. It's like there's this big unknown feeling, this big X, the unknown variable in the equation, and I feel absolutely certain the universe is going to rush in to fill it."

Amused, Nick agreed, with many fewer words.

"That's cool, man."

We separated as soon as we parked, agreeing to meet back at the truck with our bounty. I grabbed a grocery cart and walked inside, soon perusing the aisles and throwing anything into the cart that interested me: various gourmet mushrooms, vine ripened tomatoes, russet potatoes, fresh tarragon and oregano, bell peppers every color of the rainbow, spinach, lettuce, white sweet onions and several bulbs of garlic. I then moved on to the rest of the store, loading up on couscous, pasta, tortillas, wheat bread, canned vegetables, a jar of garlic-stuffed olives, organic coffee, yogurt, soymilk and a 12-pack of Heineken. Meanwhile, the lyrics to the Jane Addiction song from 1990 were circling through my head, and I had to make a conscious effort to not sing them aloud:

When I want something,
And I don't want to pay for it
I walk right through the door
Walk right through the door
Hey all right!
If I get by, it's mine
Mine all mine!

Finally, when I decided I had enough, I began the "maneuver" I had invented. I walked through an unattended checkout aisle on one end of the store and passed in front of every other register on the way to the opposite door. I casually looked around, as anyone might who has just bought some groceries and was headed to his car. It didn't seem anyone had taken particular notice of me. I reached the door, walked through the anti-theft sensors. I did not expect them to go off, as we had learned only certain items contain the chips necessary to set them off. Food, even beer, was not included. And yet I could not help but hold my breath as I walked between them.

*Hey all right, if I get by...*My heart skipped a beat, but the alarms did not go off.

Walk right through that door!

The automatic doors parted to allow me passage outside and into the open sunny skies. I felt a wave of euphoria. I was not allowed to bask long, however.

"They didn't bag your groceries?" At first, I thought the question was coming from another customer, but then I looked down and saw a well-dressed, middle-aged woman wearing a manager badge. I stared at her for a moment and considered lying. Unfortunately, no story came to mind. This is where a certain quirk of my character kicked in, one that had been with me since I was a child. I hated to lie.

"I didn't pay for them."

She looked almost sorry for me for a moment, the sides of her mouth drooping slightly in pity. Suddenly they tightened into a frown.

"Well, sir, I'm going to have to ask you to come with me."

I knew she could not bring me in by force. The San Gabriel river wasn't more than a hundred yards from where I stood. If I bolted now, I could hide there until Nick came to pick me up. But then, how would I let him know where I was...

"Sir! Come with me." Now her face was almost pleading. Somewhere deep inside, I felt compassion. Perhaps, swimming somewhere in my subconscious, was the knowledge that thefts were directly impacting her job, as she most certainly had to report these losses to her own superiors. If I was aware of this at all, however, it must have been at a subconscious level. I thought only of myself. I tried to work up a sense of self-righteousness, that I was, in some sense, a political prisoner. After all, property is theft. Who are they to incarcerate me for taking something that belonged to me as much as it did to them?

It was difficult to believe my own internal dialog or propaganda. I did feel like a criminal. In addition, the implications of what had happened were slowly sinking in. I would not be able to attend the party, that was for sure. Although this should have been the least of my concerns, it did hit me pretty hard, nonetheless. I felt a peculiar sadness that I would not be able to enjoy the 12-pack of Heineken I had placed in my cart. Suddenly, I thought of Mira and Eugene, and felt a pain shoot through my heart that felt worse than anything I had felt in some time.

The police arrived and read me my rights. I was determined to stay silent, but they didn't ask me any questions. I was handcuffed and led from the store. My mind tried to see myself through the eyes of everyone in the store who stared at me. Martyr? Revolutionary? No. Criminal.

I was loaded into the back of a police cruiser that was parked outside. There were no flashing lights, I was relieved to see. The entire back seat was hard plastic, a fact I had somehow known already even though this was my first time to see one up close. What did surprise me, however, was that there was a well in the middle of the seat where I could place my cuffed hands without too much discomfort. It seemed almost kind.

I was taken to the Williamson County Jail, booked and processed. I was allowed to keep all of my clothes on except for my shoes, which I had to trade in for a pair of slippers. This, I assumed, was meant to humiliate the prisoners. I tried to conjure up a deep thought about what Foucault might have to say about this, but just then realized I actually knew almost nothing about Foucault except some vague notion about the "panopticon."

I was led to a large cell which contained about twenty others. As might be expected, this was a diverse mix of people along with a variety of coping strategies. Some were sitting quietly, others were standing and talking with the others, making loud jokes. One guy was singing a song I didn't recognize, by an artist named DJ Screw. The only lyric I remember is "I miss my free world."

I had zero interest in socializing. I was given a thin sheet, but no pillow. Fortunately, I had been wearing a brown fleece hoody that made a fine substitute when rolled up. I laid down on the floor and completely wrapped myself in the sheet, forming something of a cocoon. I did not sleep, but I dozed in and out of consciousness countless times for the next several hours.

Occasionally I would awake fully, but I would continue to lie there motionless, hearing but not discerning the conversations happening around me. And then, maybe 30 minutes later, maybe an hour later, I'd drift off again.

I heard a clang, as the door to the holding cell opened and shut, and a voice.

"Wow, you guys give out blankets now? You didn't have blankets the last time I was here."

The voice was loud, far too cheerful for the situation, and utterly grating in its clumsy cockiness.

I knew the voice. I peeked.

It was Dale, the guy who drove us to LA for the protests over 2 years ago. He was one of the most annoying people I had ever met, and now he was in jail with me, sharing this 20' x 20' concrete box with me for the next God-knows-how-many hours. I wondered what it was in our entangled karma that made our souls destined to find one another, again and again, in small, enclosed spaces. Which one of us had a cosmic lesson to learn? Was he supposed to be learning to spend less time talking about himself, and more time listening? Or was I supposed to be learning patience, to listen with generous ears? Could it be both?

I laughed, out loud, and then suppressed my laughter. I did not want him to hear me. Technically, I shouldn't have wanted anyone to hear me, since it would be strange to hear a man laughing while lying on a concrete floor completely enshrouded in a thin bed sheet. It was just funny. I couldn't believe this was happening, and a part of me felt it was so outrageous that perhaps it couldn't be a coincidence. That maybe the universe really did have a sense of humor. And if that were the case, then maybe even the terrible situation I found myself in might not be so terrible after all.

I continued to hide from him, for perhaps a few more hours, but eventually I simply could not remain on the floor.

It was beginning to feel like "morning," which was almost a meaningless concept since none of us knew what time it was, and the lights had never gone off. I removed the sheet and sat up slowly, my bones cracking after several hours of immobility.

I didn't look at or speak to Dale, hoping perhaps my invisibility trick might work better at helping me avoid conversations than it did helping me avoid paying for groceries. Of course, it didn't work. Out of the corner of my eye, I saw him staring at me, expressionless. After an hour of this went by, I realized he recognized me, but either couldn't place me or couldn't remember my name. This was fine by me.

"Lozier!"

By the time they called my name, I was crawling out of my skin. The bail had been set at $2400. I only needed to come up with $600 of that in order to pay a bail bondsman to post bail. I didn't understand half of what was going on, except the fact that I definitely did not have $600. Maggie, Elazar and Isaac pooled their money to cover it. It was only fair, in a way, considering we were trying to function as an anarchist collective of sorts. The groceries, after all, had been for all of us. And yet, when I saw them in the greeting area, I felt the first thing I should do was promise to pay them back as soon as possible.

The person I wanted to see the most was Mira, and I was puzzled when I did not see her.

"Where's Mira?"

"She went on a roll with one of her friends. She said she'll be at the Olive House when you get home."

This stung. To "go on a roll" just meant to go for a drive on country roads, which were abundant in Williamson County, and smoke a joint. I didn't care that she was getting high, of course. That was the first thing I planned to do when I got home. However, I couldn't understand why she wouldn't want to be there when I got out of jail. I wondered if she was angry with me. I knew we shared political views, but had we ever discussed the idea of "hyper-boycotting?" Perhaps she didn't approve. I wasn't even sure I'd blame her if she didn't. When I had got out of jail in LA, I had felt triumphant. There was a huge crowd to greet us, and a buffet of reclaimed food far more abundant than our shriveled stomachs required. This time felt very different. I was alone. Whether I had been arrested for a just cause was far less clear – perhaps because it had been self-serving rather than sacrificial.

The four of us piled into Isaac's jeep and headed back to the Olive House. I told the whole story of what had happened. They asked why I didn't run, why I had complied with the manager's orders. Those weren't legal orders, you know, you could have just walked away, they explained, as though I were a child. Did I detect some judgment in their voice? Had I not been hardcore enough? I had no defense, no way of explaining my behavior. I should have run away, I decided, scolding myself now.

Mira was not there when I got home, but a glass pipe on the front porch was. Seeing some green matter remaining in the bowl, I took a few puffs until the stress in my body and mind melted away. And then I grabbed the communal tin of drum tobacco and some rolling papers and rolled myself a cigarette. My two favorite chemicals now flowing through my system, I felt immensely better. I almost forgot about the fact that Mira hadn't greeted me at the jail, or that she wasn't home even after I arrived. But as the minutes wore on, my concern and insecurity and aggravation grew.

When her friend's car finally drove up and she was dropped off, I was not in a good state. She smiled at me widely, as she always did. An outside observer might have assumed she was totally unaware anything had happened to me.

"Hey, babe!" she said, beaming.

"Hey," I responded, flatly.

"What's the matter?" Her face turned to concern, which I found insulting.

"Um, well, I just got out of jail."

"Aww, yeah I know, babe. Come here and give me a hug."

I accepted the hug, and after 12 hours of nothing but concrete and thin sheets, it felt good. But I remained unsettled, and after a few seconds I pulled away.

"I just don't understand why you weren't there," I said, studying her face for a reaction. My fear of rejection often competed with my need to speak honestly, and I felt the tug of war happening in my body.

She seemed puzzled.

"I'm sorry, I guess I didn't know you wanted me there." Now I was puzzled. "How could I not want you there?" She cast her eyes to the ground.

"I don't know. It just felt like Elazar, Isaac and Maggie took the reins and I just felt weird about interjecting myself. They didn't even ask if I wanted to contribute to your bail. I would have if they had asked!" She made eye contact with me, and I felt my emotions subside. I hugged her again. I understood her explanation to a degree, yet there was a part of me that still felt conflicted. However, I was too happy to be reunited with her to let it spoil the moment.

Chapter 17

Mira and I had another two good days together before she returned to her parents' vineyard in Fredericksburg. The beers, sex, marijuana and tobacco were sufficient to keep reality at bay during this interim period, but it did not take long after she left for reality to set in.

I sat in the living room, my eyes wandering across the eclectic items on our coffee table, taking inventory of my situation. I didn't have a job. I had almost no money. I had a room, but almost nothing in it. I recycled the same three outfits over and over, washing infrequently. I took note of the fact that I had not contributed to the cost of the "communal tobacco," so even the cigarette in my hand was in some sense not mine. I had spent so much of my time decrying the evils of private property, and yet now my obvious lack of it did not feel like something worth celebrating.

I felt utterly overwhelmed at the question of how to move forward. Even though I had been bailed out, my situation was far from over. It was just getting started. I had a court date, and between now and then I needed to figure out how I was going to handle it. It was a Class B Misdemeanor. I only knew that this was worse than a Class C. I thought I should probably hire a lawyer. This, of course, brought me back to the problem of money. I had none, and no way of earning it. I needed a job.

Since I did not have a car, I would need to find something within walking distance. This was not ideal. Georgetown was a rather small town. We lived about two blocks from the university, but downtown was another five blocks from there. There was really only one place I could think of that was reasonably close. Jenny's, a small diner on University Avenue. I walked inside, greeted by the familiar smells and sounds of a central Texas "greasy spoon." Bacon, spoons stirring coffee, hamburgers, laughter, French fries. I saw a middle-aged woman with stringy blonde hair tied back in a hairnet working the register. I stood in line behind the elderly couple paying for their meal. I noticed they left four quarters for a tip.

"Thank ya'll!" the woman said to them, smiling to reveal deep lines that told me she was a smoker. Her smile evaporated as she turned to look at me. I became suddenly aware of my clothing, which probably wasn't clean. I hoped she didn't think I was a homeless person.

"Can I help you?"

"Hi, I was wondering if you were hiring."

She considered me for a moment.

"Actually yeah. Our dishwasher just quit. Can you start tomorrow? The pay is $7.50 per hour." This actually was more than I expected, and my spirits lifted.

"Sure! That's great. Do I...need to wear anything specific?"

"Nah, you're fine. You'll be in the back." I was too happy to wonder about this response. I shook her hand and she asked me to be back the next day at 10am. Her name was Jenny.

Like most people, I had preconceived notions about what a job as a dishwasher would feel like. The perception was that a dishwasher was the lowest of the low. Not the person working the job, of course, just the job itself. A dishwasher got no respect. He, or she, simply toiled away behind the scenes, washing endless piles of filthy dishes the wait staff consistently threw their way. They were paid the least and worked the longest.

This wasn't exactly my experience. Sure, I did realize I was at the bottom of the totem pole; however there was some freedom in that too. Washing dishes really wasn't that hard. The dishwasher who filled my shoes before me had left a radio in the back tuned to an Austin R&B station. Even though I had never listened to R&B, for some reason I kept it on and within a few weeks I was singing along to 50-Cent, Ja Rule and Missy Eliot. The hours flew by. My expectations were simple and clear, and the knowledge that I was making money made it easier to face other challenges in my life.

I visited a lawyer who agreed to take my case for $500. This felt like a lot, but I also knew it wasn't much in the world of legal fees. I also knew that the future consequences of this charge on my record, if improperly handled, could cost me much more than that in the long run. He wouldn't require payment until the case was settled, which was perfect since I hadn't yet received my first paycheck.

Finally, there was the biggest challenge: my plans to move to Eugene. When I mentioned it to the lawyer, he did not sound optimistic. His answer was essentially "Let's wait and see," so I knew there were no guarantees. When I spoke to Mira about it, it became clear that she was not changing her own plans. She wanted me to come, certainly that's what she wanted. But, when I spelled it out in my mind, it came to this. Her first choice was to go to Eugene with me. Her second choice was to go alone. The possibility of remaining in Texas with me was her third choice, or maybe not a choice at all.

Although my feelings for her had not changed, my confidence in the future of our relationship was waning. I enjoyed every moment we spent together, every conversation, but when we were apart, I was finding myself more focused on taking care of my own business. This is as it should be, I realized. Each of us must be our own person, otherwise we have nothing to offer one another when we come together.

I knew I had to keep focused in terms of my political commitments as well. Certainly, there was enough to keep me occupied on that front. George W. Bush was beating the drums of war against Iraq. I was working at the restaurant the afternoon I learned that the Bush administration was going ahead with an alliance to invade Iraq without seeking the approval of the United Nations Security Council. They did this, of course, because they knew a resolution authorizing the invasion would be vetoed. I was astounded at the egotism of his decision. Every purported justification for invasion was a blatant lie. Saddam Hussein had absolutely nothing to do with 9/11. Religiously, he and Al Qaeda were on opposite ends of the spectrum. The claims of "weapons of mass destruction" were a total sham. I couldn't even blame George W. Bush or his "cronies" entirely. What he was doing would not be possible had so many prominent Democrats not lined up at his side. They should know better, I thought.

The 2003 invasion of Iraq is now almost universally considered to have been a massive mistake. No connection has been made, then or now, between the attacks of September 11 and the Saddam Hussein regime. What was most upsetting, during this time, was the support offered by Democrats, who voted to approve authorization for unilateral military action by George W. Bush, a decision with consequences that resonate even to this day. Hillary Clinton's support was particularly disappointing. It was truly unbelievable to watch as plans continued to be laid despite protests from the global community, including a near unanimous vote by the United Nations opposing the invasion. George W. Bush was clearly going to get his way, and nobody was going to stop him.

In February, a large protest was planned in downtown Austin. There were no direct actions planned, so I simply attended as a mere "participant." I was astounded, when I arrived at the Capitol Building, to see over ten thousand people gathered. Soon the crowd took Congress Avenue. An hour later, a sea of people spanned the entire street from the Capitol Building all the way to the bridge. I had never seen anything like it in Austin.

It seemed like too good of an opportunity to waste, and some of the folks from the Rhizome Collective I encountered on the bridge seemed to feel the same. We had a quick discussion and decided to try to divert the march to the offices of the Austin American Statesman newspaper, which wasn't far from the bridge. Why? Because "corporate media." We didn't need a specific grievance to know their reporting could not be trusted, and that their support for the war build- up was implicit.

I saw some younger kids, probably high school students, carrying a long banner: "NO WAR WITH IRAQ." I approached them and conveyed the plan, speaking with boldness and authority. I told them we would be leading the march. I tied a black bandana, which I had brought just in case, across the bridge of my nose and behind my head. We began marching south to the end of the bridge, while other anarchists I knew began rallying the crowd to follow us.

Initially, I had no specific plan for how to handle the line of police cars and motorcycles that were completely blocking the end of the bridge on the south side. One of the kids asked me what we were going to do, and I could detect the growing nervousness in his voice. I formed a plan in the same instant I responded – "just keep marching straight ahead." Again, my apparent confidence was enough to convince them to trust me, no questions asked.

I noticed that although the police were completely blocking the road, four lanes of traffic, the sidewalks on either side were open. I realized that if we were to deviate to either side, at this moment about 30 yards from the police, they would react and block the sidewalks. However, if we waited until the very last second, there might not be enough time for them to stop us.

I whispered to the young girl next to me.

"Keep going, but when we reach the police line, we need to move fast to the left and take the sidewalk."

We continued forward, inching closer to the police, taking care to moderate our pace so that the crowd of people remained close behind us. I could see the police becoming nervous themselves, some of them having unsheathed their billy clubs, holding them menacingly across their bodies.

When we were mere feet away, I shouted "now!" On cue,

myself and the three high school students sprinted to the left, crossing in front of the police lines and reaching the sidewalk. The crowd followed behind. As I had hoped, the plan worked perfectly. The police were not able to respond quickly enough, and the crowd streamed past the police lines.

We reached the end of the bridge and headed east to the Austin American Statesman building. For whatever reason, the police did not pursue us. We walked around the building, shouting slogans like "NO CORPORATE MEDIA" and banging on the glass windows. There did not seem to be anyone inside. This was, unfortunately, when we realized that getting past the police lines was probably the most well thought-out part of our plans. After a short while, the crowd dispersed.

That evening, reading the reports on IndyMedia, I learned that this day of action had been deemed "the largest coordinated protest in world history." In Texas alone, 5000 had protested in Dallas, and 7000 in Houston. I had never even heard of a protest taking place in either of those cities. There were half a million in San Francisco, hundreds of thousands in New York City, and a million in Rome. There had even been a small demonstration by scientists in Antarctica, making this the first protest to happen on all seven continents.

The scope of the day's protests was far beyond anything I had imagined up until that point. Surely this will stop the war, I thought. And then, a haunting thought, the near certainty that it would not. And what did that mean? Next time, could we bring out 20,000 in Austin, two million in Rome? How many millions would have to fill the streets to stop the machinery of global capitalism? The answer, it seemed, was in the question.

Finally, my court date arrived. I had managed to buy a cheap suit at the thrift store. It was too big for me. Isaac dropped me off at the courthouse downtown, and I told him I would call when it was over.

"Good luck, dude," he said, staring at me as always with his fierce blue eyes.

"Thanks."

I walked inside and found the correct courtroom. My lawyer was waiting for me. He already had news.

"Ok, I've possibly struck a deal with the prosecutors. The deal is no jail time, no additional fines. It's just one year of probation, and the charge will be wiped from your record."

"That sounds good to me," I said. "Possibly?"

He hesitated for a moment, and almost looked apologetic for the words that were to follow.

"Yeah, there's just one problem. With your record. Have you been arrested before? Like, in Los Angeles?"

"Oh," I sighed, sinking into my seat. "I forgot about that." I was doomed.

"Can you just tell me what happened? It's a little difficult to make out."

I had no way of imagining what the record might have said. I doubt there was any government form that covered that specific situation. I had been arrested, and charged, but I never gave them my name. I was booked as "John Doe." However, one of the conditions of the release, after 10 days on hunger strike, media coverage and direct negotiation with the country prosecutor, had been that we provide identification as we were being processed out. This, of course, allowed them to finally tie our identity back to our original crimes. Even though the charges were dropped, a note of some kind had obviously been made.

I didn't feel I had any option but to tell him the entire story, which he listened to in rapt amazement. This was a small-town courthouse in central Texas. It was unlikely they dealt with many former political prisoners.

"Oh-kay," he said, taking a deep breath. "Let me see what I can do with this."

He returned to the prosecutor's desk and spoke with two men in suits. I watched them follow along as he related whatever version of the story he decided to communicate. Then I saw everyone, my lawyer included, break out into laughter. One of the prosecutors shook his head and muttered something I couldn't hear, still smiling.

My own lawyer walked back, also smiling.

"Alright, that's fine. The deal is done."

One of the conditions of the probation was that I was forbidden from leaving the state without permission from my probation officer. Since I hadn't yet met with my probation officer, this seemed like a good time for me to accompany Mira on her move to Eugene. Obviously, I wasn't going with her, for good, but I could still be a part of her road trip and help her move into the place she had rented. Our plan was that I would come back to Texas after, work for a while, and perhaps get permission from the probation officer to transfer my case to Oregon. Talking about this brought back the familiar feeling of saying words I wasn't sure I believed but believing them at the time helped both of us keep going.

The road trip had its ups and downs. The scenery was spectacular. We drove through the deserts of West Texas and New Mexico, smoking bowls and listening to music and sharing laughter. When we reached Arizona, we stopped at a truck stop and spotted a picnic table with a lovely view of the desert. "Watch out for rattlesnakes," Mira laughed, half-joking, as we stepped our way among the rocks, a brown bag in her hand.

We reached the picnic table and she brought out of the bag two sandwiches as she named the ingredients: hummus, bean sprouts, avocado, tomatoes, lettuce, green onions. A vegan delight. We sat on the same side of the table, facing the western sky, and watched the sunset as we ate. Before we left, I picked a yellow brittle bush flower and handed it to her.

"I'll keep it forever," she said, looking directly into my eyes, smiling.

The idyllic moment was shattered not more than a few minutes later, when I once again offered to drive, and she once again declined. "I don't mind," she said, as she had said every time. I was realizing she didn't just "not mind" driving, she actually didn't want me to drive. I felt insulted, perhaps a bit emasculated. Did she not trust me? This turned into a huge argument, the fun times turned into silence.

We rented a small motel room just after crossing into California, which was very late that night. This should have been a fun and exciting moment, but instead we weren't speaking to each other. There was only one bed, and each of us slept on opposite sides with a yawning space between us. It was the polar opposite configuration from our last night in college. We made up, sort of, in the morning. Mostly, it just felt like we were moving on.

The drive through California was pure delight. We had lunch in San Francisco, and by the late afternoon made a stop in Arcadia for coffee. Arcadia was legendary for its weed, but of course we weren't there long enough to find out.

Finally, we made it to Eugene. I navigated the directions to her house using a printout from MapQuest we had made back at the Olive House. It was a lovely wooden house with a large porch and a tall oak tree in the yard. I imagined Mira and I sitting on that porch together having coffee in the morning, and I felt a pang of sadness. We were supposed to be doing this together, but I had ruined everything.

We met her two roommates, both women about our age, both warm and welcoming. She was shown her room, which had a lovely view of the street through two large windows. We carried inside the few belongings Mira had brought with her in the Volvo, but the bulk of her possessions were coming on a U-Haul which her parents were driving up in a couple of days. Until then, we would spend our days exploring the city, casually looking for a job for Mira, and our nights on sleeping bags.

Eugene was everything I had hoped it would be, and more, which made the bitterness of the experience compete strongly with the sweetness. It was visually beautiful, trees everywhere and mountains in the distance. The activist scene was alive, and we came across anarchist bookstores and small organic food co-ops everywhere we turned. We toured the Whiteaker neighborhood, famous for driving out the police during the riots in Eugene in the summer of 1999. It was believed that many of the participants in the Black Bloc at the WTO protests in Seattle later that year lived and organized in this neighborhood. This neighborhood was also the launching point for many tree sitting actions in the surrounding Cascadia old growth forests. Anarchy symbols were stenciled into the sidewalk and on the side of buildings. The energy of this place was palpable, and my sadness compounded.

When Mira's parents arrived with the U-Haul, their added presence was a welcomed distraction. Her parents were very fond of me, and I enjoyed their company. It didn't hurt that they enjoyed smoking a bowl with us every now and then, although when this happened her father became very quiet and her mother became extremely talkative. After we finished moving in the rest of Mira's furniture, we spent the next few days engaged in more typical tourist activities such as watching whales off the Pacific coast or visiting vineyards. Finally, it was time for me to return to Texas.

Despite the fact that our relationship had not felt perfect, saying our goodbyes felt extremely sad. Mira brought me to the Greyhound Station, and as she parked, I noticed tears welling up in her eyes.

"You won't forget about me, will you?" she asked in a tiny voice.

"That's impossible," I said, and kissed her, holding my lips against hers for several moments. "I love you. I am going back to Texas, and I'm going to figure out how to get back here with you." I had taken a flyer from a communal apartment building in Whiteaker, and when I got back, I intended to fill out an application.

"I hope so."

"I hope so, too," I responded, before correcting myself with the words that would help us get through the moment. "I know so."

And once again I boarded a bus for another cross-country trip. It had become a familiar routine.

Chapter 18

Things unraveled quickly after I returned to the Olive House. The nearly 2-day trip on the bus had given me time to do little else than contemplate how my current circumstances did not add up to the vision I had created for myself. Instead of Mira and I joyously living together in Eugene, she was living there by herself. I was stuck in Georgetown, Texas and beginning a year on probation. This was not how I had planned things. To make matters worse, the asymmetry between Mira and I was becoming apparent to me. Had the roles been reversed, I knew it was impossible I would have chosen to move to Eugene by myself. It wasn't that I blamed her for making that choice. It made perfect sense. I had done this all to myself. And yet, this, and other signs, were making it apparent to me that we were not on the same page.

On the bus, I had plenty of time to ponder related issues like our "polyamorous" status. I had agreed to it because that's what she wanted, and I wanted her. But I didn't really want to pursue other relationships. Did she? She had never indicated so, and yet that was almost more unsettling. Was it a power thing? To ensure I was never overly comfortable in our relationship? I knew this kind of thinking was crazy. She wasn't that kind of person. However, I could not deny that things felt unbalanced, and also, I was just very pissed off at life.

The night I returned to the Olive House, there was a huge party. I drank massive amounts of beer and whiskey. Technically, I wasn't supposed to be doing this since I was on probation. But I doubted they could detect alcohol in a urine sample.

A girl named Kathryn was there, with whom Elazar had recently broken up. They hadn't been together long and were trying to remain friends. I had known Kathryn at a distance for a couple of years, since she had been a student at Southwestern.

I did not know her well, but I found her attractive. To my surprise, I felt she was flirting with me. I reciprocated. She asked to see my loft, which I was able to reclaim after my return from Oregon. I let her climb the ladder first and I followed behind and then pulled the curtain closed. I turned on some Christmas lights for atmosphere. We laid on the mattress and cuddled for a moment. Then I heard Elazar's voice.

"Kathryn?" He was under the loft.

We looked at each other with wide eyes. We were silent for a moment, as though wondering if we should respond. It wasn't that we were intentionally hiding from him. I thought maybe he had picked up on things, but surely he was ok with it since they had broken up. It didn't occur to me that perhaps the breakup was still fresh for him. It didn't occur to me to think of anyone but myself.

"Yes," Kathryn responded, a bit shakily.

"Is Aaron up there, too?"

"Yeah," we both responded.

He was quiet for a moment, and I could hear him breathing. After a few seconds, which felt like an eternity, he left the room. What else could he do, really?

"I'm gonna go," said Kathryn.

"No, don't go" I replied, still thinking about myself.

"I can't do this," she said simply, smiling. "But I think you're really cool."

It felt amazing to hear this.

She slid off the mattress and onto the ladder, and waved goodbye. I returned with a half-hearted wave. Then, a moment later, I heard her climb back up the ladder, pulling the curtain back again.

"Come here," she said, leaning forward. We kissed for several seconds, and then she left for good.

While I did not initially feel bad about my decision, considering we were in a polyamorous relationship, the uncomfortable feelings grew. Later the next evening, I went to another party, and kissed another girl. It was an equally brief encounter.

The day after that, the uncomfortable feelings had become painful, and I knew I had to tell Mira. I called her early the next day but got her voicemail. I called again 30 minutes later, and again 30 minutes after that. My guilt had morphed into obsession to relieve that guilt, and she was the only one who could relieve it. Not that I could be sure she, of course. But the possibility seemed infinitely better than this uncertainty.

Finally, she returned my call. She sounded a little annoyed, I supposed because of my repeated calls.

"What's up, babe?"

"I have to tell you something."

A pause.

"Ok. What is it?"

"I kissed two girls." The words felt strange and awkward as they left my lips.

"What?" she blurted, with a hint of laughter that I interpreted as shock.

I repeated the sentence, the words still feeling unbalanced in some way.

There was a very long pause. My stomach churned in knots as I awaited her response. I worried she would hang up. Finally, her words broke the painful silence, but provided no relief.

"I don't know what you expect me to say."

"Well, you wanted us to be polyamorous."

"I wanted? Aaron, that was something we both agreed to."

"Well, I guess I didn't really want it."

"Can you stop and think right now about how crazy that sounds? You did this, not me."

We went around in circles on this point for several minutes. Eventually she said she just needed some time to think. I couldn't let it go like this, my emotions were rising, and I felt like I was about to erupt. And then I did.

"You're never there for me!"

"I am," she responded quietly, almost imperceptibly.

"No, you're not!" My voice was rising.

"Aaron."

"You're not! You say you are, but you're not! I would have never left you, never! I would have been there for you, if you made a mistake, one stupid fucking mistake. Here's the truth. I love you more than you love me. And I'm sick of it. I can't take it anymore. I don't want us anymore. It's over, goodbye."

And then I hung up.

What followed, on my end, were 3 days of depression, anxiety and suicidal thoughts. It seemed every direction I looked I saw only threats. I was facing a year in the criminal justice system. The invasion of Iraq was looming. I was struggling to scrape together with a part-time job that paid very little. I was living in Texas when I was supposed to be in Oregon. But worst of all, I had lost the love of my life.

The thoughts of suicide became so intense that I actually went to buy a gun. I had no idea how much a gun cost, or what the process of buying one was like. I would find out. I was handed a handgun that had a nice weight to it. I turned it over in my hand, looking at it, pretending to examine it as if I had any criteria whatsoever other than knowing it would do the job.

"How much?" I asked.

"$500."

I had just that in my bank account. Was there any need for there to be anything left over?

"And," he continued, "you need to pass a background check. It takes about 24 hours."

I was relieved to not have to make the decision in that instant, but I did fill out the background check. I wondered whether it would clear. I doubted it but didn't have anything to lose. On the walk back home, I wondered what some alternatives might be. I saw an Oleander tree and remembered learning in a botany class that they were extremely poisonous. "Backup plan," I noted, "oleander tea." And I thought that might make a nice name for a poem.

The next day, I returned home from work to find a voice waiting on the answering machine. I was the only one home. I pressed play.

"Hey, this message is for Aaron. This is Chuck with the Georgetown Pawn Shop, just letting you know your background check came back clear. You're good to buy the firearm, so feel free to come back in when you have a moment. Thanks!"

I felt a chill run through my body, and I deleted the message. I imagined myself walking into the store, buying the gun, walking home with it in my possession. In my pocket? In a bag? Where would I go? Would I go home to get a snack first? How did that make any sense? What meaning did time, or pleasure, or even pain have when the end of the world was imminent? Why not just immediately shoot myself the moment it was handed to me? Too risky, I thought. But the real reason was I didn't want to involve anyone else. Why create unnecessary pain and suffering in the world?

These thoughts spiraled through my head until I became dizzy. But finally, I reached the conclusion that if I was ready to end it all, what was the rush? Might as well try a little longer. If I'm ready to die anyway, I really have nothing to lose.

I carried this attitude with me the next day when I went into work. I could tell as soon as I walked in that Jenny was in a terrible mood. I steered clear of her. I finished all of the dishes early and stepped outside for a smoke break until the next batch of dishes arrived. As I sat outside, leaning against the brick wall and smoking my cigarette, Jenny stormed outside and slammed the door behind her.

"What the hell do you think you're doing?"

"Having a smoke break," I replied flatly. "I finished the

219

dishes."

Her eyes widened as though I had just insulted her.

"Well then find something else to do! Come with me!"

I put my cigarette out and followed her back inside. She was worked into a fury. She led me into the kitchen, picked up some cleaner from the bottom shelf, and started spraying the countertops.

"See," she said, "you could be cleaning the counters while you're waiting for dishes." She tossed a rag at me, and I barely caught it.

"Or," she said, slamming the spray bottle hard on the countertop, "you could be scraping the stovetop." She grabbed a metal scraper with a wooden handle that was tucked into a pocket on the side of the stove and began scraping it frantically on the stainless-steel surface, pushing bits of gristle and oily French fry crumbs into the pit at the far end.

"I'm done," I said. The words came out before my mind had a chance to contemplate the decision. "I quit," I said, noticing that the words felt good to say.

"Fine! Go!" she screamed, her smoker skin glowing red like a cigarette ember.

"I am," I affirmed, untying my apron and tossing it on the counter. "Goodbye."

I walked out the back door, hearing the last notes of a Jah Rule song playing from the little radio, and feeling a tad bit sad that I probably would never listen to another one of his songs again.

The impulsiveness of my decision scared me a little; however I knew it was necessary. I didn't mind washing dishes. In fact, I didn't mind doing extra duties in between. However, I could not accept being degraded. In that moment in the kitchen, I saw my life fork in two different directions. I could either stay on the path that had brought me here, or I could start to pursue a different one.

Chapter 19

The day I walked away from the dishwashing job a new phase of my life began. I wasted no time before looking for another job. In fact, I headed to the Career Center on campus to see if they had any openings. An index card on the job board caught my eye.

"Looking for someone to help establish an online antique business. Must have experience operating a digital camera, writing descriptions and uploading pictures to a website. Interest in history a plus. Full time – $8/hour."

I called the number and a man named Larry answered. He gave me directions to his house on the far west side of Georgetown. Isaac let me borrow his car. I drove out there to find a beautiful limestone home on several acres of land. I also noticed a large, perhaps twenty-thousand square foot metal warehouse on the property. The rolling door was up, and inside I could see porcelain antiques numbering in the thousands. A very large man in his mid-50s came outside the house and started walking down the pathway toward the gravel road where I had parked. I noticed he was very tanned and well dressed in a polo shirt and khaki shorts. Following behind was his wife, a small woman with pale skin, dark hair and glasses. She could have been a librarian.

"You must be Aaron," he bellowed, reaching out his hand. I shook it, firmly.

"And you must be Larry. Good to meet you."

"And this is my wife, Anne."

"Good to meet you," she said more quietly, but with a kind voice. I shook her hand as well.

"Well, let me show you the place," Larry announced ceremoniously. "It's really something incredible."

He led me inside the warehouse. It was, indeed, astonishing.

There were rows after rows of shelves containing all manner of porcelain items. There were hundreds of complete dish sets, each containing plates, bowls, saucers, teacups, gravy bowls and butter dishes.

"Most of these are Haviland, but there are some other manufacturers as well."

Then he led me to an area containing dozens of porcelain figurines. These were idyllic scenes of eighteenth-century aristocracy, men and women dancing or women sitting alone with flowing lace dresses.

"You can touch them, gently. But be careful. Each of these are worth hundreds of dollars."

I carefully touched the lace and was astonished. I was sure it had been fabric. It was so fine and detailed. But no, it was porcelain.

"These are Dresden," he said, "which are very rare since these pre-date World War II and most of the figurines like this were destroyed in the bombings. Let me show you something else."

He led me to another, smaller area, where the pieces were considerably more spaced out. There were all types of porcelain here, arranged on tables, including dishes, figurines and vases. And yet, there was something different about them. They were astonishing in their color and detail. The lace on the figurines was even more intricate. The scenes and patterns depicted on the dishes and vases were spectacular. They looked like they belonged in a museum.

"This is our Meissen. It is the finest porcelain on earth."

He gave me the backstory. His mother had owned a prominent antique store in Dallas but had recently passed away. He, being the only child, had inherited her business. Being a forward-thinking businessman, or so he believed, he decided to take the business online. He had recently married Anne. Together they bought the property in Georgetown and had all of the pieces moved by truck across the state.

"A lot of the pieces were damaged," he admitted, seeming embarrassed.

He had hired a company in Houston to build the website. He needed someone to take photographs of everything, upload them to the website, and write descriptions of the products. He also needed help researching the pieces, since he only knew a little. Fortunately, along with the pieces, his mother had left him an extensive library of books about the different manufacturers she carried.

I told him I had all the skills he needed. I had worked with computers all my life, and I loved history and loved to write. I promised to help him turn his dream into a reality. I was hired on the spot.

I tried not to think about whether this job compromised my anarchist principles in some way. Certainly, it was "bougie" by any definition. But I, myself, was certainly not earning a "bougie" wage. Who could I possibly be hurting by helping this guy get his online business going? And sure, when I got my degree in history, I certainly didn't expect it to be used to research porcelain manufacturers. On the other hand, it was a lot more relevant to my studies than washing dishes. And if I were getting paid to learn, I could certainly find a way to make it as interesting as possible.

I found having a steady job actually enhanced my political activities, rather than diminished them. It felt good to simply be able to pay my bills, and no longer having to worry about this freed up large chunks of my brain to focus on the revolution.

This positive change in my life even helped me to reconcile with Mira. We both apologized, although we weren't necessarily trying to get back together. She even told me she was seeing someone. I told her I was happy for her. She told me she missed me and wanted me to come visit her again as soon as possible. I told her I would work on it.

In the meantime, I began writing an article for the Eugene quarterly Green Anarchy. It was a re-work of a paper I had written in college on "eco-feminism." I argued that there were actually close connections between eco-feminism and green anarchism. Both made the connection that the exploitation of the earth was inextricably tied with the exploitation of women. Both questioned the nature of authority in general, which was perceived as masculine. I worried the article might be a little heady, but after emailing it to them I received an enthusiastic response that it would be printed in the next edition.

While I was building connections with the Eugene anarchist community online, Mira was doing so in person. One day she called and told me she had met John Zerzan at a party. My jaw hit the floor.

"Yeah, he's a funny little man. But he's cool."

She also told me she had started working with people affiliated with the Cascadia Forest Alliance who were supporting the tree-sitters. This news was equally exhilarating. Among all those involved in the anarchist movement, the tree-sitters seemed to me the purest. They believed that we as human beings were one with the earth, that there was no difference between exploiting people and exploiting the environment. And that even if we abolished capitalism, it would do no good if we continued to ravage the ecosystem. Unlike the rest of us, who dealt mostly in slogans and abstractions, the tree-sitters put their lives directly on the line. Their actions were not symbolic. The means of their protest and the goal of their protest were one and the same: to save the lives of trees.

I began saving money to visit Mira in Oregon. My usual means of travel – hitchhiking, ridesharing or the Greyhound bus – were impractical for my situation given the demands of work, on one hand, and regular meetings with my probation officer on the other. Although these meetings were scheduled, I was routinely reminded that I could be contacted at any time and required to come to the probation office. If I were to take the risk of traveling out of state, I would need to make the duration as short as possible. For this reason, I needed to buy a plane ticket.

One day, Mira called me with earth-shattering news.

"John Zerzan wants you to come on his radio show."

"Are you serious? Oh my God, I can't believe it! How did this happen?" I had to struggle to control my breath.

"He told me he really loved your article. He said if you come to Eugene, he'd like to invite you on his weekly radio show to discuss it."

This was a dream come true. John Zerzan was easily on my list of top three radical intellectuals, along with Noam Chomsky and Guy Debord. But it wasn't simply that I was going to meet him. He had asked to meet me, because of something I had written. I was going to be able to engage with him. And I was going to be on his radio show in Eugene, Oregon.

I asked for a week off, and Larry and Anne were happy to accommodate. In addition, I asked if I could work extra hours in the meantime. I suggested this as a way I could "make up" for the time off in advance. Mainly I needed the money. Again, they obliged. Because of this, I was able to purchase a ticket to Portland departing in only 2 weeks.

Mira picked me up from the airport, all smiles and kisses. As I held her again, it suddenly felt like nothing had changed. Had I just imagined the last few months? Had we ever even been apart? We loaded into her Volvo. As I sat next to her in the front seat, she reached over and grabbed my hand and held it most of the way back to Eugene.

She had been quite busy. She was now hanging out with "John" regularly as well as several others close to him. She had begun working with the tree-sitters and had made a number of supply runs to the Cascadia. She asked if I wanted to join her on another run the next day, and I couldn't say yes fast enough.

The usual division I had become accustomed to, between radical politics and the "rest of society," did not seem to exist in Eugene. The supplies we would be bringing to the tree-sitters were donated by local restaurants and grocery stores. At first, I wondered if the business owners were unaware of where their donations were headed, but that thought was quickly dashed as I saw the owners themselves sported dreadlocks, piercings and/ or anarchy tattoos. They raised their fists in the air in response to our thanks. It felt like we were all on the same team.

We collected the supplies during the day, mostly food but also basic toiletries like toilet paper, toothpaste, soap and even contact lens solution. (Even if you spent the night in a tree, you still needed to take out your contacts beforehand.) However, we would not leave until much later that night. We weren't necessarily forbidden from going to the area of the forest we were headed, but since we were technically supporting illegal activity, it was best to take precautions to avoid being spotted by local police, or the logging companies. A friend of Mira's named Sarah arrived at the house in a pickup truck with a covered bed. Everything was now in 12-gallon buckets which we loaded in the back. Mira sat in the front seat next to Sarah and I sat in the back. It was a long trip, almost 2 hours, and while Sarah and Mira chatted animatedly the whole way, passing back and forth a glass pipe, I sat in the backseat. I enjoyed my own buzz as I watched the towering evergreens race across the window, just discernible against the dark sky with the help of a full moon. I dozed off more than once before we finally rolled to a stop on a dirt road, deep in the forest.

I stepped out, and imagined I could be on Endor, or Fangorn Forest from *Lord of the Rings*. It felt as far from civilization as a human could be. The forest was alive with sound as millions of insects put on a symphony that was almost deafening but at the same time deeply soothing. The stars in the sky were abundant, even with competition from the moon. I felt embraced by the multitude of trees around me, many of which were very large and hundreds of years old in some cases. It was clear to me why these beings were worth saving.

After putting on our backpacks, we each grabbed two buckets, one in each hand. Sarah led the way through the forest, down a dark and discrete trail. The forest floor was blanketed in ferns, their soft ends touching me as I passed by. We continued for about a mile before a small campfire became visible in the darkness ahead, and we entered a clearing which was one of the base camps.

There were several folks sitting around the fire, a familiar mix of hippies and punks. There was a woman with a Mohawk and numerous piercings, a man with long blonde dreadlocks and beads. They greeted Sarah, whom they knew well, raised their eyebrows at Mira, whom they were just starting to know, and eyed me with suspicion. I didn't take it personally. It was a dance I was quite used to at this point. Experience had taught me that the less I took offense at their suspicion, and in fact demonstrated that I understood the need for the suspicion, the more quickly I would win their trust.

"I hope you guys didn't bring any more of those Monkey Bars."

Sarah smiled.

"We have a whole bucket-full," she said.

"NO!" He shouted with what felt like real anger, as his face was fiercely lit up by the fire. "I block the Monkey Bars!"

I half-understood what he was saying. The term "block" referred to a concept within consensus process. Since the idea was to make decisions by consensus rather than majority rules, any one person was allowed, if they felt strongly enough, to block a decision. Anyone could use a "block," even to stop a decision that was otherwise unanimous. The point was that every voice was important. There were no formal restrictions on how many times, or how often a person could use a block. It was generally understood that if you abused the privilege you would be ostracized from the group.

So I understood he intended to, for some reason, block receipt of the Monkey Bars. I just didn't know what Monkey Bars were.

Sarah laughed. "You can't be serious, Razor?"

I silently laughed myself, learning this man with the long beard and doubly long blond dreadlocks called himself Razor.

"I'm dead serious," he said. "Do you know what the Monkey Bars did to us last time? You don't understand. They are like crack."

Everyone laughed.

"Don't laugh! I am not kidding. You guys don't know what it's like to live for months, even years out here. All of you, who live in Babylon, where sugar is for breakfast, lunch and dinner, and everything in between, you're used to it. It's just a nice little snack. You don't worry about when you'll be able to have another one, because you can get one anytime you want. For us, it's not that way. It's sweeter than almost anything we ever have. It's amazing. And yet, when you're halfway through the bar, you start to wonder when you'll be able to have another. You can see everyone else is thinking the same thing, eying the bucket. You stash yours away and start making plans for how you are going to procure some more. Look, I know we don't believe in property, but when you bring Monkey Bars into the camp, you start to understand how people came up with the idea."

I was intrigued how this small anarchist community in the woods was already grappling with such profound questions about how to deal with the reality of scarcity according to anti-oppression, anti-hierarchical principles. Clearly the subject of this controversy was something major.

"What are Monkey Bars," I finally asked. Everyone looked at me.

"You've never had a Monkey Bar?" Razor asked,

dumbfounded. I shook my head. "Ok, so they're like these vegan cookie bars. They're made of, like, coconut and oats and chocolate and nuts and angel cum – I don't know what they put in these fucking things, but they are out of this world."

"They're really good," Mira agreed.

"They're not good, they're dangerous. And we can't have them in our camp. You need to take them back."

"Let's see what everyone else thinks," Sarah suggested.

"I already said I was blocking it!"

But now he was smiling. He reached into one of the buckets, pulling out one of the gooey cookie bars, and consumed half of it in one bite. He closed his eyes, reveling in their sweetness.

Past the campfire we found another clearing where perhaps a dozen tents were set. Mira had brought a tent for the two of us, and it took us some time fumbling in the dark to get it set up. Then we unfurled our sleeping bags inside. Mira gave me a kiss goodnight and then turned to sleep. I lay awake for a while, looking up through the mesh top at the night sky. I felt a blend of wonder and anxiety. On the one hand, I was amazed at the beauty of the old growth forest at night. On the other, I was struggling with mixed feelings and uncertainty about my relationship with Mira. Two months ago, I had written it off. I assumed she had as well. We had both dated since that time. As I understood it, she had a regular partner. But they, of course, were polyamorous. I wasn't necessarily interested in being the third spoke of a love triangle. I actually wasn't sure I wanted to rekindle a relationship with Mira at all. But I wanted to be with her now, for the moment, for however long it might last

I awoke at what felt like an early hour. The sun was up, but still low in the sky, and streaks of pink against the blue were visible between the trees which towered overhead. I could hear activity. I turned and saw Mira was no longer in the tent. It was chilly. I could see clouds form when I breathed out. I was already wearing black jeans, but I dug in my backpack and pulled out my hoodie as well. I carefully placed on my contacts, which took longer than usual because I didn't have a mirror to assist me. Finally, I emerged from the tent.

There was a lot going on at the camp. There were small fires as well as camping stoves where people were making oatmeal or coffee. Others were carrying back clothes they had washed in a nearby stream, preparing to hang them up to dry. A few others were standing and talking intently. One of them carried a clipboard. I overheard one of them say something about a blockade. I tried not to pay attention, as I didn't want to be mistaken for a CI.

"Hey, sleepy head." A familiar voice. I turned and saw Mira walking toward me with two steaming metal camping cups. She handed one to me. Coffee. There was no cream or sugar, but I didn't care, it was hot. I sipped it with delight.

"So, we've divided up the new supplies into week rations, which we will be bringing out to the sits." She gestured behind her and I saw several 5-gallon buckets which she and Sarah had already prepared. I suddenly felt bad for sleeping late, but I wasn't sure I could help it. I had always been such a hard sleeper. I didn't even remember her getting up from the tent.

"Ok, sounds good!"

"You finish your coffee and then we'll head out." She smiled and leaned in to give me a kiss on the cheek.

When it was time to leave, we each took a bucket in each hand, and I was surprised by the weight.

"It's quite the hike," said Sarah, "but we can take as many breaks as you need." Why was she singling me out?

She wasn't wrong. I did, in fact, feel like the weak link of the group, asking them to stop several times. Mira was doing fine, but I supposed that was because she got a lot of exercise working at the plant nursery. Sarah didn't even seem fazed, looking strong in her overalls and not even a hint of sweat. I supposed my lifestyle of drinking, smoking pot and working on a computer wasn't the best preparation for hiking miles in the woods, carrying a heavy bucket in each hand. My back hurt most of all, but my forearms burned as well. When I saw Mira give me a look I interpreted as disappointment, I vowed to stop less and complain not at all.

We reached the first sit. Only I wouldn't have known it if Sarah hadn't pointed it out. I arched my head back and saw, over a hundred feet in the air, a wooden platform that could have been the bottom of a very small tree house. We set our buckets on the ground and stretched our relieved shoulders. Sarah fetched a walkie talkie from her backpack and turned it on. There was a moment of static before she pressed the button and spoke into it.

"Ground to Sleeping Bear, come back."

Another moment of static, and then a female's voice.

"Sleeping Bear, go ahead."

"Hey girl, it's Sarah. We got your groceries." More static, and then an exclamation of pure joy.

"Woohoo! I'm dropping the rope now."

While we waited, Sarah explained the name Sleeping Bear came to her after being woken up one night, while sleeping on the platform, by an unexpected visitor. She opened her eyes and saw a black bear in the tree with her. The bear stared at her for several minutes before moving along.

As I was listening to the story, a thin, colorful rope with a carabiner tied into the end lowered into our field of vision. Sarah attached the carabiner to one of the bucket handles, then radioed back.

"You're all set!"

The rope pulled tight and the bucket was lifted into the air, slowly, continuing its journey all the way to the platform.

We hiked further, to the next sit, and repeated the process until all of the buckets were gone. I was impressed by the efficiency of the operation and felt a sense of reverence for the people on the platforms, whom I was never able to see. These were quiet warriors, nearly invisible, in possession of unimaginable bravery. I tried to imagine the terror they might experience when the logging companies arrived on their doorsteps, and bounded on all sides, the countless hours of anxiety blended with boredom as they waited for this moment to come.

We returned to camp by a different route, following a dirt logging road. We came across another group of protesters who were digging a trench across the full width of the road. Already it was about 3 feet deep and wide.

"Hey, guys!" Mira greeted them. "What'cha up to?" One of the guys answered.

"Sabotage!" We laughed. Of course, he was serious. He wore glasses, a long, floppy Mohawk and a sleeveless shirt that read "DIRTY DEEDS DONE DIRT CHEAP."

He explained how they were planning to cover the trench, once it was wide enough, with quarter-inch plywood. He motioned toward a pile of wood and other supplies hidden off the side of the road, covered in brush. The plywood would be just stable enough to hold the dirt and gravel they would cover it with, in an attempt to make the trench imperceptible to trucks bringing in logging equipment.

"It won't stop them," he admitted sadly, "but it will slow them down. If we slow them down for long enough, maybe we can stop them."

"Well, I like your shirt," Mira said.

He responded by singing the AC/DC lyric.

"Dirty deeds and they're done dirt cheap!"

John's Zerzan's weekly radio program, "Anarchy Radio," was broadcast from a building on the campus of the University of Oregon in Eugene every Tuesday night. Mira and I arrived there fully baked after smoking a bowl of high-grade marijuana on the drive over. I was excited and nervous, and wondered whether it had been a good idea to enhance an experience that was already guaranteed to be intense.

We entered the building and found a proctor sitting at a desk near the entrance, reading a book.

"Hi," said Mira, "we're looking for the radio broadcast room." He didn't look up from his book.

"Down the hall and to the left."

We followed his directions and entered a room by a thick metal door with a glass window. Seated next to a microphone was John Zerzan, a small man with a long face and a white beard that came to a point. His hair was also white, with short bangs that cut a horizontal line across his forehead. Had he been wearing a black suit rather than a simple blue button-down shirt, I might have mistaken him for an Amish man. He smiled at us with kind eyes behind his glasses.

"Rose Marie!" He greeted Mira with a hug. I had forgotten she was using this pseudonym more often, and this was probably the only name he knew her by. Then he looked at me.

"And you must be Blackbeard."

I shook his hand.

"Yeah, I know it's not much of a beard, and it's more brown than black, but I've used this name since middle school." He just smiled, and I realized my explanation was superfluous. Being high sometimes made me extra talkative, but not always about interesting topics.

"Well," he said, "let me go over the logistics before we get started." He showed us how the microphones worked, about how closely we should speak to them in order to ensure optimal volume.

He explained the basic structure of the show. The first segment was devoted to local news around the town. The second to specific "direct-action" news. For example, he might discuss a new tree-sit that had been established. Although these actions occurred deep in the forest, they were considered public. The tree-sitters wanted the logging companies to know they were there, and it was also in the tree-sitters' best interest that others in the local community knew they were there. But there was another type of direct action, in which the actions occurred in secret and for which responsibility was only claimed anonymously, or on behalf of an organization whose members operated underground. These included, especially, the Animal Liberation Front and the Earth Liberation Front. Since these were decentralized entities, organized anonymously not according to a hierarchical structure but rather a shared set of ideals, anyone sharing those principles could act independently – or in a small group – and write a public claim of responsibility. That public claim of responsibility, more often than not, came through John Zerzan.

In the final segment of the show, we would discuss my article.

When the time arrived, John pressed a button, and I heard the disclaimer.

The views of the following program do not reflect the views of the University of Oregon, it's faculty, staff or students. The opinions are entirely those of John Zerzan.

After this, John pushed another button or two and some punk music began playing. I did not recognize the band, because I knew absolutely nothing about punk music. I had tried, unsuccessfully, to become a fan but never got very far. I liked At the Drive-In, as well as another obscure band, Fifteen, Maggie had introduced me to. That was about it. Mira was like me, more knowledgeable of reggae than punk, and so the three of us sat in awkward silence while the song played.

Finally, John introduced the program. I was impressed by the ease of his delivery. He spoke casually, as though speaking to a group of people in the same room. I noticed he had a slight lisp which I thought was cool. It reminded me of Isaac Brock from Modest Mouse. (Modest Mouse, incidentally, was my favorite band at the time.) It also made him seem disarming, which was a curious contrast with his reputation: one of the most dangerous minds in America. A friend of Ted Kaczynski.

John talked about a local benefit for Cascadia Forest Defenders, happening at a bar in "the Whiteaker." He also talked about a speaker coming to talk at the University of Oregon. When John initially described his work, I assumed he was endorsing the talk. He did, after all, seem to be an environmentalist. And yet, John commenced to criticize him harshly for the next 15 minutes. John's use of the word "liberal" was unambiguously derogatory, and I got the feeling he felt, as some anarchists did, that liberals were a bigger threat than conservatives. John's basic problem with this intellectual was the same basic problem John had with almost everyone on earth: they believed in civilization.

In his more charitable moments, he might say people "believing in civilization" was like fish "believing in water." It wasn't something they had ever thought to question. Only John would have to quickly explain that the difference here was that fish need water. We don't need civilization. From the first moment humans switched from hunting and gathering to farming, something changed. The idea of control emerged, and the necessary separation between oneself and one's external environment. This separation was fueled by the introduction of language, which separated the idea of a symbol from its object. Humans began to spend more time in the world of symbols, less time in the world of objects, and this itself evolved into the idea of class. From here, Zerzan connected with Marxist theory.

Obviously, I found these ideas very appealing. But just as obviously, any solution to the "problem" of civilization seemed quite out of reach. For this reason, I had a little bit of a hard time understanding why John seemed so critical of any intellectual who did not go all the way down the same rabbit hole as deeply as he did. Surely there was value in creating alliances.

Once John finished his rant, he began his direct-action report. Two new tree-sits, Cascadia Forest Defenders. Three tractors burned at a construction site, Earth Liberation Front. A dozen pigs liberated from a pig farm, Animal Liberation Front. It felt eerie hearing him announce these actions on the radio and knowing that until this moment he might have been the only person who knew about the actions besides the people who committed them. It was a feeling I hadn't had since my hacker days in middle school. A feeling that, at any moment, a squadron of black-clad police might burst through the door, guns drawn.

Of course, I loved this feeling. I loved feeling like I was in the "center" of things. I wanted to be dangerous. I wanted to be a threat to the state. I hoped they had a file on me. I had never harmed another human being, and I had no intention to, except in self-defense. I wanted my voice and my ideas to be my danger, my threat to the state.

Once he finished the report, he transitioned to the final segment.

"Ok, and we have Blackbeard and Rose Marie here to discuss Blackbeard's recent contribution to Green Anarchy magazine, which I consider to have been the key piece of the issue." Mira and I made eye contact and she gave me what seemed to be a proud grin.

I answered some basic questions about the article and explained it had basically grown out of a paper I had written for a feminist theory course I had taken my last semester of college. I wanted very badly to seem smart. I discussed theorists whose work I had barely read. In some cases, not more than a few pages. Sometimes, when attempting to describe my concept of a certain philosopher's contribution, I felt what I was actually doing was describing my own ideas and attributing them to another. I had done well in high school and college not because I worked hard, but because I was able to reason through the answers – and that worked as well for me for calculus as it did for history. Of course, the truth probably was most people didn't read half the things they claimed and understood them even less. In fact, the more esoteric and inaccessible the work, the more it was revered. Take Deleuze and Guitarri's *Thousand Plateaus* for instance. I couldn't make heads nor tails of it, but by the number of times I cited it, you would think I read it at night like a bedtime story. The sad truth was I just wanted to seem deeper than I really was.

And so, the interview ended and judging by our faces we all felt it had gone well. We sat politely as John ended the show as it began, with punk music I didn't recognize, but I bobbed my head to the beat anyway.

Mira had one last surprise for me. The following evening there was a free screening of *Mardi Gras: Made in China* at a park in the Whiteaker. The organizers had learned from Mira that I had been involved in making the documentary. She said they really hoped I could come, and also allow people to ask questions about the film. It was yet another boost to my ego. This visit to Eugene had certainly invigorated me. I began thinking about moving to Austin. I could do more there and be able to participate more deeply in the anarchist community. It wasn't Eugene, but given my current circumstances, it was probably as close as I was going to get for a while. I might as well make the best of it.

Mira drove me back to the airport, and as we got nearer, I noticed tears rolling down her cheeks. I grasped her hand.

"What's wrong?"

"You know what's wrong," she said, half smiling, half frowning. "I'm going to miss you."

"I'm going to miss you, too. In a year, I will come up here to meet you." That familiar feeling of words feeling untrue. She felt it too.

"I don't think that's going to happen."

There was a long silence, quiet except for her occasional sniffle. I felt two simultaneous urges, each as strong as the other. On the one hand, I wanted to argue. To insist that I was coming. To proclaim that I did intend to repair our relationship. On the other, I felt the urge not to argue, to let the words stay where they were. To let the truth be the last word, no matter how painful it may be. In the end, the urge to remain quiet won out. It was one of the saddest moments of my life up to that point.

Mira parked at passenger drop off, leaving the car running and the hazard lights blinking. I got out and grabbed my large backpack from her backseat. She got out and walked in front of the car toward me. She wasn't looking at me. She was looking at something in her hands. She extended it toward me. I saw it was the dried, yellow brittle bush flower I had picked for her in the desert of Arizona. I was taken aback by the fact that she had really saved it all this time. I took it, and her eyes were still cast downward, welling with tears. Finally, she made eye contact, and I saw her eyes were red and her eyelashes had clumped together. I gave her a kiss. A long kiss. Our last kiss.

Chapter 20

I followed through on my decision to move to Austin. Elazar had been looking for a place, so I asked if I could join him. He agreed. He also invited his friend Denise whom he had gone to high school with. She also agreed. Elazar found a place that was perfect, except for one problem – it only had two bedrooms. I offered to take the living room. I put up bookshelves for walls which gave me some semblance of privacy. This left a small dining area, the kitchen and the bathroom as the only common areas in the house. That was ok with us. It was located on Rainey Street, which was near Cezar Chávez and I-35 on the west side. We were a block from the Barton Springs trail, and five blocks from 6th Street.

I kept my job in Georgetown working for Larry and Anne. We had made tremendous progress since I started with them, cataloging, photographing and writing descriptions for hundreds of items. We were now getting regular orders. Not enough to break even, perhaps, but headed in the right direction. Larry and Anne were thrilled and extended a full-time position to me at a raise to $10/hour. With my share of rent only being $350, I'd be able to cover my bills and pay for gas and buy a six pack of beer every now and then. That was all I needed.

I was able to meet more people in the activist scene in Austin, but we spent more time drinking than protesting. The truth was, we were in something of a slump. This was the summer of 2003. Many of us had witnessed the largest international protest in world history, followed 3 months later by a nearly unilateral invasion of Iraq by the United States. There was a sense of hopelessness. At least, I felt hopeless and I assumed others felt the same. If it had been possible for us to stop it, where had we gone wrong? Should the protests have been larger? Would yet another million or two have made any difference? Surely not.

As anarchists, of course, we believed we knew the answer. It was not a worldwide protest that was needed. This was only symbolic, a minor disruption at best. No, what we needed was a worldwide, general strike. Only if every worker refused to work would the machine come to a true halt, and in that revolutionary moment, an anarchist society could be built from the bottom up.

Feeling you knew the answer didn't make things feel less hopeless. It made them seem more so. Millions may come out for a few hours, even a day, but would they put their livelihoods on the line? And for what? A revolutionary ideal, a theory? The more I thought through what would be required, the amount of education that would need to happen, the minds that would need to change, the task seemed impossible.

Needing something to put my energy into, I began applying myself more fully at work. I dove into the books covering the history of the various porcelain manufacturers whose goods we carried. I used this knowledge to write detailed articles about them which I published on the website. These articles were effective in attracting visitors to our website, some of whom became customers.

I remember one morning coming to work and seeing Larry in a frenzy, waving some papers in his hand. I couldn't tell if what he was about to tell me was going to be a good thing or a bad thing.

"We just got an $8000 order. Do you think this is fake? Do you think this is a scam?"

He handed me the papers, which were the printed order. It was too long to fit on a single page. It was three. I looked at the name and address and there didn't seem to be anything out of the ordinary. But it was a lot of pieces, and my first thought was how long would it take to pack that many.

"I don't know," I said. "It looks like it could be real. I could give the guy a call and find out more."

"Yes, please do," Larry said, and I noticed a smile slip. "This could be really great for us if this is real."

It was real, and it did take a very long time to pack. Almost an entire work week, starting Monday, finishing Friday. I knew we would have to insure everything. I thought a bit sadly about the fact that some percentage of these pieces would get broken. We hadn't dealt with many orders, but we knew that much. And then I felt even more sad to think, now that more and more people are ordering things online, isn't it inevitable that we will lose most antiques in the world to "breakage." We had dishes that had survived the bombing of Dresden but would not survive the age of e-commerce.

It was the first time in my life that I was getting paid to do something I actually enjoyed. My ultimate goal in life was to become a writer. Well, here I was writing. Sure, it wasn't the kind of writing I wanted to be known for. But it sure beat washing dishes. I began throwing myself fully into the articles I wrote for the website, articles about porcelain manufacturers. Whenever possible, I drew in details from other events happening in history at the time, and how those events influenced the development and manufacture of porcelain and fine china.

Still, I did feel myself to have something of a double identity. Around Anne and Larry, I was the rising leader in their new business. I was the scholar who talked to them at lunch about antiques, their history and their value. But as soon as I got off work, I became Blackbeard again. I sometimes stopped to get a six pack before making the 30-minute drive back to Austin. When I stepped into my home, I was among revolutionaries. And the revolution was always at hand.

My writing caught the attention of the web development company in Houston that had built Larry and Anne's website. I received a call from one of the owners, a Russian man by the name of Gary. He was an extremely authoritative and smooth talker. I was intimidated by him. I didn't have the slightest idea why he wanted to talk to me. When I realized he was offering me the chance to write for other websites at the rate of $50 per 500 words, I jumped at the offer immediately.

This began taking up my time in the evenings. And so I developed a very standard routine for the week. In the morning, about 7am, I got up and dressed and headed out the door by 7:30. I stopped halfway, in Round Rock, to get a cup of coffee from Seattle's Best. (Hey, at least it wasn't Starbucks.) I began forming a crush on one of the baristas, but never got up the courage to ask for her number. I arrived at Larry and Anne's by about 8:15 and got to work. Sometimes they would take me to lunch at Larry's country club. Once I got off work, I headed home, usually picking up a six pack along the way. Once home, I might spend 30 minutes chatting with my roommates before packing up my laptop bag and heading out the door. I had a coffee shop I liked, on Congress Street a few blocks from the Capitol. (Also with a cute barista, but I knew she was married. Her husband worked there too, and he was cool.) My favorite part about the coffee shop was they served alcohol. So once I arrived there by about 6:30 I might start with a cup of coffee but ended up ordering one or two Lone Stars after that. Once I had written at least one article, I headed home and continued drinking until bed.

Drinking, you could say, was integral to my routine. After a few months of this lifestyle, I realized I could not remember a single day in which I had not drank at least six drinks. I thought back to that moment in Boston when I walked past a liquor store and realized I could not resist the desire to go inside. I'll worry about that later, I had thought.

Was now "later?"

No, not later enough.

Although my full-time job, part-time writing gig and drinking were taking up the bulk of my work week, I was still devoting the majority of my weekends to activism. Protests had slowed down, and so I spent my time volunteering for various anarchist initiatives such as Inside Books, which sent books to prisoners. Or Bikes Across Borders, which brought bicycles to border communities in Mexico. I spent one full weekend hauling a trailer full of bicycles to McAllen, Texas, leading a caravan of a dozen other vehicles. Rather than cross the bridge with the full trailer, however, we parked our vehicles and rode all of the bicycles across, one by one. In this way, we avoided the usual import tax. Some of us had to make multiple trips. Once all the bikes were across, I brought the truck back over.

I was also spending a lot of time writing articles for IndyMedia.org. I had become a part of the "global collective," meaning I had permission to contribute, approve and publish articles to the global site. (IndyMedia.org was the global site, but there were over a hundred local sites, e.g., austin. indymedia.org, london.indymedia.org, chiapas.indymedia. org and so on.) I was forming close relationships with editors and contributors around the world. I even developed a virtual crush on Clara, a highly articulate and prolific contributor from the Netherlands. It wasn't uncommon for there to be heated debates about whether or not certain articles should be revised or outright rejected. Clara often stepped in as the voice of reason and resolved conflicts. She was slow to take sides, but whenever she did, her position carried significant weight and generally directed the final outcome.

One day we received an announcement which made me sit up in my chair. The WTO was meeting in Cancun, Mexico. Organizers on the ground were organizing a response. Security forces were making plans. The meetings would be held on the resort peninsula. This was the area most tourists thought of as "Cancun." In reality, most of the residents lived inland, in Cancun City. Authorities were establishing a heavily fortified security fence across the border between these two worlds. The plan did not even need to be stated. Converging in Cancun, City, protesters would march directly to the fence, dismantle it and continue on toward the convention center.

This was only the second time the WTO had met since 1999 in Seattle. The other meeting was in Doha, Qatar in 2001, which was hardly amenable to large-scale protests. But Cancun was in driving distance from Chiapas, arguably the true birthplace of our movement. Mexico had a vast progressive community and a strong history of militancy, as well as tragedy. Four dead in Ohio was a refrain bringing to mind the greatest massacre in the US during its radical phase. In 1968, 2 years prior to the incident at Ohio State, a massacre in Mexico City left hundreds of protesters – in truth, an indeterminate number – dead. Those who still chose to participate in radical politics in Mexico knew they did so at some risk to their own lives. Higher stakes meant deeper commitment.

On top of this, this was the first major anti-globalization protest since September 11. It was exciting to think about returning to our roots. Perhaps it was a chance to distract ourselves from our abysmal failure at stopping the march of war, now raging in both Afghanistan and Iraq. But in truth, the issues had not changed. Workers were still being exploited, farmers were still losing their land, and the environment was still being decimated. It felt good to think about uniting with workers and farmers in Mexico to resist the faceless, multinational organizations that dehumanized them as well as us. I navigated to Expedia and purchased a round trip ticket for the first week of September.

Shortly after, both Maggie and David had purchased tickets as well. And I learned Rolando would be flying up from Venezuela. As word continued to spread, I realized this would be a highly international event. An entire contingent of farmers from South Korea would be attending. I knew that protests in South Korea were highly militant, with Molotov cocktails regularly being showered upon police lines. All the most well-known names were also planning to attend, such as Starhawk,

Lisa Fithian and Rick Rowley (maker of This is What Democracy Looks Like). All signs pointed to this action becoming the next Seattle.

David, Maggie and Rolando met me at the airport. We took a taxi to downtown Cancun City. Despite the similarity in name, it was nothing like the Cancun most tourists experience. Instead of resorts and swimming pools and beaches, there were dirt roads, street vendors and concrete buildings. This was Mexico. We arrived at Parque de las Palapas in the center of town which was filled with hundreds of activists. The majority were Mexican, although there were plenty of white and Asian faces as well. Some were sitting in circles, embroiled in passionate conversations and debates. Others were constructing signs, banners or puppets. One side of the park was filled with tents where activists were camping. A man pushed a cart with a sign that read "Tacos y horchata." My mouth watered.

Maggie introduced us to a group she had been camping with. Many of them had come from out of town, mainly Oaxaca or Mexico City. They were dressed like gutter punks, wearing black skinny jeans and hoodies, covered in handmade patches affixed with safety pins. Some wore Mohawks or piercings. "This is the Mexican Black Bloc," Maggie informed me.

There were, in fact, two distinct Black Blocs at the convergence, and they began to be referred to as either the "Mexican Black Bloc" or the "International Black Bloc" (the latter composed mostly of Americans, but some from Europe as well.) Maggie, whose Spanish was much better than my own, explained that it had been agreed upon that the Mexican Black Bloc would be taking the lead in the next day's march. We were there to provide support, but not to provoke confrontation ourselves.

"Fine by me," I said. Frankly, it sounded exciting.

I spent a fairly restless night sleeping in a tent with two strangers. I had brought a sleeping bag, but no pillow. It was hot and humid. I was excited, yet uncomfortable. At one point,

I exited the tent to take a walk. Most were sleeping, but a few were sitting around campfires, smoking joints and drinking beer. I recognized the group as being the same Maggie had introduced me to earlier. We made eye contact, and I waved. They called me over to join them.

I did my best to converse with them in my broken Spanish. They passed me a joint, and after a few tokes my Spanish seemed to improve. I asked them simple questions, like where they were from or if they had children. I wanted to engage in deeper conversations. My vocabulary was not extensive enough to ask the questions I really wanted to ask, in Spanish or English. I wanted to coordinate with them to overthrow the capitalist system. How does one begin such a conversation?

On the walk back to my tent, feeling buzzed and staring up at the stars, I felt a familiar feeling of wonder – not unlike the feeling I felt on the rooftop in Boston a year earlier. The potential of life seemed endless. How did I end up here, in Mexico, getting ready to battle alongside fellow revolutionaries from around the world? Had I made all the right decisions, or all the wrong ones? I didn't know how to answer the question. I only knew I was grateful. And with this feeling of gratitude, I crawled back into the tent and quickly fell asleep.

The next morning, I could smell tortillas. I emerged from the tent and was nearly blinded by the intensity of the sun. It was not yet 8am, and yet the temperature was already over 90 degrees. Breakfast was being served for free by local activists. I stood in line with a mix of punks, hippies and academic-looking folk.

There were also a sizable number of independent documentary filmmakers and other photographers. I felt a little annoyed by their numbers, in fact. Even David and Rolando had brought cameras and planned to use the footage to make films. I appreciated the importance of the work they were doing, but I also saw them as detracting from our numbers. They supported our cause, as well as our tactics, but they were not willing to place themselves on the front line. I had begun to quietly resent anyone, in fact, who supported our cause but was unwilling to fight alongside us at the barricades.

It is important to understand that in my mind, our actions were not intended to be symbolic. The most common question or criticism I received from other activists was how violence could possibly change people's minds? But I was not trying to change anyone's mind. That time had passed. Anyone was welcome to join us, but they had to understand we in no way saw ourselves as "petitioning the government for a redress of grievances." To put it bluntly, we wanted to overthrow the government. And not only our own government, but all governments. We wanted to be the spark that would set alight a worldwide revolution. This obvious point was what most people missed. Anarchy means "an absence of government." It is treated as a synonym for chaos, and so when people saw us do things like smash windows or slash police car tires, they assumed this chaos was our ultimate goal. But actually, it was just a means to an end. We did not want chaos or violence, in the long run. We simply believed violence was necessary to overthrow a state built on violence and maintained with violence. What we truly wanted was a world free of oppression and violence and theft. We wanted to live in a world where people lived together in peace and harmony with their natural environments. Anarchy, after all, is a utopian philosophy.

The crowd continued to gather until I estimated its size in the thousands. There were people of all ages, races and social classes. The "South Korean" contingent was extremely recognizable. They all wore identical clothing. Khakis and brown vests. They carried loud drums and marched in unison. They struck me as highly disciplined. I wondered what they had planned.

Finally, the march was underway. Maggie and I marched together in what had been designated the "international Black

Bloc." We locked our arms and marched in roughly identical rows. To our right were the Mexican Black Bloc. They marched separately, many of them wielding large sticks. They shouted slogans in Spanish. We chanted our own, in English. But in one moment, we all came together in unison to chant the anthem from Chile that now had become a rallying cry in support of the Zapatistas: *El pueblo unido jamás será vencido*. The people, united, will never be defeated.

We filled a wide street and proceeded downhill. I soon saw our destination. A red fence blocked our progress forward, as this road continued onto the resort peninsula where the WTO meetings were being held. To call it a "fence" is something of an understatement. It was over 12-feet tall, reinforced with chain-link and metal bars. Behind this fence was a contingent of riot police. Behind them, another fence. And in front of the fence, where we were headed, were more than a hundred riot police in full gear, behind transparent shields, nightsticks in the ready position.

As we came closer, I wondered what would happen. A part of me assumed it would be the same routine I had experienced many times before. We would approach dangerously close to the police lines. Many of us would get in the police's face and scream insults. A few brave souls might even get in a shoving match. This would go until the police began to act upon us, with tear gas or pepper spray or simply by moving toward us and swinging their batons. Then most of us would scatter and regroup elsewhere. A game of cat and mouse would ensue for the remainder of the day and possibly into the night. This is not what happened.

Rather than slow down, the Mexican Black Bloc seemed to increase their speed and collided right into the police lines. There was immediate chaos. Protesters struck police with their sticks, and the police retaliated. Some protesters armed with crowbars began breaking apart concrete and passing to others who hurled them at police. To my horror, many of the police picked them up and threw them back. I feared for my life.

The International Black Bloc joined in. There was a sense of jubilation and I saw many exchange smiles at one another. We were getting to see how real revolutionaries fought. Perhaps it was only because we were in Cancun, but an uncomfortable comparison came to mind. It felt like tourism. I stood in bewilderment as I watched the events unfold before me. I saw Maggie shoving at the police lines beside the others. At one point she pulled on a shield and others joined in. They managed to wrestle it from the officer, and someone held it up to loud cheers.

I was suddenly faced with the prospect of doing something I had never done before – strike another human being. I saw a stick had been discarded on the ground. It was embedded with nails, and I was careful not to puncture myself as I positioned it in my hands with a firm grip. I looked through the crowd at the police line not more than a few feet in front of me. I imagined myself moving forward and striking. Could I deflect the shield in such a way that I could strike the police officer directly on the head? That seemed most effective. Then I looked through the shield, at his face. I realized then how small he was. His face was brown, an indigenous face. His eyes were wide with fear. I intuitively knew he was a poor man. The idea of me, a white man, striking an indigenous man in another country – for any reason whatsoever – was unthinkable. I couldn't do it. I dropped the stick to the ground and exited the crowd.

I watched from a distance as the battle continued. I tried to rationalize the fact that I had abandoned my comrades, that I was shirking from battle. Rather than think more deeply about whether I actually believed in violence, I focused on what I saw as fundamental impracticality. It was impossible that we would make it to the WTO summit from here. Even if somehow the anarchists managed to totally send the riot police into retreat, they would still have a fence to tear down. This would give the police time to send reinforcements. But even if they didn't, another contingent already stood at the ready behind the first fence. If the anarchists made it past them, they would have another fence to tear down. And then, they had something of a mile march before they would make it anywhere near the actual delegation. There would be endless opportunities for the state to halt our progress. There were at most a few hundred of us. In order to achieve our aim, we would need many thousands.

Concluding this fight was a lost cause. I convinced myself I was justified in not participating.

As I was considering these thoughts, I noticed some of the South Korean contingent were climbing the fence. Two of them managed to reach the top and sit. One wore a white sign around his neck that read, in red lettering, "WTO Kills Farmers." The police swung at them with batons but could barely reach, and then the anarchists pushed them back. They raised their fists and chanted something I could not hear. Then suddenly I heard screams as one of the men tumbled off the fence and into the crowd of protesters.

There was chaos as more protesters rushed in his direction to find out what had happened, and for a while the intensity of the fighting increased. Had they shot him? But I didn't hear a gunshot. Soon an ambulance arrived. The crowd parted to allow two paramedics to reach him and place him on a stretcher. They carried him out, and I saw his hands were bloody and covering his chest.

Eventually I would learn this man's name was Lee Kyung-hae. He was a farmer from South Korea. He died by his own hand, a knife to his heart. His suicide was an act of protest. Initially, I felt bewilderment. I sensed many others felt the same way. It was not a form of protest most of us in the West were familiar with, at least not intimately. Certainly, we had all seen the black and white photograph of the monk in Vietnam who set himself on fire in protest at the war. But this was the second death now in our movement. The first, Carlo Giuliani in Genoa. And now, Lee Kyung-hae.

He achieved a martyr status immediately. That evening, activists began making signs in honor of him. These included many "WTO Kills Farmers" signs like the one he had worn. Others began bringing flowers, candles and other symbolic items to the place where he had died and constructed a memorial. And others began fervently planning an action avenging his death. Yes, he technically committed suicide, but we felt really it was the economic policies of the WTO, which had threatened the lives of so many farmers like him, that were to blame for his death.

I began to notice something I hadn't witnessed before. A leadership seemed to be forming in the camp. As opposed to open spokescouncils, which had been the norm in most actions before this, they were holding private meetings. Since this was a clear deviation from the principles of consensus decision-making which had been our guiding force since Seattle in 1999, some explanations were sought by several of us who voiced concerns about this.

I remember Lisa Fithian providing the explanation. She was an activist I recognized from almost every protest I had been to. She also now lived in Austin. She was a slight woman, certainly not imposing. Her skin was sun-worn, as though she had spent a certain amount of time in the desert. The truth was probably that she spent so much time outside at protests. She had very thick blonde hair that was cut basically into a mullet. She spent a lot of her time with the Black Bloc anarchists, but she didn't dress the part. She usually wore a simple T-shirt and jeans.

A dozen of us were gathered around Liza and a few others from the emerging leadership to ask why the meetings were being held in private.

"Basically, there were concerns about power dynamics. We

have many people of color involved in these actions, indigenous and campesinos, many of whom live locally and will more directly bear the brunt of any retaliation – including retaliation that may happen long after we are gone. We concluded it was not truly equitable to hold a spokescouncil composed of a mix of white *norteamericanos* and people of color, so they elected representatives among themselves and invited a few of us to join."

It made a bit of sense, at least in terms of the logic I operated under. Who was I to say anything in a spokescouncil meeting here? What did I know of the condition of people who actively lived, worked and organized here? It did make sense that they should be the ones who made the decisions about what we do or don't do. What right did I have to introduce any proposal of my own, or raise objections to ones they might make?

Still, something didn't sit right with me. I tried to put my finger on it. It was something about Lisa. I couldn't explain it, but for some reason I didn't believe that she had just been "invited" to join. I didn't know much about her, but I did know she was the kind of person who always wanted to be at the center of things. Our movement had always proclaimed itself to be nonhierarchical, and yet I couldn't help but feel she wanted to be a leader.

I also wondered at the idea of the "indigenous and campesinos" having representatives dictate their actions. We balked at the idea of having leaders or representatives among ourselves, but somehow, we ignored this when it came to thinking about power dynamics among the Mexican activists. Why would the principles of decentralized and nonhierarchical organization not apply to them also? It reminded me a bit of the double standard we had subconsciously applied to the Mohawks in Akwesasne. We uncritically assumed the leaders who claimed to speak for them did, in fact, speak for them.

Chapter 21

The natural result of these secret planning sessions was that most people had no clue what, if anything, had been planned for the next day. Rolando and I, along with his new girlfriend, Katrina, decided to try taking a trip into the resort area where the meetings were being held. It was an interesting paradox. Obviously, the resort peninsula was not closed. Protesters were not allowed to enter it as protesters, but why couldn't we be tourists? We decided to find out.

"Should we try to dress, I don't know...more mainstream?"

Rolando and Katrina laughed. Rolando playfully tugged at one of my dreadlocks.

"It's no use," he said.

We caught a bus in town and paid a few pesos for fare. The three of us sat down, a bit nervous. I looked around to see if there were any other activists on the bus, but no one seemed to fit the part. They appeared, judging by their uniforms, to be workers commuting to their shifts at some of the many hotels and resorts that lined the beaches. Maids, janitors, bellhops. I wondered why they weren't joining in the protests, when certainly their lives were far more directly impacted by the policies we were protesting than ours were. They can't afford to, I thought. We had the privilege of taking time off work, flying to a foreign country and risking arrest. Even 10 days in jail would not fundamentally change the course of our lives. This was not the case for everyone. And so, I thought, this was the very best use of my privilege – to speak and act on behalf of those who were too oppressed to do so themselves.

Or was I just falling into the same trap I had just been criticizing in my head the night before? I sighed deeply and leaned my head against the window, noticing we had passed easily into the "red zone." Suddenly, in sharp contrast to the widespread poverty that had surrounded me the last 48 hours, I saw perfect white hotels lining sandy beaches. White bodies were sunbathing, strolling in the waves or playing beach volleyball. I saw familiar restaurants: Hooters, Bubba Gump Shrimp Co, Señor Frogs. Aside from a prominent billboard that read "Cancun Welcomes the WTO Fifth Ministerial," there was no way anyone could have known this was anything other than a typical September in paradise.

Finally we saw the *Cancún Centro de Convenciones* – a massive convention center at the easternmost tip of the resort peninsula.

"This is our stop," Rolando said, smiling with a perfect Che Guevara grin.

Katrina reached for her backpack, which was open, and looked at Rolando. She didn't say anything, but I could tell something was wrong. I glanced at the backpack and saw for myself. A gas mask was inside. Rolando shrugged at her as he stood up and ushered the three of us off the bus.

"Why did you bring a gas mask?" she shrieked at him once we were alone at the bus stop, baking beneath the tropical sun.

He shushed her.

"Lower your voice," he said gently.

"Why did you bring a gas mask?" she whispered this time.

He held his arms in front of him, devoid of explanation.

"In case they use gas," he said simply.

Katrina laughed and looked at me.

"Well, what about us?"

He took a moment and realized what her question meant. He looked at both of us and broke out into another of his irresistible smiles.

"Well, they probably won't use gas. Let's go."

It was a strange and surreal feeling walking among a mix of tourists in bathing suits and delegates in suits. I noticed the men and women in suits wore badges which read OMC – the Spanish abbreviation for the WTO. I was surprised to see that not all of the delegates were white. And then I remembered there were delegates from all over the world, including South America and Africa. I briefly felt a similar dilemma to the one I felt when facing the police lines. These people were the enemy. I was here to stop them. Physically, not symbolically. Well, here was my chance. What was I capable of? And on the other hand, I looked at their faces and did not see enemies. I saw only human beings. Aged, intelligent, often kind faces. I knew in that moment I didn't have a fraction of the life experience these people did. Nor, if I was honest, did I fully grasp the intricacy or complexity of the work they did. What was truly contained in my mind beyond simple slogans, such as people before profits? Sure, I wanted justice and peace. But did I truly know the steps that needed to be taken from here to there?

I shook these thoughts away like mosquitos. It seemed like this was happening more lately and I couldn't afford to let myself get distracted in this way. I returned my mind to the basics. As an anarchist, I was opposed to all forms of coercion and violence. This seemed to me a fundamental truth. Obviously, the ideal form of society was one in which violence had been overcome, or at least reduced to a manageable scale where it could be met by community self-defense. This was a goal worth fighting for because of the very real violence, oppression and exploitation that was affecting millions of people around the world. And the violence of capitalism affected the First World as well, though in more subtle ways. In the place of the club or the gun, we were battered by clocks. Rather than treated as mindless workers, we were treated as mindless consumers – and we played our part well. There was no doubt we were privileged. Anyone working in a factory in China would give anything to trade places with the most mundane life of an office worker in Illinois. And yet, the system as a whole was dehumanizing, degrading and destroying all life on the planet. In the end, this was all I needed to know or understand.

Suddenly, I saw two people I recognized.

"Lisa! Starhawk!"

I had spoken to Lisa just the night before, but I had not seen Starhawk since the direct-action training in Los Angeles. She had become something of a celebrity since then, appearing on numerous independent documentaries. A part of me was a little star struck, no pun intended. I completely lost my composure and rushed toward them.

I wasn't expecting the response I got. They looked at me fiercely, scolding. They did not say anything, just looked back at the ground and raced past me. Rolando approached and looked at me concerned, placing his hand on my shoulder.

"What are you doing, man?" he said quietly.

I immediately felt like an idiot. I knew then there was a clandestine action planned. I had just potentially outed them to the police. Their names were recognizable as organizers. And now that I looked around, I realized there were in fact police everywhere. Stationed in groups of two to three on virtually all street corners. As far as I could tell, however, none of them had taken note of my gaffe.

"Yeah," I replied. "Sorry, I just wasn't thinking."

After walking around another half hour, aimlessly, we heard some commotion about a quarter of a mile down the main road. Someone was playing drums, others were shouting. A crowd began gathering. We began running in that direction. Rolando pulled his camera out and began filming. Police sirens began within seconds, and two trucks full of riot police passed us. This was a geographically tiny area. They had enough resources to have police ready at virtually any location.

We made our way through the crowd to find a few dozen activists who had taken the street. Half of them were sitting on the ground with their arms locked, and the other half were dancing, waving signs or playing drums. Lisa and Starhawk were there, of course. I realized this was most likely the action that had been planned in secret. I was disgusted. We had perhaps 10,000 activists ready to act on the other side of the peninsula, all of whom had been excluded from this secret action. And because of that, we had so few numbers here that the action could not possibly be anything more than symbolic. In 15 minutes, all of them would be arrested, and business would continue as usual. I wanted no part of this.

As we walked back to the bus stop, a black van pulled up and three police officers stepped out holding semi-automatic rifles. They surrounded us and directed us up against a brick wall.

Rolando looked at me with serious eyes that said, let me handle this.

My Spanish was nowhere near good enough to follow everything he said to them. For a moment, I thought he had convinced them to let us go. Then they asked to see his backpack, and my stomach dropped. Sure enough, they pulled the gas mask out. Katrina and I looked at one another, scared. Rolando didn't miss a beat. He kept talking to them, intently, keeping eye contact, and making passionate gestures with his hands. The police officers occasionally looked at one another, but I couldn't read their expressions. Then they looked back at him. After some time, I realized he was not arguing about the gas mask, he was arguing for the cause. Occasionally they would raise their eyebrows or nod their heads, and I began to feel he might actually be recruiting them to our cause. Finally, they placed the gas mask back in the backpack, handed it to Rolando, and left.

"What did you say to them?"

"Just that we are all on the same side," he said simply.

I awoke in my tent the next day just as unsure what the day would bring as I had been the day before. I knew there was going to be a march to the fence. The second one, in fact, as the first fence had been breached on the first day and the police had been unable to repair it.

After a gathering in the park consisting of tens of thousands of people, the march commenced. The sun bore down on us as we marched, chanting in English and Spanish, winding through street blocks. We reached the fence and stopped at Lee's memorial. A hush fell on the crowd, as we collectively and wordlessly agreed to a moment of silence in his honor.

The crowd continued through the break in the fence, some of the anarchists pulling it apart wider to allow more people through at a time. The next fence was another 100 yards away, and there we saw twice the number of police as last time – except this time they were on the opposite side of the fence.

The events that followed, once we arrived at the fence, all felt highly orchestrated, although once again I was not a part of the orchestration. Those of us in the Black Bloc were told by Fithian and others to stay back. A call was made on the megaphone for women only to step forward. Maggie joined this group, leaving me behind to watch. Bolt cutters were passed around, and they began snipping away at the chain-link fence. I was simultaneously excited and perplexed. I was eager to dismantle the fence, fight past the police, and make our way to the convention center. And yet, the fact that the police were standing passively by on the other side, watching, felt strange to me.

Several minutes later, a large rope appeared. The diameter was as wide as a tennis ball, and it was over 100 feet long. It was affixed to the fence by several of the women, and once secured, it began to be pulled and stretched out into the crowd until it became taut. I instinctively grabbed a section of the rope, and along with dozens of other activists, began pulling. With our combined force, the fence ripped apart easily. I heard a loud metallic creaking as the metal bars bent and twisted. The fence, which had appeared impenetrable moments before, was now in shambles.

Now those of us in the Black Bloc began locking arms. Several others armed themselves with pipes and sticks, ready to breach the fence and engage with the police. Here again, Fithian and the other leaders with megaphones held out their palms, standing between us and the breach in the fence.

"Please, we have all agreed, all of us women organizers, indigenous leaders, campesinos and the Koreans, we have all agreed that this will be a nonviolent action." This was promptly translated into Spanish.

The response was a chant arising from the Black Bloc.

"Lee! Lee! Lee!"

The situation was tense, with the sudden "organizers" trying to stem the tide of anarchists. Pleas continued via megaphone, and eventually, the Black Bloc stood down. Multiple effigies were burned bearing the acronyms for the WTO. A few more speeches, and the protest was over. I walked back to the camp knowing that some excellent footage had been captured that might inspire the world; however I felt only used and excluded.

Mere weeks after arriving back in Texas, Maggie and I attended a screening of the film Kilometer Zero at Monkeywrench Books, Austin's anarchist bookstore. I felt annoyed when I saw Lisa Fithian there, but I smiled politely anyway.

The film, which David and Rolando had worked on along with Rick Rowley, was well made as usual. I even made an appearance or two. Despite the clean narrative, however, I felt the film was an overly sanitized version of the more complicated reality I felt on the ground.

After the film, there was a question-and-answer period. One person asked, "There seemed to be some violence. Who was throwing the rocks?"

Lisa piped up. "The police! It was crazy, the police just started throwing rocks at us out of nowhere."

"That's not true, the Black Bloc was throwing rocks," Maggie countered.

"Yeah," I said, "the Black Bloc was throwing rocks, but some of the police threw the rocks back at us."

Lisa's face turned beet red and she said nothing. Here we had a fundamental disagreement about public relations. Lisa's philosophy was to blame all violence on the police, to paint all protesters as peaceful – even though she knew this not to be the case. Maggie and I, on the other hand, were open and honest about the reality of violence. Certainly, a lot of violence was instigated by police, but not all of it. Not only were we not ashamed of this, we were proud of it. We had long ago accepted the fact that the capitalist system could not be overthrown nonviolently. People would have to fight. A lot of people. And if we wanted more people to join us in this fight, we would have to be honest about the fact that we were fighting.

With all of these thoughts fresh in my mind, I went home that evening and wrote a scathing critique about the actions in Cancun, and how "leaders" were emerging that threatened to undermine the decentralized, nonhierarchical principles of our movement. I placed these concerns in the context of the upcoming protests against the FTAA in Miami, which I predicted would be a disaster. I fired the essay off to John Zerzan, and it was promptly published in the next issue of Green Anarchy.

Chapter 22

As much as I wanted to attend the protests against the FTAA in Miami 2 months later, the mundane struggles of life under capitalism prevented me from doing so. I simply did not have enough vacation time or money after my international excursion to Cancun. Dean and David, however, were planning to attend, and I vowed to support them every way I could. I had been devising in my mind a fairly simple and inexpensive way to construct protest "placards" that could double as effective shields against riot police. I made a trip to the local hardware store and bought a sheet of plexiglass, a roll of contact paper and several feet of nylon straps. I brought these materials to a friend of mine, Joe, who worked on the landscaping crew at the university. He was also an active member of the American Indian Movement.

He invited Dean and I to his home, where he had a fully outfitted workshop in his backyard. When I arrived with the materials, I was shocked to find a native Texas javelina, a wild pig, hanging from a tree. Joe, a middle-aged Apache man wearing a red bandana and with long black hair in pigtails, was busy at work cleaning out the intestines. His hands were covered in blood and guts. I almost vomited at the sight and the smells.

Joe looked at me and laughed. "What, you ain't never cleaned a javelina before?"

"No," I admitted, suppressing a gag reflex.

He laughed again, grabbing a towel from a nearby table covered in knives and other cleaning implements.

"C'mon," he said, motioning toward a nearby wooden shed, "let's see what you got."

We stepped inside his workshop, which smelled of sawdust and motor oil. I laid the materials down next to the table saw.

Dean, holding the sheet of plexiglass, carefully leaned it against the wall.

"So, what is it you're wanting to make again?"

"Protest signs," Dean said.

"For the protest against the Free Trade Area of the Americas in Miami next month."

"What's that?" he asked.

We proceeded to give him our rant against capitalism and globalization, which by this time we had down pat. We explained that global free trade agreements such as the FTAA, which would expand NAFTA to the entire western hemisphere, were formulated at the behest of multinational corporations in pursuit of ever-expanding profits. These profits were obtained at the direct expense of poor workers, indigenous communities and the environment. Because these were undemocratic entities, answerable to no one, the only way they could be defeated was through direct action to physically stop the meetings from taking place. He nodded as we spoke, taking everything in. After we had finished speaking, he paused for a moment, and then looked at the sheet of plexiglass.

"So, what's that for?"

Dean and I looked at each other, turning a bit red. We hadn't exactly explained our true intentions.

"Well," I began slowly, "we want the signs to be really sturdy."

"So, you want to make shields," he asked, grinning widely and showing his teeth.

Now Dean and I just laughed. Busted.

"Hey, I'm in the fucking American Indian Movement, boys. You don't think I know about this shit? Now let's make your shields."

He was an expert craftsman. He cut the plexiglass into two identical pieces, each about three-and-a-half feet tall by two-and-a-half feet wide. He then used a grinder to carefully round out the edges. He affixed the contact paper, smoothing out any air bubbles. This was so we could paint slogans on them, such as "Down with the FTAA," giving them plausible deniability as protest placards. Finally, he used a sort of punch to place holes in the plexiglass, which fit a grommet he used to attach the nylon straps. He then showed us how they could be held tightly against the arm. Each shield had two straps – one through which our upper arm would pass, and the other to be gripped by the hand.

He handed them to us, and we tried them out. We were gleeful at the results. These were first rate shields, and yet from a distance they looked like normal poster boards. These were sure to make the other anarchists jealous. I only wished we could construct a hundred of them and hand them out at the protest. Even more, I wished I could go myself.

We thanked Joe profusely for his help. I offered to pay him a little for his time, but he refused. In fact, before we left, he opened up a freezer he kept in his workshop and pulled out two large Ziplock bags and handed one to each of us.

"Javelina sausage," he said.

I was sitting on the porch at the Olive House enjoying a hand-rolled cigarette and a Lone Star tall boy when Dean's Honda Civic pulled in front of my house a week later. I smiled and stood to greet him. I was excited to hear about his experiences in Miami, but when I saw his face, I could tell something was wrong. He got out of his car and when he saw me smiling, he tried to smile back, but looking at his eyes it was obvious his thoughts were a million miles away.

"Hey, Dean, it's good to see you. Is everything ok?"

"Uhhhh," he responded with a long groan. "Shit, man. We've got a lot of catching up to do."

I could tell he had too much energy to sit, and while this was not an uncommon experience with Dean, this was on a level I had not seen before. I offered him a Lone Star and a cigarette, both of which he accepted gratefully, and suggested we go for a walk.

"Ok, man. All I have to say is shit was fucked in Miami. It was fucked. I don't even know where to start."

"Relax," I replied calmly, giving him a supportive pat on the shoulder, "just take as much time as you need and start wherever you like."

"Ok," he said again. "Let's see. Well, basically, the police were all over us from the word go. I would say they outnumbered us two to one. The first day, they completely surrounded us. Nobody could do anything. And they were super aggressive. Pushing and shoving and pepper spraying anyone that got out of line. It felt like being in prison."

"Jesus."

"Yeah. And they were attacking anyone with anything that remotely looked like a weapon. Even people holding flags with poles that were too thick. David and I got spooked, and so you know those shields we made? The first chance we got we dumped them at a construction site."

Selfishly, I was disappointed to hear this. I had spent a fair amount of money on the materials and was honestly hoping he would bring them back.

"Oh, so you got rid of them?" I tried not to let my disappointment come through in my voice, especially since he seemed so shook up, but probably I did not succeed.

"Well, actually, we tried to get them back. After the protest, this was after dark, David and I went to retrieve them at the construction site. We got out of the car and went to climb the fence, since we had thrown the shields on the other side. Next thing we knew, *womp womp!* Sirens went off and we saw blue and red lights everywhere. There were three police cars that just came out of nowhere."

"Oh, shit," I said, finally understanding the gravity of the situation.

"Before we have a chance to react, five or six police officers jump out of their vehicles with their guns drawn."

At this point he made eye contact with me, making sure I understood what he was saying.

"Guns drawn," I repeated.

"Guns drawn and pointed right at our heads. One of the cops came right up to me and screamed 'Get down, get the fuck on the ground right now or I'll blow your fucking head off!'"

I couldn't believe what I was hearing, and if it had been anyone telling me this story other than Dean, I might not have believed it. But Dean was not one to lie, or even exaggerate.

"So we are on the ground, face to the asphalt, and I have my hands behind my neck like this." He interlocked his fingers behind his head, looking at me. "We lie there for a while as the police make calls on their radio. Five, maybe 10 minutes later another car arrives, this one unmarked. Two guys get out wearing FBI jackets."

"No!"

"Dude, listen."

We stopped walking for a minute as he faced me directly. I could see Dean's hand was trembling as he took another drag from his cigarette.

"I am telling you, this really happened. It was the scariest thing I have ever experienced in my life. I know it sounds like some crazy activist fantasy, but I promise you, I swear to God, this is exactly what happened.

"The next thing I know, they grab us by the collar and tell us to get up. David and I are separated by the FBI agents, who then pull out files and drop them on the hood of their cars. I saw my name on one. And Aaron..."

He stopped at this point, just looking at the ground. I felt my stomach drop as I experienced something approaching a brief out of body experience as though I already knew what he was going to say next.

"The other one had your name on it."

As terrifying as this whole experience had been for David and Dean, in the end they were not arrested. Hearing all of this was a harsh collision with reality for them both, and in a way, it was for me too. However, since I had not experienced this personally, I had the privilege of maintaining a certain psychological distance. I wouldn't admit it to Dean or David out of respect, but secretly I was excited by the idea the FBI had a file on me. In my mind, it meant I was doing something right.

For Dean and David, however, having experienced this traumatic event first-hand, I got the distinct impression it was far less exciting for them. From that point forward, neither of them had much interest in participating in mass actions. I didn't blame them, but I certainly wasn't going to let it stop me.

Chapter 23

I did not attend any major actions for the next several months. I split my energies between working for Larry and Anne during the work week and writing and editing for IndyMedia.org on the evenings and weekends. I was forming strong bonds with other members of the Global committee, including Clara in the Netherlands and a fellow by the name of Peter in the UK. We had vigorous discussions on all manner of issues surrounding anti-capitalism and the advancement of our global revolutionary movement. While our stated purpose was to be servants, stewards of the global website which was the hub of now hundreds of local IndyMedia subdomains, I could not help but feel I was an important member of the anarchist movement worldwide. The work gave me a tremendous feeling of satisfaction and a sense of leadership – however unanarchist this might seem.

One project I took personal interest in was the lack of an IndyMedia outlet in Venezuela, which in my view was further along the revolutionary path than any other region in the world. Of course, my view was not necessarily a popular one among anarchists, but I was largely influenced by Rolando's passionate emails to me on the subject. Two years prior, in 2002, there had been an attempted coup led by the opposition forces which had resulted in 19 deaths. A documentary had been released the following year, The Revolution Will Not Be Televised, which dramatized these events in gripping detail. The documentary asserted that this coup was nothing more than an attempt by capitalist forces, with the covert assistance of the CIA, to overthrow a democratically elected leader. Chávez, far from being the dictator the opposition considered him to be, was a noble and selfless figure who was fighting for the rights of the poor.

The criticism among anarchists was that Chávez was ultimately an instrument of state power. On the global IndyMedia listserv, this claim was bolstered by the participation of a self-proclaimed anarchist collective in Caracas, El Libertario. Each time an earnest attempt was made to establish an IndyMedia center for Venezuela, an anonymous representative of this group made an appearance. They asserted that no IndyMedia site should be established for Venezuela if, in any way, it lent support to Chávez's "Bolivarian revolution." This led to a great deal of confusion among the members of the global committee, for most of us were, in fact, anarchists. Rolando fed me bullet points, which I summarized in my own emails to the group, such as the following:

"There is an element of class here. El Libertario is a university group, with lots of internet access, and lots of time. So, they have had the ability to inundate their message in both Spanish and English on the IndyMedia lists. And the people actually trying to get IndyMedia Venezuela up and running, or the pro-Chávez, simply cannot compete. In Caracas, El Libertario is often referred to as anachistas en papel – 'Anarchists on Paper.'"

Despite support from Clara and Peter, we could never come to a consensus, and so the site failed to materialize.

Frustrated by these efforts and compelled by continued pleas by Rolando to come visit him, I made the decision to take a sabbatical from work for the month of October and bought a plane ticket to Caracas. Larry and Anne were perplexed by my decision, a confusion I was unable to remedy due to what I considered a necessary secrecy surrounding my true intentions. I played it off.

"I have a friend who lives there. I just think it will be a fun adventure, and maybe I can do some writing."

Larry, who was a strong Bush supporter and knew nothing of my politics, pressed.

"But Aaron, it is extremely dangerous there. Venezuela is a

dictatorship. There are protests all the time and people have been killed."

I shrugged it off.

"My friend Rolando says it's not so bad."

In the end, there was nothing they could say that would change my mind. Since I was such a vital part of their business, they felt they had no choice but to give me the month off.

As the plane made its final descent into Caracas, my eyes were glued to the window. It was much as I had imagined. The downtown area was pristine, at least from a distance. It could have been any major city in the United States. The difference was the landscape that surrounded it. Caracas was more or less seated in a valley, surrounded on all sides by mountains. And on the sides of every mountain were where the poor lived – millions of impoverished people who had constructed their communities quite literally out of shipping pallets and cardboard.

Once the plane had landed, I made my way through the airport. I carried everything in the same backpack I had used in my backpacking adventure in Europe several years prior, so there was no need to stop at baggage claim. The last email from Rolando had contained instructions about his friend Carlos who would be picking me up. Rolando himself was not in Venezuela. He was touring in South Africa, showing his own film about the Bolivarian revolution he had started at Emerson. Knowing he would not be meeting me at the airport, and that instead I would be in the hands of a stranger in the most foreign country I had ever visited, made me feel a bit uneasy. I assured myself this was all a part of the revolutionary adventure.

I exited the airport and saw that night had fallen. There were many other travelers around me, and the correspondence of class and race division was immediately evident. Those with darker skin wore simpler clothing and tended to carry more makeshift luggage, whereas those with lighter skin were dressed in fine clothes and name brand luggage. I remembered what I had learned in my Latin American history classes about the Spanish conquest, and how the divisions between the Spanish (the conquerors) and the indigenous and creole (the conquered) were still present after 500 years. The fact that support for or against Chávez fell along these same lines left me no room for doubt as to which side I wanted to be on.

"Aaron?"

I heard a voice say my name as it would be spoken in Spanish, with an accent on the second syllable. I turned and saw a tall, sturdily built man with dark skin and kind rounded features. He smiled, and I immediately felt at ease?

"Carlos?"

He nodded his head. I reached out my hand to shake his.

"Mucho gusto. Me llamo Aaron." Since he already knew my name, I felt embarrassed, and tried to acknowledge it in my broken Spanish. "Pero, tu lo sabes." But you already knew that.

He directed me to his car, a 1990s era Honda Civic, where I loaded my backpack into the trunk and sat in the passenger seat. He disengaged the parking brake, and we exited the airport. The windows were down, the air was hot and the sounds of traffic and honking horns were everywhere as we headed toward the city.

I did my best to speak only in Spanish, but Carlos himself often repeated himself in English whenever he could tell I did not understand – which was often. He was excited I had come to Venezuela to learn about the political situation and the Bolivarian revolution. He talked excitedly about his own family history. He came from a long line of communists, he told me. Chávez, he said, was a man of the people. He recounted in dramatic detail the initial coup attempt in 1992 led by Chávez. The president at the time, Carlos Pérez, had gone back on his campaign promise to oppose the IMF. Widespread protests had resulted, followed by a repressive military crackdown. Carlos told me there had been massive protests in his hometown of Maracaibo, which his parents had brought him to. I saw tears well up in Carlos' eyes as he described the scene he saw as a teenager of millions of his fellow countrymen taking the streets and remaining there for several days. In the end, Chávez was arrested. But when he was released from prison 6 years later, he had reached celebrity status. He ran for president and won easily in 1998.

We reached Carlos' apartment building in the middle of downtown Caracas, a high-rise building over 30 stories high. We took the elevator to the fifteenth floor, followed a narrow hallway and entered his one-bedroom apartment. Once inside, I saw many bookshelves filled with books on political theory, all, of course, written in Spanish. A poster of Chávez hung on the wall, a portrait of Che Guevara on another. It was clear to me that Carlos was a committed revolutionary, and knowing his parents were themselves communists, he came by it honestly. We retired early, and I laid on a mattress in the living room he had prepared for me. My heart thumped with excitement as I laid in the dark and heard the street noises outside, and it took me hours to fall asleep.

When I awoke the next morning, Carlos was sitting on the couch reading. As soon as I opened my eyes, he looked up from his book. He seemed to have been waiting for me, and I wondered what time it was. I glanced at a clock and saw it was almost 10 AM. He made a comment in Spanish I did not understand but sensed was a commentary on how late I had slept. He was ready to take me on a tour of Caracas.

Rolando would not be arriving until the next day, so we spent a long leisurely day exploring the city while Carlos gave me a dense education of both history and the current political situation. I was thankful that we started with breakfast, which we got at a nearby food stand not far from his apartment. This consisted of empanadas, filled with meat, beans and rice, as well as a tall glass of the freshest orange juice I had ever tasted. We finished this off with small shots of espresso in tiny plastic cups. My entire breakfast cost less than two dollars. I realized the $1500 I had saved for the trip might go further than I realized.

We toured the city on foot, exploring the university as well as a number of city historical monuments, some of them dating back hundreds of years. Graffiti was ubiquitous. There were political slogans, some of which I recognized from my time in Cancun (El pueblo unido jamás será vencido) but the most common graffiti, by far, consisted simply of one of two words: Sí and No. I asked Carlos about it.

"This is from the referendum in August. Ever since Chávez came to power, the opposition has sought to remove him by any means possible. In 2002, as you know, there was the attempted coup, with the support of the CIA. After that failed, this year they managed to push forward a referendum. Many international observers came, including your former president Jimmy Carter. Chávez won the referendum easily, and all observers agreed the process was a free and fair one. So the graffiti was to indicate support for either position – 'Sí' to remove him, 'No' to keep him."

Understanding the context now, I looked again at all of the graffiti and felt sadness. It was not obvious to me whether there were more No's than Yes's. Instead, I saw mainly a country that was deeply divided. Despite my inclination that one side was on the right side of history, and the other was not, I could not help but feel some deep internal pain at the awareness that there were two sides so deeply dug into their positions that they were willing to do anything to prevail over their adversaries.

The highlight of my tour came when we reached Parque Central in the heart of Caracas. Here we came across a colorful mural which Carlos told me was painted by a good friend of he and Rolando, Ian Pierce. The title, displayed in red lettering on a white background, read "Venezuela: Una Memoria Viva."

Venezuela: A living memory.

The scope of the mural was far beyond what I initially perceived it to be, for while I initially only saw the first 20 feet or so, as we continued walking, I realized it wrapped around a corner and continued for at least another 100 feet. It was a full history of the country, starting in the indigenous period. The illustrations were dramatic and heart wrenching. It covered the period of the conquest, depicting conquistadors in armor with skulls for faces. It depicted death and slavery. It continued into the period of Simón Bolívar, the liberator and namesake of the Bolivarian revolution, who led the fight for independence against Spain. From there, it covered the dark periods of neocolonialism, in which Venezuela was ruled by numerous dictators who served at the behest of global powers, including the United States. There was a large barrel labeled "Oil" upon which a general sat. When we reached the period of the 1980s, I saw two illustrations that caught my eye. One was of a man sitting on a couch wearing a T-shirt that read "I LOVE MIAMI." Next to him sat a bag of McDonald's. There was a television where his head should have been. But above this haunting image, a man with thick curly hair who reminded me of Bob Ross sat in a window strumming a guitar. A cartoon bubble emanated from his mouth, which contained colorful images of sunshine, farmers and a white dove.

"Who is he?" I asked.

"Alí Primera. He was a communist musician who wrote and performed beautiful songs of resistance which for us was a light in a very dark time. He was like our Bob Dylan. You should find his song about Che Guevara."

Rolando arrived the next day and met us at Carlos's apartment. The relaxing pace of things I had enjoyed with Carlos up to that point abruptly ended. Rolando's face was glowing, and I imagined this is what Moses must have looked like after returning from the burning bush. His curly black hair was now replaced with dreadlocks, which were pulled back with a colorful scarf in Rastafarian colors.

"Aaron-mon," he greeted me, giving me a huge hug. "I am SO glad you are here. Now that you are here, I can tell you what I have planned. We are going to tear down the fucking Columbus statue."

Evidently this was a plan he had concocted while traveling in South Africa where he had heard a song by Burning Spear called Christopher Columbus. Rolando gleefully sang a few verses for me.

> Christopher Columbus is a damn blasted liar
> He's saying that, he is the first one
> Who discover Jamaica
> I and I say that,
> What about the Arawak Indians and the few Black man
> Who were around here, before him

At this last line, he laughed.

"There were, of course, no Black men in Jamaica before Christopher Columbus came. But that isn't the point."

The plan was to have a rally at the Columbus statue, which I had already seen during my tour with Carlos. It was hard to miss, rising as it did 40-feet high in the center of a prominent traffic circle. The action would take place on Columbus Day, which had been renamed by Chávez to "Día de la Resistencia Indígena" (Day of Indigenous Resistance) 2 years prior. Rolando's dad had procured hundreds of feet of thick rope from some friends in the commercial fishing business on the northern coast. While plans for the rally had already been made public, the intentions to dismantle the statue were completely secret. My skin tingled with excitement knowing I was now part of the inner circle of a clandestine action.

During the following weeks, I participated in many meetings with activists all around Caracas. I learned more about the group Libertario which had been sabotaging our efforts to establish an IndyMedia center for Venezuela. Each person I met with expressed disgust for this group, which some claimed to consist of only three or four people at most. I also encountered heavy critique of the anarchist movement in general. For them, the mere fact that this small group could make such a big impact represented for them a deep flaw in the anti-globalization movement of the First World, and a fundamental lack of understanding of Latin American politics. Most of the activists I encountered did not seem to have any interest in fighting it. They had their own "independent media." They had no desire to be "recognized" by the larger movement. I felt humbled by this and found myself spending less time talking and more time listening.

At last, the day of the action arrived – October 12, 2004. Rolando's father drove us to the action in a pickup truck he had borrowed from a friend. The fishing rope filled the bed of the truck and was concealed with a large tarp. We parked as close as we could to the statue. There was a large grassy area around the statue where hundreds had already gathered. I wondered quietly whether the statue would actually fall and thought with some trepidation how embarrassing it might be if it turned out the statue could not be pulled off of the pedestal.

There were a number of speeches given by various activists, all in Spanish. I struggled, without much success, to understand everything that was being said. At best, I recognized certain key phrases about indigenous rights, neocolonialism, support for Chávez and contempt for the opposition and the United States government.

Rolando gave the last speech, and while I again had trouble following the specifics due to my limited fluency in Spanish, it was obviously a fiery one. As I watched him bellow into the megaphone with the sunlight hitting his face, I was struck with the sense that I was witnessing him in his full power. His passion, quite frankly, intimidated me. His own commitment to the revolution made me aware of the limitations of my own. The last month I had spent in Venezuela, however inspiring, lacked the comforts of home. How much was I really willing to sacrifice for the greater good of all of humanity? However much, it was clear to me that it in no way compared to what Rolando was willing to put on the line.

At the conclusion of his speech, time seemed to suddenly speed up. Rolando's father removed the tarp from the back of his truck and Rolando and several others immediately began unloading the rope and hurried to carry it to the base of the statue. Now everyone knew what was happening. A friend of Rolando's, also with dreadlocks, tied the rope around his waist and ascended the statue with athletic precision. Another followed behind, and the two of them tied the rope around the neck of Christopher Columbus, to the cheers of the crowd. I began to feel both extremely invigorated and extremely nervous. The illegality of our action, which had thus far been discussed in secret whispers, was suddenly on full display. I began wondering about the police. There were none in view. And while I assumed the President of Venezuela would support us, I understood the municipal police were under the control of the opposition. Would the national guard, under the control of Chávez, come to our defense? And if so, how exactly would things play out given there might be two possible armed responses to our action, with opposing agendas and allegiances?

Once Rolando's friends had descended the statue, the crowd began stretching out the rope. I held a digital camera in my hand, and took several pictures, but then was faced with the decision of whether to record what was happening or to participate. I chose to participate. I dropped the camera into my bag and rushed forward to grab a section of the rope before it became taught. At the slightest tug, it seemed, the statue came crashing down headfirst. It had been so easy.

There was an immediate reaction of jubilation by the crowd, and I felt a surge of adrenaline unlike any I had known before. This statue had stood here for a hundred years, and now it was gone. I did not think of myself as destroying history – I was a part of it.

Time sped up even more after this point. I approached Rolando to find out what was next, and he rapidly explained that Chávez was at this very moment giving a speech at the municipal palace, and that we would bring the statue to his doorstep. I had the sudden image of a cat bringing a dead mouse to its owner. Would he be proud of us?

Several people, using the bits of rope still attached to the statue, dragged it into the street and the rest of us followed. Drums and songs and chanting accompanied a festive atmosphere as we wound our way against the flow of traffic, and were greeted by blaring horns, fists shaking in the air, and stares of dumbfounded astonishment. As exciting as this moment was, my feelings of trepidation grew beneath the surface. I did not see any police, yet somehow this felt more foreboding than comforting.

We reached the palace. Looking through the crowd, I saw at the entrance to the palace a line of soldiers armed with semi-automatic rifles. My stomach dropped. I had the vivid understanding that I was no longer in the United States. Nor was I participating in a media-saturated international action. The real-ness of the situation took hold of my mind and body. Everything in my vision took on a grainy character, and I felt the metallic taste of fear on my tongue. Shots were fired. I looked around, expecting to see blood or falling bodies but did not. Moments later I realized, with minimal relief, that we were being fired upon with rubber bullets. I heard a rapid series of muted thumps and heard the hiss of tear gas canisters, and then the acidic smell and taste. The crowd ran in every direction, in panic, and the statue was abandoned at the steps of the palace.

I was terrified of being arrested, or worse, and so I ran. Fortunately, I knew where I was and was able to make my way back to Carlos' apartment. There I sat and waited for a number of hours, hoping against hope that Carlos and Rolando had escaped safely.

Finally, they arrived, unharmed. I learned that five people were arrested that day, including the two who had ascended the statue. Rolando had not been connected to the action, even though he had been the one who organized it. I also learned that it had not been the municipal police who had attacked us, but Chávez's National Guard. Chávez himself denounced the action as the work of "anarchists."

There were protests outside the jail for days afterwards, and over 90 people signed a statement claiming responsibility. Rolando encouraged me not to sign the statement, and to avoid the protests due to the potential higher consequences I might face.

"They might want to make an example of you," he said.

Instead, I focused my energy on writing a detailed article about the event which I submitted to the IndyMedia global committee under my "Blackbeard" pseudonym. It was immediately promoted to the top story. While I may not have had success in helping to establish an IndyMedia center, for the moment the attention of anarchists worldwide was on the dramatic events in Venezuela.

Chapter 24

I returned to Austin riding the greatest high of my activist career to date. I brought back a bottle of rum concocted from the sugar cane fields of Simón Bolívar and threw a party at my apartment. All of my friends came, including Dean, Maggie, Isaac and Elazar. I told them the stories of my adventures in Venezuela while songs by Alí Primera and Burning Spear played on my laptop. At this moment, anything seemed possible. I felt sure I was ready to dedicate my entire life to the revolution. In a drunken haze, I fired off an email to Larry and Anne letting them know I was quitting my job. I could no longer afford to devote 40 hours a week caring for bourgeois antique porcelain. I would make ends meet with my web content writing, but most of my time would now be devoted to organizing.

At one point, I noticed Maggie step outside to take a phone call. Moments later, she came back in and pulled me aside.

"Hey, I hope it's ok, but I invited a few friends over."

"Of course!" I actually found it a little odd that she felt the need to check with me.

There seemed to be something more she wanted to say. Then she did. "They just moved to town from Columbus, Ohio. They are with ARA and came down here to help organize."

"ARA?"

"Anti-Racist Action."

I was sure I had heard the name before but did not know very much about them.

"Oh yeah? What are they into?"

"They're fucking hardcore," she said. "These people don't talk, they act. They have been putting their assess on the line to physically confront Nazi skinheads and the KKK in the streets. They have stories you would not believe. Some of them decided to move to Austin because they heard about our community here and want to organize an ARA chapter here. A few of us have been meeting with them while you were gone, and they have ideas on how to reinvigorate our community."

I was intrigued. While my recent participation in the protests in Cancun and Venezuela had been personally invigorating, I was aware that the anarchist movement in Austin had grown a bit stale and seemed directionless. In the last few years, our anti-globalization focus had been fractured by the September 11 attacks, forcing much of our energies toward anti-war efforts. And while that had been a worthy target of our energies, it was all-too-obvious that even massive mobilizations had done nothing to slow down, or in any way impact, the invasions of Afghanistan and Iraq. There had not been a major protest in Austin in almost a year. Despite that fact, reports were coming out about widespread abuse and torture of prisoners of war in Iraq, particularly the Abu Gharib scandal. Pictures were circulating in the media of a prisoner draped in a black robe and hood being forced to stand on a wooden crate with strange wires attached to his hands – presumably he was being subjected to electrical shocks. Never had the need for resistance been clearer, and yet it felt like we were doing nothing about it.

Fifteen minutes later there was a loud knock. I opened the door and saw three men. Two of them, to my untrained eye, looked like skinheads. I vaguely remembered hearing about "anti-racist skinheads," but I had never met any in real life. One would have to study their tattoos carefully to realize the Nazi symbols were overlayed with ban circles. The other, however, who stood in the middle, looked more like a motorcycle gang member than anything else. He was short, but physically imposing. He had long black hair and an equally long gray beard. He had dark brown eyes and stared right into mine, grinning diabolically. He reached out his hand and introduced himself.

"Hi, I'm Gerry."

I shook his hand and told him my name. He made eye contact with me again only briefly before walking inside and joining the party.

While Gerry's demeanor was quiet, even brooding at first, he loosened up quickly after a few drinks and became the life of the party. He regaled us all with his war stories fighting Nazi skinheads and other white supremacists in Columbus. In fact, it seemed after a while that it was his party, and everyone there gathered around him, drinks in hand, listening with astonishment at his tales of glorified violence.

"Two years ago, in York, Pennsylvania, there was an all-day street battle between the anti-fascists and several white supremacist groups. Matt Hale, leader of the racist World Church of the Creator, was giving a speech at a fucking library. But out in the streets was where the real action was. The Aryan Nation, the National Alliance, the Hammerskins, they were all there. On our side, we had over two hundred anti-fascists, outnumbering them two to one. There was our group from Columbus, other ARA chapters, the Barricada Collective from Boston."

This caught my attention.

"The same Barricada Collective that organized the Black Bloc in DC against Bush's inauguration?"

Gerry paused, seemingly annoyed at the interruption. I suddenly wondered if my intention in asking the question was simply to signal my own bona fides. Despite myself, I realized I wanted his acceptance.

"Yup, that's the one." He cleared his throat and continued. "Anyway, we basically spent the whole day hunting these groups and beating them with chains and crow bars and anything else we could get our hands on. The pigs, of course, were on the side of the white supremacists, and defended them at every turn.

"At one point, we cornered a group at their vehicles and started smashing their windows and beating their cars with tire irons. One of them jumped in his pickup truck and drove through the crowd. A fucking 8-year-old girl was struck and broke her arm. Then the pigs did what pigs do. They charged all of us, swinging their batons, even beating the fucking 8-year-old girl. I would have intervened, but at that moment I had a national guardsman pointing a fucking grenade launcher right in my face. I looked at him and realized he was crying because he knew he was doing a bad thing."

There were more stories like this, and eventually I got tired of listening to them. I stepped outside to smoke a cigarette. While a part of me was as entertained by his tales as anyone else, I was also processing complicated feelings of doubt. I had difficulty relating to the degree to which he glorified violence. I myself had never struck another human being – not a cop, not a Nazi, not even a high school bully. When I had a clear opportunity, in Cancun, I froze. I wondered about whether my reluctance pointed to my own lack of commitment, or worse, a deep cowardice. Revolutions are never pretty, I reminded myself. If I am truly committed to seeing this through to the end, I thought, sooner or later I would have to take this step. And while I knew this rationally, I could not imagine myself hurting or killing another human being in the name of any cause.

Despite these internal conflicts, I was certainly not ready to step away from the struggle. Since it seemed ARA had now become the center of anarchist activity in Austin, I soon joined the chapter myself. We held weekly meetings at Rudy's Barbeque on Guadalupe Street. Even attending regular meetings was a new thing for me, as all of the meetings I had attended up to this point had been on an ad hoc basis. ARA was organized. We had an agenda, and with the exception of Gerry's rants (which were common) we generally stayed on topic. Maggie was a meticulous note taker and agenda keeper and was one of the few of us who had the guts to tell Gerry to shut up when he went too far off the rails.

I knew most of the people who attended the ARA meetings from previous actions, but there were some new faces. One was Scott Crow, a tall slender man in his mid-40s. He was softly spoken and extremely intelligent, and I took an immediate liking to him. There was another man in his 30s who simply went by the pseudonym "Justice." There were also young people. There was a girl named Charlie, who was still in high school. She was pregnant, a fact that might have led me to feel concern for her except for the fact that she was so intelligent and self-assured. Then there was another young girl, Teri, who was 19. She wasn't particularly intelligent, and frequently had trouble following our conversations. Mostly she just nodded and agreed with everything Gerry said but would occasionally add a remark of her own that was completely off base. I questioned the value she brought to our organization, or worse, whether she might be a liability. But in the end, my deep-seated belief that the more bodies we had in the street the better won out over any quiet concerns I might have had.

Election day arrived, as it often does, on my birthday – November 2, 2004. I had paid only passing attention to the lead up, catching only a few minutes of a debate here or there. I had no particular opinion about John Kerry except that I knew him to be an establishment Democrat. This time I decided not to vote. However, I sincerely hoped and also believed that George W. Bush would be defeated. I could not imagine, after dragging us into two wars against nearly unanimous objections of the international community, and the largest coordinated global protests in history, that he would win a second term. But win he did. Once again, it was by a slim margin. However, it was not "too close to call," and I watched with sickness as Bush gave his acceptance speech to a crowd of enthusiastic supporters.

I slept late the next day. When I woke up, I called Maggie and she told me some of the ARA folks were having coffee at a place across the street from the Capitol Building. Feeling some company might make me feel better, I got dressed and headed out. I caught a bus at the stop near my apartment and sat in the back brooding and writing in my journal while I watched the familiar landmarks on Guadalupe Street pass across my field of vision. I got out in front of the Capital, and across the street immediately spotted Scott, Maggie, Gerry, Teri, Charlie and someone else I didn't recognize sitting at a table outside.

I approached and offered a glum greeting.

"What's up, guys?"

"Hey," Maggie replied lamely.

The others just stared into their coffee, with the exception of the new person I hadn't seen before. She had dark skin. I imagined she was probably Latina, though she might have just as easily been black. She had long black dreadlocks decorated with all manner of glass beads and metal rings. She had big brown eyes, which made direct contact with mine. My heart rate increased noticeably, and I felt my palms grow sweaty. I dried a hand on my hoodie and reached it in her direction.

"Hi, I'm Aaron."

She smiled, and I suddenly noticed her tiny silver nose ring. She took my hand and shook it tenderly.

"I'm Lucia."

"Go get some coffee," Gerry interrupted gruffly. "We have things to discuss."

After ordering an Americano and bringing it back to the table, I pulled up a seat next to Lucia. Gerry continued talking, and everyone else listened with rapt attention.

"Yeah, it fucking sucks that that war criminal got re-elected, whether it was legitimate or another stolen election. The fact remains that the whole system is a sham. We don't end wars by electing a nicer fascist. We end wars by fucking grinding the machinery to a halt. So it's time to stop crying in our coffee and start planning our response."

The effect of this speech in improving my spirits was

considerable, and I noticed I was not alone. Suddenly frowns were replaced with tentative smiles. Gerry had a way with words, crude as they may have been. There was something comforting about his no-nonsense, in-your-face New Jersey accent. I felt he had something I didn't. Unbridled audacity. There were only a handful of us sitting at this table, and yet just in this moment I felt we had the power to set the revolution alight all by ourselves.

"Let's take the streets," Lucia suggested.

"Sure," Gerry said. "But we need numbers. How do we get numbers? We have about 6 weeks until January 20th. How do we get ten thousand people to join us?"

No one answered. The only time I had seen these kinds of numbers in Austin had been February the previous year, during the protests against the Iraq war. While it felt significant in the moment, this had only been a flash in the pan. I had never seen anything like this before, or since, in Austin. And if I was being honest, I really did not understand how it had happened. Certainly, large coalitions of mainstream activists had been involved in the process. Anarchists themselves rarely planned such large actions. We simply attended, planning our own convergences which rarely brought more than a few hundred into the Black Bloc. A couple of thousand at the most.

"We need to inspire people," Lucia said. "We have to make the revolution fucking sexy. Everyone is pissed off. We need to give them hope. We aren't like those big boring socialist organizations that no one cares about. We actually have a message. Everyone wants to be a part of the revolution, they just don't know how."

"Everyone doesn't want to be a part of the revolution," Maggie remarked sarcastically. "That's the problem. They need to be educated. That takes a lot longer than 6 weeks."

"Sometimes people need to be inspired before they have the desire to seek out that education," Scott suggested. "I think Lucia is on to something. If we can get our message out, especially right now, I do think people will respond."

"I could plan a walk-out at my high school," Charlie suggested. "I know a lot of people would be down for it."

"That would be badass," I said. "Let me know if you need help making flyers."

"We could storm the Capitol Building," Teri said. There was the usual need to let her down gracefully.

"Maybe one day," Scott said smiling, placing a hand on her shoulder. "Just probably not this action."

She looked embarrassed. The conversation moved on.

Gradually a plan began to come together. We knew we would not seek a permit for our day of action. As anarchists, we would never do anything to legitimize the state's authority. Nor would we plan a single action that could be disrupted. Instead, we would plan multiple actions, each appealing to their own cohorts and drawing their own numbers. First, we would organize the obvious rally at the Capital, which would draw those in the mainstream. At the same time, we would plan a "critical mass," a protest made entirely of bicycles, which would begin at the University of Texas. The high school walkouts would be organized by Charlie. She would start with her own high school, though she knew students at other schools she felt confident would want to participate. All of these actions would culminate at the Capitol grounds. Then, without warning, we would bring everyone into the streets and take Guadalupe.

"This is a good start," Gerry said. "But we want to push things further. We need to make sure there is a clear revolutionary, anti-capitalist presence. And that is going to be our job."

Obviously, that meant a Black Bloc. But rather than announce it, we would plan it internally at our ARA meetings.

Chapter 25

Lucia and I became close friends and partners in crime. I was inspired by her fresh attitude, as she had only recently become interested in anarchism. She offered a unique perspective. In her mind, anarchy was "sexy," even fashionable. We sat in my apartment drinking Lone Stars and sharing a bowl one Saturday morning as we made plans. Most of our planning meetings involved lots of alcohol.

"We shouldn't pretend we don't care about fashion," she said. "Of course we do. Do you think when someone in the Black Bloc is shopping for hoodies, bandanas and skinny jeans they don't realize how fucking cool they're going to look? Of course we care about fashion. It's just a different kind of fashion. It's cooler, it's revolutionary, it's fucking sexy."

I felt like she was speaking out loud a hidden secret. Of course, she was right. Certainly, I had thought about these things, but to speak them, it seemed, would be to risk ridicule from others who would consider such things shallow, even capitalist. I found her honesty refreshing.

"People don't care about politics," she said, "they want to be sexy and cool. They want to make out."

"Make out, not war?"

Her eyes got wide and she stared at me for a few seconds, her mouth open in surprise.

"Did you just make that up?"

I shrugged.

"Yeah."

"That's brilliant! Make out, not war! Let's put that on a fucking poster and make a thousand copies. No, ten thousand copies. Let's put it everywhere!"

I got out my laptop and we searched for artwork. We found a black and white drawing of two people kissing. Lucia loved the fact that the gender of each figure was ambiguous. We altered the title somewhat, to "Walk Out and Make Out" in honor of the high school walkouts. Beneath the drawing, we wrote:

A new era of resistance against Bush and his wars begins with a kiss.
Anti-Inauguration Day
January 20, 2005
Capital Building @ 4:00pm.

We formatted it such that four small flyers could be cut from a single piece of paper. This would allow us to make as many copies as possible at the lowest cost. We stood back and admired the final product.

"It's beautiful," she said. "I feel like we just made a baby."

We laughed. It was a joke, but truthfully, I was falling for her. I was afraid to bring it up, however, in case she didn't feel the same way. I was deeply enjoying the creative energy we were displaying together and didn't want to do or say anything that could jeopardize it.

The next several weeks were packed with activity. Rather than keeping the organization of the "J20" actions within ARA, we created a separate "spokescouncil" meeting and invited various organizations to participate. We began holding this meeting every Tuesday night at Plaza Santillo on Austin's east side. The meetings grew week after week as representatives from various leftist organizations began attending. What started as a handful of ARA folks expanded to a large circle of attendees numbering in the dozens. Still, it was exciting to know that myself and my friends had been instrumental in forming this group. Using the skills I had learned from working for Larry and Anne, I put together a website, austinspokes.org, which I used to publish information about the upcoming actions, downloadable flyers and a statement of our principles of unity.

The focus of the ARA meetings, therefore, became increasingly focused upon our specific contribution: the Black Bloc. Here, once again, Gerry took the lead.

"There are going to be thousands of people on the streets," he proclaimed confidently. Lucia and I looked at each other, knowing this statement to be true and also knowing it would in large part be due to the thousands of flyers we had distributed around the city. "This is our chance to show everyone what a disciplined Black Bloc looks like. We aren't fucking around, and the police won't be either. When you show up on J20, I want all of you to be dressed identically. That means black pants, black hoodies, black masks. No cute patches or spikes or brightly colored hair. We need to be identical. At least, as much as possible."

"Second thing," he continued. "We need to train. No military just recruits soldiers and sends them into battle assuming they will know how to comport themselves. We are no different. I know most of us have been in a Black Bloc before..."

"I haven't," Teri interjected.

Gerry paused and glared at her.

"We know that, Teri. That's the point. Whether you have been in a Black Bloc or not, that doesn't mean you know how to behave – how to hold a line when you have riot police charging you, or horses or motorcycles trying to break you apart. That takes discipline, training, practice."

"So we need to practice," I suggested.

"Exactly. And not just once. We need to start training 3 days a week until the day of the action. We don't have a lot of time. But we have a unique opportunity here to recruit, and I for one don't want to miss the opportunity."

We began meeting at Rosewood Community Park on Austin's east side. Scott and Maggie had acquired a number of sturdy wooden poles which would eventually form the structure for four banners that would surround us on all sides. We spent hours practicing various maneuvers. We started simply, just practicing marching in sync. We then practiced turns, whereby the side of the square would become the front. We practiced transforming into a wedge formation, which could be used to penetrate police lines.

It was interesting to me how quickly we had all become comfortable with military terminology, a language Gerry was very accustomed to using. At one level, I wondered if this conflicted with my core values as an anarchist. After all, I had never imagined that our purpose was to construct a mirror image of the forces we were organizing to oppose. Did we really expect to win by simply becoming a more effective version of the police and military? I knew such a notion would be laughable, if it weren't so tragic.

When we weren't practicing maneuvers in the park, attending meetings or passing out flyers, Lucia and I were busy constructing banners which would compose the perimeter of the Black Bloc. We took a large piece of black fabric and painted a pink, heart-shaped anarchy symbol. This complemented the "make out, not war" theme which had caught fire in Austin. We saw our little quarter-sheet flyer with the two androgynous figures kissing practically everywhere we went.

Lucia and I arrived on the Capitol grounds together, dressed in all black with our faces covered. We were half an hour early, but there were already a few hundred people present. We were able to quickly identify our ARA crew by their identical clothing and the large banner with the anarchy-heart symbol, and another that read "NO WARS, NO PRESIDENTS." Despite his black garb, Gerry was easily identifiable due to his short stature, wide girth, flowing beard and long hair. He was holding a megaphone and giving an impromptu speech.

"The time has come to stop crying and start organizing. In the past year, the left has been mired in debate about who or what white male candidate to support, as though if we were to vote green, vote Democrat, support this or that party, the occupation of Iraq will end. This is a lie. This has always been a lie. In the end, we are faced with two facts.

"Number one, no candidate that the ruling class seriously put forward was ever willing to, or capable of, ending the war and occupation.

"Number two, the ruling class is unwilling to allow free and fair elections in this or any other country.

"Therefore, the only remaining path is direct resistance. We are no longer willing to be channeled into responsible or respectful protest, electoral politics or civil obedience to an absolutely illegitimate and genocidal authority. We must take to the streets, not just today but every day. We must shut down business as usual until the ruling class has absolutely no choice but to concede to our demands!"

His speech was met with raucous applause. I had to hand it to him. Gerry could rile up a crowd. He was right, of course. In my view, the Democrats and Republicans were (in the immortal words of Bill Hicks) nothing more than the puppet on the left versus the puppet on the right. In fact, this illusion of "two sides" was not an accident. It was an intentional strategy cooked up by the ruling class – the rich, capitalist owners of the "means of production" – to keep the people fighting against one another rather than recognizing the reality of a common enemy. It was brilliant, actually. This is why electoral politics could never end war, environmental devastation, the widening gap between the rich and the poor, sweatshops, foreign occupations, torture or the increasing "McDonaldization" of our planet. Only revolution could do that.

As more people gathered and listened, it was my turn at the megaphone.

"Today is not about John Kerry. Today is not about George W. Bush. It is about your power. You have the power to end wars. You have the power to end wage slavery. You have the power to stop the destruction of the environment. Today we will take to the streets and show the government, and all governments, what the power of the people looks like."

My words, which flowed spontaneously, were met with more applause, and I felt my skin tingling with the recognition that I was channeling a message much greater than myself. I continued. "Peace is stronger than war. Justice is stronger than oppression. And love is stronger than hate. Let us show the world, and one another, that we are stronger than the system we oppose!"

More applause. As I handed the megaphone to the next speaker, I glanced to my side and noticed Lucia was staring at me adoringly. She came closer, wrapped her arms around my neck, and planted her lips firmly on mine. Moments later, I noticed others doing the same. Women kissing men, men kissing men, women kissing women. I felt a tremendous sense of joy and power in that moment. I felt unstoppable.

Suddenly we heard another wave of sound coming from about a block away on 11th Street, which ran directly in front of the Capital. It was the sound of chanting and cheers interspersed with the rings of bicycle bells. I turned and saw hundreds of people on bicycles, many of them bearing signs such as "NO WAR" or "NOT MY PRESIDENT." This was the critical mass! And before I had a moment to process this, I saw a crowd of over a hundred high school students coming from the opposite direction, crossing the Capital lawn and heading in our direction. I estimated the total crowd to be over five thousand.

Lucia and I rejoined the ARA group which was now organizing into a bloc – a quite literal "block" actually since our four banners, reinforced with thick poles, were of equal length and enclosed us on all sides. We instinctively turned to Gerry, who held one of the corners. If we were the soldiers, he was our commanding officer.

"It's time to take the streets, ladies and gentlemen."

We marched carefully toward 11th Street, keeping our steps in rhythm. Someone began a chant I had never heard before.

When I move, you move
Just like that
When I move, you move
Just like that
A-P-D
Step the fuck back!

We met no resistance as we stepped into the streets and proceeded South on Congress. The police presence was strong, composed mostly of officers on foot as well as a large contingent of motorcycle cops. However, they remained on the periphery, ensuring we remained on course toward the bridge. There had been some negotiations between the police and other organizers, not affiliated with ARA of course, that the march would end there and then disperse. We, however, had different plans.

Our objective was to set an example of militancy and autonomy for the other demonstrators which we hoped to build upon in future actions. Therefore, we would not follow the rules, even if breaking them meant doing something purely arbitrary. Our hope was that others would join us, and one disruption could provoke a response by police that would then lead to further disruption. In our minds, the day could hardly be considered a success if we did not at least try to kick the ant pile over.

As we approached 3rd Street, only a few blocks from the bridge, Gerry called out.

"Steady...Steady..."

And then, at the exact center of the intersection, he yelled.

"Now!"

In perfect synchronization, each of us turned 90 degrees and the right side of the bloc became the front. We headed west down 3rd Street. The police were totally unprepared for this, and we passed their sparse lines with ease. Many, but not all, of the other demonstrators followed us. I noticed many journalists, both mainstream and independent, following along on the sidewalk and snapping pictures. As planned, we were now the center of the action.

I heard the loud roar of police motorcycles revving up their engines in an attempt to intimidate us. Our pace began to increase, and our formation morphed from a square to a trapezoid as Gerry yelled for everyone to slow down and keep things tight. Now there were dozens of police charging us, their batons out. One of them pushed Scott, who was holding the left flank.

"Get on the sidewalk!"

Our formation disintegrated under the pressure and now everyone was running. We regrouped at the sidewalk on the corner of 3rd and Colorado, and I looked back to see that most of those who had begun to join us had now returned to the main march, presumably under pressure from the police. The smallness of our numbers, not more than two dozen, became quickly evident.

With the police pushing us from behind, we continued down Colorado and turned back east on 1st Street to rejoin the march. The most resistance we could muster was to walk slowly, on the sidewalk, as the police barked at us to pick up the pace. Finally, we reached Congress again, and I saw the bridge over the Colorado river was filled with a sea of protesters, and there was a heavy police presence pushing people onto the sidewalks, using bicycles as shields.

We rushed to the focal point of the confrontation, but here it was unclear what we should do. From my vantage point, there were nowhere near enough people challenging the police's orders for resistance to make logical sense. The vast majority of protesters were complying. And so, when ordered by a large police officer to "Get on the sidewalk," I did as he said.

At that moment, I saw Teri rush a police officer and strike him in the chest. I was astonished. Without hesitation, the officer removed what looked like a gun and pointed it at her. He pulled the trigger, and a sinister coil of metal wire proceeded from the barrel and became attached to her shoulder. I heard a loud clicking sound and saw her drop to the ground. She began shaking, as if she were having a seizure. I had never heard of a taser gun before, much less seen one. Chills ran down my spine at the gruesomeness and strangeness of what I was witnessing.

There were loud screams as another kid charged the police and suffered the same fate. I did not recognize him but based on his appearance I assumed he was one of the high school students. Several other police had drawn their tasers at this point and were pointing them at demonstrators. Everyone, anarchists and non-anarchists alike, complied with their orders and returned to the sidewalk as the arrests were made. The only resistance, at this point, were loud shouts and insults from the demonstrators standing on the sidewalk. I saw Gerry among them, as well as Maggie and Scott.

I marveled at the fact that those of us who had instigated all of this had avoided arrest. In the end, it was the youngest and least experienced who would be spending the night in jail while the rest of us enjoyed beers and laughs at the inevitable celebration that night. I felt a tremendous sense of guilt. How was it possible that Teri did not understand that all of our talk about fighting the police had been just that – talk? Our goal, all along, had been to get as close to the line as possible, but not to cross it. How did she not realize this? But the more I thought about it, the more I realized she could never have known this. She took us at our word. She must have assumed, as she charged the police with the ferocity of a warrior, that her comrades would have been at her side, doing the same. She didn't have the experience we had. She didn't understand how heavy the consequences for "assaulting a police officer" would be. We did, and that's why all of us leaders, who she looked up to, would be walking free while she was now facing consequences far heavier than she could possibly comprehend.

Chapter 26

As exhilarating as the momentum leading up to the Inauguration Day protests had been, particularly the inspiring and creative organizing strategies Lucia and I had implemented, the emotional crash immediately following was just as profound. Our plans to push what otherwise would have been a peaceful demonstration into more radical territory had landed two young people in jail facing serious charges. While I felt largely responsible for this, this sentiment did not seem to be shared by the other members of ARA. In their minds, the "state" alone was to blame. We held a fundraiser to help cover their legal expenses, but it did not take long before our attention was pulled into determining what was next. We had to keep the momentum going, one way or the other.

An opportunity presented itself only a month later, when the Austin IndyMedia Center hosted a IndyMedia conference at the University of Texas. While I initially expected it to be a regional event at best, I was soon contacted by some members of the global committee from Europe I had been working with the past couple of years. Clara and Peter both emailed letting me know they planned to fly in and asked if they could stay at my apartment. I happily agreed.

I held a kickoff party the night before the conference. I purchased large amounts of beer and liquor as well as an eighth of the best weed I could get my hands on. As I was cleaning up early in the evening, I heard a knock at my door. I opened to see two people I had never met before – a middle-aged woman with glasses and a lanky young man with long hair and a boyish, clean shaven face.

"Blackbeard?" the woman asked sheepishly.

"Clara! Peter!" I gave them huge hugs, absolutely thrilled to be meeting them in person for the first time. They came inside with their heavy backpacks and we spent the next hour talking excitedly. I shared with them the recent events of the Inauguration Day protest, and they told me about other exciting things happening in the UK and the Netherlands regarding squatter rights. We caught up on the situation with Venezuela IndyMedia, which unfortunately had not been making much progress.

Soon others began arriving. Everyone from ARA came, as well as many IndyMedia folks and others from across the anarchist community in Austin. A couple of hours later, there must have been fifty people spilling out of my small, one-bedroom efficiency apartment and filling the courtyard. I felt proud to be the center of attention, and even prouder that the majority of attendees knew me only as "Blackbeard."

"Blackbeard, do you have any more cups?"

"Blackbeard, where can we go to buy some more beer?"

"Blackbeard, do you know what bus we can take to get to campus tomorrow?"

I had a distinct feeling that I had arrived as a major organizer in the global anarchist movement. Feeling overwhelmed with emotion and excitement, I decided to take a quick breather outside by myself. I filled a plastic cup with my favorite cocktail, Makers Mark with coke and a squeeze of lime, rolled a cigarette and stepped outside. I wandered out of the apartment complex and toward the street. I spotted an unmarked white vehicle I had never seen before, parked on the road right outside my apartment, with two men sitting in the front seat. One of them held what looked like a laptop, which luridly lit the inside of the otherwise dark car. There was no question in my mind that this was law enforcement, and my apartment was now under surveillance.

I returned to the party, telling no one what I had seen. I was, however, mostly quiet and reflective for the rest of the night. I wrestled with a mix of emotions. I knew there was no reason for me to be surprised. David and Dean's experience in Miami confirmed that the FBI knew who I was. How could they not? I had been on John Zerzan's radio program, for God's sake. I had participated in virtually every major anti-globalization or anti-war convergence in north America in the previous 5 years. I had spent the past few months practicing quasi-military maneuvers in the park with a prominent radical leftist organization. And now I was hosting a party for anarchist organizers from all over the world. If I weren't on law enforcement's radar by this point, their radar was clearly broken. And yet there was a difference between understanding all of this theoretically versus seeing it with my own eyes.

This was one of the obvious costs of the life I had chosen, and I imagined it would only get worse. The only question was whether it was worth the cost. This question, at this moment, was more difficult to answer than I might have anticipated 2 years prior. Was justice worth the cost? Was fighting for indigenous and workers' rights worth the cost? Was stopping war worth the cost? The answer to all of these questions, for me, was unambiguously yes. There was only one problem for me, and that was the fact that I could not draw a clear line in my mind between the actions I was participating in and the goals I aspired to achieve. Taken in isolation, I could consider the fact that I now most likely had a file with the FBI as evidence simply that I was now in good company along with great men such as Martin Luther King or Malcom X. But if I was being honest with myself, it was obvious that such a comparison was deeply flawed. Not only was the scope of my influence not even remotely close to what these people had accomplished in their lives, I was not even sure everything I was doing was pointing in the same direction.

The Inauguration Day protest in Austin was clearly my greatest accomplishment as an anarchist organizer. Of course, I had not accomplished it on my own, but I knew both Lucia and I had been key players in bringing it to life. But if this was my greatest accomplishment, what had I accomplished exactly? Had the inauguration been delayed by even 5 minutes? Had it resulted in even one less bullet fired, or bomb dropped in Iraq or Afghanistan? Clearly not. In fact, the only tangible difference we had made in anyone's lives were the criminal records two teenagers would now be carrying with them for the rest of their lives. A peaceful demonstration would have been one thing. Even widespread civil disobedience resulting in increased, sympathetic attention to our cause might have resulted in some impact, however miniscule. But we had accomplished neither of these things. We had, instead, introduced just enough chaos to cause damage to two people's lives and largely negative attention in the media. So, was it really worth it?

While the IndyMedia conference provided a much-needed distraction from these nagging questions, once it was over and everyone went home, I became more restless than ever. My alcohol consumption skyrocketed, and I found myself drinking all day, every day. Lucia and I often drank together. We had become somewhat romantically involved since the "make out" in front of the Capitol Building, but the relationship was complicated from the beginning. Like Mira, Lucia wanted an open relationship. I did not, but I acquiesced once again. Secretly, I resented her for this. My anger and frustration led to more drinking.

I did not seem totally alone in this habit. Alcohol was served at the BBQ restaurant where our ARA weekly meetings continued to be held, and many of us drank during the meetings. Once the meeting concluded, we would often continue the "meeting" at Lovejoy's, a bar on 6th Street. These discussions were often loud and chaotic. The topics of discussion would wildly wander between ideas for future actions, to philosophical discussions about how to spark a global revolution, to simply listening to Gerry ramble on about his own war stories about attacking

Nazis in the streets – violent scenes retold in gory detail. But one night, Gerry finally came forward with a coherent proposal.

"Have any of you heard of David Horowitz?"

We had not. Gerry continued.

"He was a radical leftist during the 1960s and 70s. He was a communist who used to work with the Black Panthers and claimed to be personal friends with Huey Newton. Which personally I doubt. But sometime in the 1980s he went batshit crazy and swung all the way to the right. He is now an anti-gay, Islamophobic, war-mongering piece of shit. And he is going to be speaking at UT in a few weeks."

We were silent, at first. It was clear what Gerry was insinuating, and yet it was a suggestion most of us had never considered before. The idea of disrupting this one man's speech placed things in a very different light. Up to this point, for basically the last 5 years, all of our efforts had been focused upon impacting big, global events. International trade agreements and wars. Clearly our influence on these events had been minimal. There had been a few symbolic victories here and there, but nothing substantial enough to truly alter the course of events. Our numbers, however large, were never enough to pose a real challenge to the capitalist war machine which had seemingly unlimited resources at its disposal.

This, however, was different. If everything Gerry was saying about this man was true, and I had no reason to doubt it, then he was a worthy adversary. Unlike the big anonymous institutions like the WTO or the IMF/World Bank, here was a human being with a real name and face who was going to be appearing at a specific place and time within our own city. Presumably, there would be no real security to speak of. It would be an easy matter to show up, slip right into the audience, and then shut his speech down. Using our network, it would be an easy matter to draw in twenty or thirty participants at the very least. While this might make for a very ineffective Black Bloc on Congress

Avenue, these numbers would be more than enough to totally spoil Horowitz's plans.

Everyone was on board, but I wanted to learn more. The next day, I spent some more time researching David Horowitz on the internet. The outlines of his biography offered by Gerry were basically accurate. He came from a long line of Marxist radicals, but after the death of a close friend – he believed at the hands of the Black Panthers – his views began to transform. He was undoubtedly right wing now, and it did seem to be true that he was guilty of a number of anti-gay and Islamophobic remarks. But what Gerry did not go into at the ARA meeting was Horowitz's current focus – freedom of speech on college campuses.

David Horowitz was the founder of the Center for the Study of Popular Culture. A spin-off group, the Students for Academic Freedom, had taken Horowitz's ideas and composed what they called the "Academic Bill of Rights," composed of eight principles. The gist of this document was the argument that universities should not discriminate against faculty or students on the basis of political or religious beliefs. In addition, there should be a "view toward fostering a plurality of methodologies and perspectives." I read through the entire document, noticing that I myself could not find a single point I disagreed with. The seventh principle stopped me dead in my tracks.

"An environment conducive to the civil exchange of ideas being an essential component of a free university, the obstruction of invited campus speakers, destruction of campus literature or other efforts to obstruct this exchange will not be tolerated."

Horowitz's speech at UT was, in fact, part of what he called the "Academic Freedom" tour, and his stated purpose was to promote the Academic Bill of Rights. The fact that our plans were an obvious violation of the principles he was promoting would not have bothered me except for two things. First, that I myself could not find fault with the principles he espoused.

And second, that I could not see how our disruption of his speech could fail to prove him right in the eyes of any unbiased observer.

I raised these objections at the next ARA meeting, and was quickly shut down by Gerry, who launched a passionate rebuke of my concerns.

"If you think he really cares about 'academic freedom' you're a fucking idiot. It isn't about that. This talk about 'academic freedom' is just good old-fashioned Orwellian double-speak. He doesn't care about freedom of speech. The only thing he cares about is silencing speech. Gay speech, lefty speech, Islamic speech. This is how fascism works. It doesn't start with brown shirts and swastikas and parades. That is where it ends. It starts here, with people like David Horowitz who spread lies and propaganda. Hate speech is not free speech. This is a fair and justified case of the need for community self-defense. We must shut down his speech to protect real free speech, the speech of the poor and oppressed who don't get to go to fucking college."

Everyone else either agreed or were too afraid to get a similar tongue lashing from Gerry and kept quiet. I decided, finally, that it wasn't for me to decide for the group which actions were justified or not justified. Despite my concerns, I conceded silently that everyone else must be right. After all, if we had been on the right side of history thus far, why would this case be any different?

We agreed it would be best for us to split into smaller groups of two or three people and arrive on campus separately to avoid drawing attention to ourselves. Several people brought air horns stashed in their backpacks. Others, just cell phones.

Lucia and I arrived at the lecture hall together and sat near the back. It was the first time I had stepped foot on a college campus since I graduated 3 years prior. It felt strange. I was in a familiar environment, the classroom, which brought back positive memories. This was the place I had aspired to be throughout my entire time in middle school and high school. I loved to learn. Education, for me, represented an escape from the world I had been born into. It held out limitless possibilities for my future, the promise of new ideas, new places, new opportunities. It represented freedom, debate, the celebration and elevation of the human spirit. However, I was not here for any of those reasons. I was here to create a disruption. I watched as a dozen or so students filed in with their backpacks. As they took their seats, some of them retrieved notebooks and pens. They reminded me of myself only a few years ago.

David Horowitz entered the lecture hall on time and was greeted with polite applause. I saw people from my group scattered throughout, and noted that, predictably, they kept quiet. I was a bit alarmed to see Teri sitting beside Gerry. She was still facing charges for assaulting a police officer. This was the last place she should be right now, I thought.

In addition to my ARA comrades, I noticed another contingent of about fifteen members of the International Socialist Organization (ISO) were present, filling an entire row. As anarchists, we had a complicated relationship with the socialists. Our ultimate objectives were quite different; however we often found ourselves on the same side of any given battle.

Horowitz approached the podium, and after a few taps at the microphone, began speaking.

"Thank you everyone for being here. As most of you probably know, this lecture is part of a series of talks I am giving on campuses across the country as part of what I am calling the 'Academic Freedom Tour.' It is my belief, and I think a lot of you shared this belief, that no student can get a good education if professors are only telling you half the story."

A cell phone rang. I saw it was coming from one of the members of our ARA group. Horowitz stopped speaking and cleared his throat disapprovingly as the teenage boy dug into his pocket, smiling mischievously, and silenced the phone after several rings.

"Please do me a favor and silence your cellphones to prevent any further disruptions," the speaker said. "Continuing on..."

Now there was a blast from an air horn. Horowitz turned to one of his aides and asked him to contact campus security. In the meantime, he attempted to continue his lecture, but he was unable to get a complete sentence out before there was another cell phone ring or air horn blast.

"Tell us how you betrayed the Black Panthers," Gerry called out.

"Sir," Horowitz responded, "we will have a question-and-answer period after the lecture. I ask you kindly to please keep your comments to yourself until that time. If you do not follow the rules, I will ask campus security to remove you from the lecture and you may be arrested."

"Wow, you really believe in free speech," Gerry retorted. But as usual, he knew where the line was and how far he could go before crossing it. He sat down and did not say anything else.

"Are you going to do something," Lucia whispered to me.

"Not yet," I said.

What was I waiting for? I had an airhorn of my own in my backpack. I simply couldn't bring myself to use it. Confronting a human being, as opposed to a big anonymous concept or institution, was a double-edged sword. Yes, it was easier to make an impact. In fact, that impact was all too clear as I could tell David Horowitz was becoming increasingly angrier and unhinged with every disruption. The problem was, I actually felt bad for him. Certainly, I did not agree with many of his views. And it might even be that his "Academic Bill of Rights" masked more nefarious objectives than what it stated on the surface. But wouldn't it be more effective, I thought, to hear what he actually had to say, and then address our concerns in the question-and-answer period? If we believed we were in the right, why wouldn't we choose rational debate over childish tactics which only served to bolster his argument?

Several officers from the UT Campus Police arrived in the lecture hall. By this time, the members of ISO were standing and holding up signs. One read "Horowitz is racist." Another, "Hate Speech is not Free Speech."

David pointed at them and spoke to the police.

"Officers, arrest them. They are disrupting my speech. I am an invited speaker on this campus, and I have a right to deliver my lecture free from disruption."

The officers explained that they could not arrest them as long as they were remaining quiet, since they were not breaking any laws. This response was met with loud applause from all of the protesters, who I now realized far outnumbered the actual students who had come to hear the lecture. Those few, however, were becoming increasingly agitated. A few of them gave us harsh looks. One even spoke up at one point.

"Can you people please shut up and let us hear what he has to say? You guys are the problem. What are you so afraid of?"

This stung. Everything felt messy. On the streets, the lines were all clear. We, the protesters, were the good guys. The bad guys, the politicians and the capitalists, were hiding away in hotels and convention centers and government buildings. The police were their henchmen, defending their interests. And so, I personally did not think of the police as the enemy but as defenders of the enemy. We had to fight the police, not because they were our enemy, but because knowingly or unknowingly, they were defending everything we opposed. The people, however, all those standing on the sidelines, were never the enemy. They might not understand our purpose, they might not even agree with us, but I always believed we were fighting for their rights as well as our own.

In this situation, it was much harder to convince myself I was one of the good guys.

As the air horn blasts and cell phone rings continued, arrests began to be made. A total of six members of our group were arrested, including once again, to my horror, Teri.

Chapter 27

I was sickened by everything that had taken place that evening, but felt it was utterly impossible to talk to anyone in ARA about it. I holed myself up in my apartment for a few days, doing little else besides sleeping and drinking.

In addition to my growing existential crisis, I was facing another crisis as well. I was running out of money. I hadn't had a full-time job since I returned from Venezuela. I had been able to make ends meet by doing some web content writing, but due to the fact that almost all of my attention the last few months had been devoted to organizing, protesting and drinking, the work had all dried up. My rent was $450 a month, a bargain for Austin even at that time. However, I only had about $500 in my bank account. This was a tough spot to be in, considering I was spending at least $10 per day on alcohol.

Therefore, I was facing another hard truth about my activist lifestyle. Although I was spending my life dreaming anarchist dreams, the reality was that I still very much lived in a capitalist system. That meant I alone was responsible for earning and income and paying my bills. No one else would or could take care of these things for me.

Days turned into weeks, with no change in my financial outlook other than its continued deterioration. I paid my rent, barely, but only had $20 remaining. I resorted to a popular practice in the anarchist community, dumpster diving. I had very little success in finding food. I noticed, as well, that the practice felt very different when it was done out of necessity rather than as a political statement. I didn't feel like a revolutionary. I just felt broke.

This opened up a new front in my existential crisis, the feeling that perhaps I was wasting my life. Here I was, a man in my mid-20s with a college degree. In fact, the first person in my family to earn a 4-year degree. And yet, what was I doing with it? Making flyers? Painting banners? Searching for ways to provoke the police, seemingly for the pure thrill of it? What had it gotten me, or anyone else? No wars had been prevented; no sweatshops had been shut down. I was being surveilled by the police, maybe the FBI, but really, I was no threat to the establishment. Did I want to be? Was that my mission in life, to one day grow up to be another Gerry, leading young people to accumulate criminal records like some nefarious pied piper?

What about my relationships? Here again, as I looked at my life over the past 5 years, I saw nothing but failure. The majority of my romantic encounters had been drunken flings. The few more significant relationships, particularly Mira and Lucia, had been built upon radical notions of free love that in my heart I did not buy into. I had no problem with the idea of polyamory, but I knew, for me, I wanted a committed relationship. I wanted to get married and have children. In the anarchist community, these were subversive thoughts I dare not utter to another.

One day, I mustered up the energy and courage to call Gary, the owner of the company that had originally built Larry and Anne's website. I asked if he had any jobs available.

"We are set at the moment in terms of web content, but I will be sure to let you know if anything comes up."

I paused, knowing there would be no coming back from the question to follow.

"What about a full-time job?"

"Here in Houston?"

"Yes."

He laughed.

"I have been hoping for this for a long time. You are a multi-talented guy and I think there are a lot of ways we could use you down here. Let me discuss this with my partners and I'll get back to you soon."

There was nothing inherent about my decision to move to

Houston that necessitated my departure from the anarchist scene. After all, there were anarchists in Houston too. I told myself maybe when I got settled in down there, I would connect with that community. However, a part of me knew I wouldn't. It was true that I needed a job, but I was beginning to feel the need for much more. I wanted to build a future. I wanted a career. I wanted to build a life that might one day include a family. I wanted to be a provider. I wanted to be needed by others.

I escaped Austin by packing everything in my car, leaving my apartment with the last month's rent unpaid, and pouring the last of my funds into my gas tank. My friend Valerie was also living in Houston at this time, attending Baylor Medical School. Her boyfriend kindly agreed to let me live on his couch for a couple of months while I got on my feet.

I settled into a simple routine that I found to be healing to my mind, body and soul. Having not even enough money to pay for gas, I woke up an hour early and took the bus to work each day. Upon arriving at the final stop, I found a local Mexican restaurant where I could buy a cheap breakfast of potatoes, eggs, refried beans and tortillas. It was only a few dollars, but they gave me so much food I was able to save part of it for lunch. All told, I was living on about five dollars a day.

I took great pleasure in the work I did. I divided my time between doing content writing and some coding. What I had learned from my father at an early age was coming in handy, and my contributions were quickly recognized and valued by the owners of the company. I had to admit it; it felt good to put in an honest day's work, and to not feel that each day was no longer an uphill struggle to change a world that simply seemed uninterested in the changes I proposed.

Without money for alcohol or other entertainment, when I wasn't working, I was writing. I purchased a black and white composition notebook and filled page after page with my thoughts and reflections on my recent past as well as my present situation. I felt I had so much to get out on paper, I wrote in the tiniest print I could manage. I was letting out emotions and doubts about my activist life I had bottled up for years.

I still spoke with my friends and comrades fairly often on the phone or by email. One day after work, Lucia told me about a major upcoming action in Houston, a protest against Halliburton. Halliburton, of course, was the infamous military contractor in Iraq, the same company that had made Dick Cheney incredibly wealthy. The action was being billed as a "day of rage," with anarchists coming from all over the country. It was crazy to me that all of this was happening in Houston. I had been involved in the "scene" in Texas for years and I had only heard of one other protest in Houston that entire time.

I was non-committal. It was taking place on a weekday, which meant I would have to take a day off work. Ordinarily, this would not have been a question for me. However, I realized I really didn't want to request a day off. I had just been handed a major project, and I felt a strong desire to prove myself to my employers. I was responsible for reorganizing an entire website, an effort I had begun throwing myself into with full commitment. I was even working evenings and weekends on it, even though that's not something they had asked of me.

The day arrived. While waiting at the bus stop, I got a text from Lucia letting me know she and the ARA folks were caravanning to Houston. She wanted to know where they could meet me. Not knowing what to say, I ignored it. The bus arrived, the air brakes hissing as it came to a stop. I stepped aboard.

Later that afternoon, I checked Houston's IndyMedia website.

16 Arrested, Dozens Trampled by Horses

I read through the accounts. There were only a few hundred protesters, but evidently, they had come ready for action. There had been considerable confrontation, a breakaway march and even some penetration into the Four Seasons Hotel where Halliburton had been meeting. Scrolling through the pictures, I recognized many faces. Some members of ARA had been arrested and charged with assault. Why hadn't I been there? It was the first major protest since 2000 I had skipped without good reason.

It was surreal hearing my coworkers talk about the protest, which had easily made the local news headlines that day. It was especially awkward when they mentioned the "anarchists," who they believed lived only to cause trouble. If there were any good intentions or beautiful ideals behind their actions, it was certainly lost on my coworkers. I felt the urge to educate them, but instead kept quiet.

Up to this point, I had been able to convince myself my move to Houston was motivated by financial reasons. This was no longer a convincing alibi.

When I returned home from work, I decided to take a long walk, bringing my composition notebook with me. The time had come to decide what I really believed. I found a quiet spot in a nearby park and sat under a tree, shading me from the intense Houston sun. I opened the notebook and placed the pen expectantly on a blank page. I closed my eyes and sat in quiet reflection.

My ideals, my hopes and dreams for the human race had not changed. I still believed in justice and peace. I still believed every person on the planet had the right to live a life of meaning and purpose. I felt sadness for the millions of people born into poverty, destined for a long, hard life of toiling away in sweatshops just so they could produce cheap goods, which people like me could purchase one day and throw away the next. I grieved for the ongoing destruction of the rainforests, which were being clear cut so that cattle could be raised – only to be slaughtered for fast food companies producing low cost, nutrient poor food for the impoverished people in my own country. I felt deep anger when I thought about the pain and terror and grief being inflicted upon the people of Iraq and Afghanistan, whose lives had been turned upside down in retaliation for the events of September 11, a tragic moment for which they bore absolutely no responsibility.

What had changed, however, was my belief that the sorts of actions I had participated in and helped plan for the last 5 years were leading in a direction that would remedy these tragedies. By dressing in black and orchestrating arbitrary confrontations with the police, who exactly were we attracting to our cause? Increasingly, what I saw were young, impressionable people in search of belonging, willing to risk a future they could hardly comprehend in pursuit of approval from older people who had done very little with their own lives.

I could no longer ignore the desperate direction the anarchist movement seemed to be taking. The events in Seattle in 1999 had certainly seemed glorious. For all its flaws, the demonstrators had not only shut down the meetings, but for the first time drawn attention to issues of social and environmental justice to which most of us had been completely oblivious. When I compared this to the recent shameful action on the campus of UT, it did not even seem like the same movement.

In one sense, the changes that were happening in the anarchist movement were easy for me to understand. In the 5 years since Seattle, we had been successful only in generating violent spectacles in the street. Neither war, nor globalization, had slowed in the least. I understood that the anger and frustration I felt as a result must be shared by others in the movement. The temptation to engage in smaller actions where our impact could be felt more easily made perfect sense. If we couldn't stop the next WTO meeting or the next war, we could easily stop a conservative from speaking on a college campus.

In believing that "history" was on our side, I realized we were in some sense no different from the past and present crusaders who believed "God" was on their side. As anarchists, we did not recognize any authority greater than ourselves. As a result, literally any action we decided to take was, by definition, justified. I was beginning to understand the folly of this world view. In theory, anarchists rejected the communist notion of the "vanguard," the idea that the most "class conscious" elements of the working class must lead others into the revolution. In practice, however, it was hard to see how we did not implicitly subscribe to this notion. Without the idea of "vanguardism," the "Black Bloc" tactic made no sense. We had nothing close to widespread support, even among most demonstrators. Only a fraction of the population was willing to participate in protests of any kind, and of those that were, almost all of them believed in peaceful protest. We had taken it upon ourselves, however, to ensure peaceful protests did not remain peaceful. We knew better than everyone else what forms of protest were justified or not justified, and these rules were being written and rewritten with every passing moment.

I still believed another world was possible, but I no longer believed it could be accomplished through secrecy, provocation and violence. I was finally willing to acknowledge something I had probably known for a long time. Only openness could lead to justice. Only nonviolence could bring about peace. Only dialog, including cooperation with those with whom we disagreed, could reveal the truth. These were hard truths to swallow, because here there were no easy answers. To the extent there were any answers at all, I knew I could never pretend to be the one who possessed them.

There I was, left with nothing but hopes and desires for the world, and for my own life, and not the first clue how I might bring any of them to pass.

Finally, my pen began moving across the page.

"I cannot say that where I am at right now is exactly where I have always hoped to be. But this is where I have ended up. My present situation is the logical result of all my past decisions. The thing for me now is not to lament where I could have been, nor to break myself in the attempt to instantly seize by force the things I could have earned. My life now is a somewhat knotted mess of debt, desires and obligations. With patience and faith, I have begun slowly to loosen the threads separating into the component fibers, until I shall see clearly what there is to be done.

"What does faith mean to me? I have for a long time disposed of this word from my vocabulary, associating it with my tortured efforts at believing something that made no sense to my mind. Faith was enduring the torture, taking it as a positive sign. Now I have begun thinking differently about the world and have in fact begun to see it as crucial to my life.

"Faith is the unfaltering exercise of good will in one's actions, a commitment that remains even when the rewards are not immediately obvious, even when life seems poised to strike a faithless blow. Faith in oneself, faith in the universe, faith that we exist for a purpose even if that purpose is unknowable. Coarsely put, to try one's best.

"And when you fail, to try again."

Afterword

In the fall of 2005, 6 months after my last protest, I met the woman who would soon become my wife.

Brianne was unlike anyone I had known in the past 5 years. While she and I shared our admiration for the 1960s, the music and the ideals of peace and love, we had come to quite different conclusions. Brianne could not understand how violence had any place in political protest. "If you use violence," she asked, "how are you not just like them?" She believed the means of change had to be aligned with the goals of change. External change must be motivated by inner change. If you want to overcome hate in others, you must first overcome hate in yourself.

I resisted these arguments for some time. However, not only did I not convince her, I became less convinced myself. The more time and space that separated me from my involvement in radical politics, the more I began to see my own motivations more clearly. I had been selfish and self-righteous. I wanted so badly to be a leader, but never a servant. My desire for a community had been authentic, but my desire to provoke a violent revolution had more to do with a search for excitement and meaning in my own life than it did any solid convictions.

In these 5 years, I accumulated many experiences but little understanding of myself. My sense of right and wrong was twisted beyond recognition. Wrong was only something that existed in others, in institutions and abstractions. It was not something that could possibly exist in myself, because I opposed those very institutions and abstractions.

Looking back, it is easy for me to see how my increasing drug and alcohol use contributed to my moral bankruptcy. This became clear after 5 years of marriage. Trying to maintain my daily drinking habit and my own sense of self-righteousness was simply incompatible with the level of thoughtfulness and humility required to nurture a healthy relationship. And so, in 2011, I became sober with the help of Alcoholics Anonymous.

Conducting a "searching and fearless moral inventory" of myself forever changed my attitudes about my behaviors, my intimate relationships and the world around me. It wasn't that I no longer recognized the fact of inequality and injustice in the world. However, I began to recognize the difference between the things I could change and the things I could not. I came to see that attributes of my own character – honesty, humility, forgiveness and compassion – had to become the well from which all of my actions sprung. The ends could never justify the means, because my own mind possessed an infinite capacity for justifying anything that served my own selfish interests.

The deeper I dug into understanding myself and my past behavior, the more difficult it became for me to see the world in black and white terms. Meanwhile, the rest of the world moved rapidly into deeper and more violent polarization. Following Donald Trump's election in 2016, I began noticing a surprising trend in street protests. The right wing was showing up with its own type of "Black Bloc." Instead of black, however, it was red, white and blue. Yet there were more similarities than differences. They too were coming to protests with shields and armor, with the express purpose of physically confronting the groups now known as "Antifa." The more I thought about it, the more I realized the most surprising thing. Not that this was happening at all, but the fact that it hadn't happened sooner.

For every action, there is an equal and opposite reaction force. Social movements, in other words, are not exempt from the laws of physics. In this way, groups like Antifa and the Proud Boys may be more alike than they are different. Both believe in the utter rightness of their cause. Both believe history is on their side. Both believe they have a duty to physically confront their enemies in the streets. Both believe that justice will not be achieved until the "other side" is completely annihilated.

Anti-Hero

Neither sees the other side as human beings.

During my involvement in the anarchist Black Blocs in the early 2000s, we operated mainly in obscurity. I was astonished at how often I would participate in large, dramatic confrontations that were hardly covered at all by mainstream media. Today, Antifa is a household name. Many liberals seem to take their namesake at face value. Anti-Fascists. I am often amazed by the fact that otherwise intelligent friends of mine seem to miss the obvious point that simply calling oneself "anti-fascist" does not make it so. Of course, I am anti-fascist. My concern, however, drawing from my own direct experience, is that those in the Antifa share a mindset whereby anyone who stands in their way, anyone who criticizes their tactics, is by definition a fascist. I am sure, simply by writing this book, this label will soon be applied to me.

If there is any chance that I, myself, can contribute to the "another world" I once so strongly believed was possible, I believe it can only happen because I decided to tell the truth. I am still liberal to this day. As such, it does no good for me to criticize groups like the Proud Boys. Only criticisms from conservatives themselves have any hope of landing. I hope that my criticism of Antifa, which comes from my own direct experience of movements such as theirs, can contribute to the de-escalation that is desperately needed in the coming years. I applaud Antifa's passion and commitment, but I condemn their propensity for violence that is motivated by unreflective self-righteousness. I defend their right to believe in anarchism or communism or any ideology, but I condemn their belief that these ideologies should be imposed upon anyone else by force.

I write this in the recent aftermath of the 2020 election. Joe Biden has been declared the winner, but Donald Trump himself and many of his supporters are deeming this a "stolen election." Obviously, I know how they feel. I can relate to their desire to take the streets, to use violence to right the wrongs of the vast

318

political machinery that feels far beyond their control. It is just as easy for me to place myself in the boots of an Antifa foot soldier, who feels now is the moment to stop a fascist coup, to engage in a new Spanish Civil War playing out on the streets of Portland, DC or New York City. How exciting this must all seem for those who share this extremist mindset. Whether I have been changed by age, or marriage or sobriety, I cannot say, but seeing an increasing number of people willing to physically hurt one another in the streets does not make me feel excited. It only makes me feel sad.

I am sure I will be accused of drawing a false equivalency, reminding people of Trump's remarks in the aftermath of Charlottesville about there being "fine people on both sides." Of course, I have my own political opinions. I believe in universal healthcare. I believe systemic racism exists and should be dismantled. I believe in equal rights for all. If I were forced to choose, I would certainly side with Antifa over white supremacists. But this is a false choice. I believe it is possible to be anti-racist and anti-fascist and still believe Antifa is doing more harm than good. That is, in fact, what I believe.

If I have accomplished anything in the writing of this book, I hope it has been to raise awareness about the human story behind every extremist mask. I do not believe anyone is evil. People commit evil deeds, certainly. However, more often than not, they believe they are doing the right thing. They have been hurt themselves. They have been confused. They have been unable to find or hold on to love. They have failed to achieve the life they thought they deserved. And so, they lash out at the other – the enemy they consider to be at the root of all evil in this world. It takes many of us a long time to realize the enemy is within ourselves. In that way, I truly believe we are all the same.

CULTURE, SOCIETY & POLITICS

The modern world is at an impasse. Disasters scroll across our
smartphone screens and we're invited to like, follow or upvote,
but critical thinking is harder and harder to find. Rather than
connecting us in common struggle and debate, the internet has
sped up and deepened a long-standing process of alienation and
atomization. Zer0 Books wants to work against this trend.
With critical theory as our jumping off point, we aim to publish
books that make our readers uncomfortable. We want to move
beyond received opinions.
Zer0 Books is on the left and wants to reinvent the left. We are
sick of the injustice, the suffering and the stupidity that defines
both our political and cultural world, and we aim to find a new
foundation for a new struggle.

If this book has helped you to clarify an idea, solve a problem or
extend your knowledge, you may want to check out our online
content as well. Look for Zer0 Books: Advancing Conversations
in the iTunes directory and for our Zer0 Books YouTube channel.

Popular videos include:

Žižek and the Double Blackmain

The Intellectual Dark Web is a Bad Sign

Can there be an Anti-SJW Left?

Answering Jordan Peterson on Marxism

Bestsellers from Zer0 Books include:

Give Them An Argument
Logic for the Left
Ben Burgis
Many serious leftists have learned to distrust talk of logic. This is
a serious mistake.
Paperback: 978-1-78904-210-8 ebook: 978-1-78904-211-5

Poor but Sexy
Culture Clashes in Europe East and West
Agata Pyzik
How the East stayed East and the West stayed West.
Paperback: 978-1-78099-394-2 ebook: 978-1-78099-395-9

An Anthropology of Nothing in Particular
Martin Demant Frederiksen
A journey into the social lives of meaninglessness.
Paperback: 978-1-78535-699-5 ebook: 978-1-78535-700-8

In the Dust of This Planet
Horror of Philosophy vol. 1
Eugene Thacker
In the first of a series of three books on the Horror of Philosophy,
In the Dust of This Planet offers the genre of horror as a way of
thinking about the unthinkable.
Paperback: 978-1-84694-676-9 ebook: 978-1-78099-010-1

The End of Oulipo?
An Attempt to Exhaust a Movement
Lauren Elkin, Veronica Esposito
Paperback: 978-1-78099-655-4 ebook: 978-1-78099-656-1

Capitalist Realism
Is There No Alternative?
Mark Fisher
An analysis of the ways in which capitalism has presented itself
as the only realistic political-economic system.
Paperback: 978-1-84694-317-1 ebook: 978-1-78099-734-6

Rebel Rebel
Chris O'Leary
David Bowie: every single song. Everything you want to know,
everything you didn't know.
Paperback: 978-1-78099-244-0 ebook: 978-1-78099-713-1

Kill All Normies
Angela Nagle
Online culture wars from 4chan and Tumblr to Trump.
Paperback: 978-1- 78535-543-1 ebook: 978-1-78535-544-8

Romeo and Juliet in Palestine
Teaching Under Occupation
Tom Sperlinger
Life in the West Bank, the nature of pedagogy and the role of a
university under occupation.
Paperback: 978-1-78279-637-4 ebook: 978-1-78279-636-7

Ghosts of My Life
Writings on Depression, Hauntology and Lost Futures
Mark Fisher
Paperback: 978-1-78099-226-6 ebook: 978-1-78279-624-4

Sweetening the Pill
or How We Got Hooked on Hormonal Birth Control
Holly Grigg-Spall
Has contraception liberated or oppressed women?
Sweetening the Pill breaks the silence on the dark side of hormonal
contraception.
Paperback: 978-1-78099-607-3 ebook: 978-1-78099-608-0

Why Are We The Good Guys?
Reclaiming Your Mind from the Delusions of Propaganda
David Cromwell
A provocative challenge to the standard ideology that Western
power is a benevolent force in the world.
Paperback: 978-1-78099-365-2 ebook: 978-1-78099-366-9

The Writing on the Wall
On the Decomposition of Capitalism and its Critics
Anselm Jappe, Alastair Hemmens
A new approach to the meaning of social emancipation.
Paperback: 978-1-78535-581-3 ebook: 978-1-78535-582-0

Enjoying It
Candy Crush and Capitalism
Alfie Bown
A study of enjoyment and of the enjoyment of studying. Bown
asks what enjoyment says about us and what we say about
enjoyment, and why.
Paperback: 978-1-78535-155-6 ebook: 978-1-78535-156-3

Color, Facture, Art and Design
Iona Singh
This materialist definition of fine-art develops guidelines for
architecture, design, cultural-studies and ultimately social
change.
Paperback: 978-1-78099-629-5 ebook: 978-1-78099-630-1

Neglected or Misunderstood
The Radical Feminism of Shulamith Firestone
Victoria Margree
An interrogation of issues surrounding gender, biology,
sexuality, work and technology, and the ways in which our
imaginations continue to be in thrall to ideologies of maternity
and the nuclear family.
Paperback: 978-1-78535-539-4 ebook: 978-1-78535-540-0

How to Dismantle the NHS in 10 Easy Steps (Second Edition)
Youssef El-Gingihy
The story of how your NHS was sold off and why you will have
to buy private health insurance soon. A new expanded second
edition with chapters on junior doctors' strikes and government
blueprints for US-style healthcare.
Paperback: 978-1-78904-178-1 ebook: 978-1-78904-179-8

Digesting Recipes
The Art of Culinary Notation
Susannah Worth
A recipe is an instruction, the imperative tone of the expert, but
this constraint can offer its own kind of potential. A recipe need
not be a domestic trap but might instead offer escape – something
to fantasise about or aspire to.
Paperback: 978-1-78279-860-6 ebook: 978-1-78279-859-0

Most titles are published in paperback and as an ebook.
Paperbacks are available in traditional bookshops. Both print and
ebook formats are available online.
Follow us on Facebook
at https://www.facebook.com/ZeroBooks
and Twitter at https://twitter.com/Zer0Books